HOW YOU CAN
THE LOOTING

T0007211

WHO
STOLE
MY
PENSION?

HOW YOU CAN STOP
THE LOOTING

WHO STOLE MY PENSION?

ROBERT
KIYOSAKI

EDWARD
SIEDLE

PLATA®
PUBLISHING

Published by Plata Publishing, LLC

CASHFLOW, Rich Dad, and CASHFLOW Quadrant, the B-I Triangle and Rich Dad's Tetrahedron are registered trademarks of CASHFLOW Technologies, Inc.

   are registered trademarks of CASHFLOW Technologies, Inc.

Plata Publishing, LLC
4330 N. Civic Center Plaza
Suite 100
Scottsdale, AZ 85251
(480) 998-6971

RichDad.com

First Printing: January 2020
ISBN: 978-1-61268-103-0

Printed in the United States of America

012020

In the decades to come
we will witness hundreds of millions
of elders worldwide,
including America's Baby Boomers,
slipping into poverty.

"Too frail to work and too poor to retire"
has become the new normal.

The looming global pension crisis doesn't affect only
active workers and retirees...
entire families, young and old, will bear the financial burdens
of an aging world population.

TABLE OF CONTENTS

CHAPTER ONE

A Teenager Focused on
Pensions and Retirement Plans?

The year The Beatles released the love song *When I'm 64* I was a teenager already thinking about aging, elder care, and retirement.

A teenager thinking about getting old? That seems unlikely.

Let me explain.

I spent my teenage years in Uganda, East Africa with my father until one day in July of 1971 he failed to return from a journey—a safari, as we'd say in Swahili—to a remote part of the country.

He and I had celebrated my 17th birthday a few days before he disappeared.

My father was an American doctor of gerontology teaching at Uganda's Makerere University and conducting field research into care of the aged—the elderly—in African traditional societies.

Why did he choose to study how Africans took care of their elderly?

Because in the mid-1960s, my father had a vision and realized that America's population demographics—the massive Baby Boom generation—meant that in the decades to come, as 80 million hippies got older, our nation would have to care for them.

For the first time in history, this young nation—a nation which celebrated youth—would have to deal with an invasion of elders.

And America, he knew, was not prepared.

You could say he foresaw the American elder care and retirement crisis we are struggling with today.

Perhaps how African societies traditionally cared for their elders might provide answers, he thought.

My father traveled extensively throughout remote parts of Uganda—which we used to call "the bush"—meeting with missionaries and others caring for the elderly who could not care for themselves. The book he completed about his work immediately before his disappearance was presciently entitled, *The Last of Life: Old Age, Missions and Missionaries in Uganda*. Through his research and travels he had developed a wide

1

network of reliable contacts who kept him informed as to happenings in the bush.

Years later, I learned he used the intelligence network he developed to also provide information to our government.

In 1971, when he disappeared in the garrison town of Mbarara, he was investigating rumors that Idi Amin, the new President of Uganda, had killed hundreds of his own army soldiers stationed at the garrison— without firing a single bullet.

My father's disappearance alerted the world for the first time—as it was immediately reported in *Newsweek* magazine—that Idi Amin was *brutal*, a murderer who would go on to kill an estimated 500,000 of his own people.

As the child of a single parent, I had to return to the United States and live with relatives I barely knew.

Since my father had "disappeared" and was "presumed" dead but his body had not been found, his estate could not be probated, his life insurance benefits would not be paid, and even Social Security Survivor Benefits were unavailable. In short, I was not only orphaned but penniless.

Worse still, since, while in Africa, my initial attempts at home schooling soon turned to no-schooling—I had never gone to 10th, 11th or 12th grades.

Don't get me wrong. I had learned a lot through reading late at night in my bedroom and helping students with their projects at the African university. But there was no obvious place for me in the traditional American educational system.

The grim reality was that, absent a miracle, I would have to spend the next three years of my life completing high school.

Thankfully, a high school guidance counselor knew of an experimental "early college" in the Berkshire Mountains of western Massachusetts called Simon's Rock—a college that accepted high school aged students.

A helping hand.

A girlfriend drove me to visit the school, since I had only a learner's permit at the time.

Another helping hand.

This most unconventional student was accepted by this remarkably *innovative* school and given a full scholarship for my first year.

A path forward, a way out of a hopeless situation, had emerged. I never graduated from high school—I never even got a high school diploma—but was accepted as a sophomore at an early college!

By the end of my first year at Simon's Rock, things had changed for me.

A Ugandan Commission of Inquiry concluded my father had been captured by Amin, tortured, and murdered because of his intelligence work. And, although his body was never found, his estate was able to be probated; his life insurance benefits came through, as did Social Security Survivor benefits.

Through diplomatic channels, the Ugandan Government offered an ex gratia settlement—without admitting responsibility for the murder—and paid reparations.

While I was excited to be a member of the trailblazing first class to receive a Bachelor of Arts degree early from the school, I never graduated from Simon's Rock.

As you can possibly imagine, once the immediate crisis of my father's disappearance and murder passed, completing my college education was not an immediate priority. However, after a two-year break, I graduated at the top of my class from another college and then law school.

This past May—46 years after I attended Simon's Rock—I was awarded an Honorary Bachelor of Arts degree from the school that had meant so much to me.

In summary, every piece of the tumultuous first years of my life left a lasting impression on me. Through my father's work, I was introduced to aging and elder care issues at a very young age. And, as a result of his murder, I experienced first-hand the value of America's Social Security system and the benefits it provides, not only to elders in retirement but to their survivors, children, and the disabled in critical need.

I also learned early in life how to be tenacious in protecting what's most important, such as health, family, and, yes, wealth.

The first forensic investigation of my lifetime—into the disappearance of my father—was not completed until decades later in 1997 when I returned to Uganda and, with the assistance of the

American intelligence community and Ugandan military, sat face-to-face with my father's murderer at Luzira Maximum Security Prison. My investigative efforts did not bring my father back. Guided by his murderers I dug for, but was unable to recover, my father's body. But I did find the answers I desperately needed about how and when he died, as well as the satisfaction of knowing I had done all I could.

Over the past 35 years, as a former U.S. Securities and Exchange Commission lawyer and corporate whistleblower securing the largest government awards in history (totaling $78 million), I have pioneered the field of forensic investigations of the money management business. These days when I'm asked to explain what I do for a living—in terms anyone can understand—I say: "It's like the television show *CSI: Miami*. Each episode of the show typically opens with the discovery of a dead body and the job of the forensic investigators is to figure out whether the death was due to natural causes or foul-play. In my work, the 'death' I'm investigating is a dead, or seriously sick, pension or investment. The question is, did the pension fail due to natural causes (such as unforeseen stock market declines), or was there foul play? The wrongdoing I look for is undisclosed conflicts of interest, hidden and excessive fees, or outright violations of law. More often than the public or even victims ever imagine, the injury or damage is caused by wrongdoing—unethical, self-dealing Wall Street investment firms who drain client accounts for their own benefit."

"It's a wealth transfer game these guys play: your wealth gets transferred to them."

To date, I've undertaken deep-dive forensic investigations into well over $1 trillion in retirement plans and uncovered hundreds of billions of dollars successfully stolen without a gun or a whimper from the victims, including pensions set aside for government workers, as well as corporate pensions sponsored by some of the world's largest employers.

I know what makes even the biggest, supposedly well-managed pensions and other retirement plans falter and fail. And I know what you can do—what you need to do—to keep the pension you were promised from being stolen.

We all deserve a safe and secure retirement. This book was written to bring you one step closer toward that goal.

Why My Poor Dad Was Poor

In 1972, I was flying off an aircraft carrier in the South China Sea. I was a 25-year-old, military academy graduate, a U.S. Marine 1/Lt, flying helicopter gunships in a fake war known as Vietnam.

Making matters worse, I had volunteered for the Marines. I was draft-exempt. I did not have to fight. I could have been a third mate, sailing on an oil tanker for Standard Oil of California, making a lot of money. I was draft exempt because of the magical three-letter word: O-I-L. More specifically, the oil industry. As a civilian third mate for Standard Oil, my draft classification was non-defense vital industry.

So why did I volunteer to fight, when other draft-age people were protesting the war, burning their draft cards, staying in school for a student deferment, or running to Canada to avoid the draft?

The federal military academy I graduated from was the U.S. Merchant Marine Academy at Kings Point, New York, one of the five federal service academies, of which West Point, Naval Academy and the Air Force Academy are the most well-known and come under the Defense Department. The other two academies are the Coast Guard Academy, under the Treasury Department, and my school, Kings Point, the smallest of the five federal academies, under the pruview of the Department of Commerce. Although the smallest of the academies, Kings Point graduates were the highest paid of the five academies, and some of our graduates earned over $100,000 a year, tax-free, if we sailed in the war zone. Not too bad… back in the 1960s.

My Bachelor of Science Degree was in Ocean Transportation… specifically the transportation of oil. For one year, while a student at the academy, I was sailing as an apprentice for Standard Oil between California, Alaska, Hawaii, and Tahiti. When I graduated from the academy in 1969, Standard Oil offered me a job as a third mate on that same run between California, Hawaii, and Tahiti. I would work for seven months and take five months off.

So why did I volunteer to fight, when I had a dream job, with a bright future?

There were many reasons. One is that we were told that two brothers would not serve in the war zone at the same time. My younger brother thought if he was there, they would not send me. I thought the same thing. That was not true. We were both in the war zone at the same time. When I tried to get my brother out of the war zone, my commanding officer just snickered. His only words were: "Grow up. You don't really believe everything our government says, do you?"

My brother and I had five uncles who served in World War II. One uncle fought against the Japanese and was captured, a POW on the infamous Bataan Death March. That uncle was one of only two Japanese Americans captured by the Japanese.

We saw serving our country in time of war as a family tradition. I knew I would not feel good about myself saying to those same uncles, "I'm draft exempt." Yet, that was not the true reason I volunteered for the Marines.

Looking back, I guess I was just curious. The Vietnam War split the country into pieces, groups, and factions. There were the hippies, and there were the draft card burners as well as the stay-in-school group (not for higher education, but for "student deferments") and those who heard the cry "America, love it or leave it"—and left. Since I had no strong views on the war, I just volunteered.

Why the Marines? In those days, most draftees were sent to the Army. My logic was that if I was going to war, I may as well fight with those who wanted to fight, so I joined the Marines.

In 1969, I left my cushy job as third mate on a Standard Oil tanker and took a cut in pay from $47,000 a year to $200 a month. In 1969, my poor dad was earning about $20,000 a year as Superintendent of Education, so my starting pay was 250% more than his pay as an adult. Poor dad could not understand why I was taking a cut in pay, to $2,400 a year, to fight in Vietnam. Nor could I.

I purchased a used red sports car and drove with the top down from San Francisco, California to Pensacola, Florida, home of U.S. Naval Aviation. I must admit, I did wonder if I would ever see America again, so I wanted to take the time to see this beautiful country, one last time… just in case I did not come back.

A Wake-Up Call

Vietnam was a great experience. It was my wake-up call. After flying a number of combat missions—seeing real war, not John-Wayne wars—I did as my commanding officer suggested: I began to grow up. I was no longer a kid, a college graduate blinded by U.S. propaganda, singing *God Bless America* as I waved the Red, White, and Blue, defending the Vietnamese from communism and the U.S. agenda.

When someone asks me, "What was Vietnam like?" I suggest they watch *Good Morning Vietnam*, starring Robin Williams. The sadness portrayed in that movie was my reality.

In Vietnam, I stopped drinking America's Kool-Aid. I was not angry, just disillusioned. And I was disappointed in myself for being so damned gullible. I did not hate my enemy. My respect for the Viet Cong and the North Vietnamese grew as I realized they were just like me, trapped on opposite sides, shooting each other because we were being shot at, killing because we were being killed.

I did not hate my fellow Marines. In fact, my love for my men intensified. I soon found myself fighting harder, not for the USA but for my men, my flight crew, and our troops on the ground. As a pilot, I had one job, and that job was not to kill. My job was to bring my crew home alive, which I am happy to say, we accomplished. Everyone came home alive and in one piece.

Not all pilots felt as I did. There was always the pilot who was looking for "hero medals," because medals meant promotions up the ladder. They were the most dangerous pilots because they thought only of themselves and were out for glory and ego. We all know people like those pilots. The world is filled with them. There was a book written for this type of person: *Looking Out for Number One.*

Some of my lonelier days on the carrier were spent standing on the deck, waiting and hoping a missing aircraft and crew would miraculously return from over the horizon. They never did.

Thank god someone built the Vietnam Memorial in Vietnam, so I could finally say good-bye to friends who never returned.

How Do You Spell War?

There is a lot of time to think on board an aircraft carrier. While we flew regularly, there were often weeks between combat missions. There is a lot of down time, with books to read and old movies to watch.

The flight deck of a carrier was a giant running track, so we stayed in pretty good shape, taking laps around the deck. The food was not great but there was always a lot to eat, so the running helped.

One day, during a long period of nothing, I recalled a lesson I learned at the academy, during one of my classes on oil. I remembered my instructor asking, "How do you spell war?"

If it *wasn't* W-A-R, then my classmates and I were stumped.

His answer: "O-I-L." Why I remembered that class at that time in Vietnam I do not know. I suspect it was because I was questioning why I was fighting in Vietnam in the first place.

The instructor, a Navy Lieutenant Commander who was our instructor in Naval Warfare, was lecturing on the history of warfare in the 20th century. His lesson: World War I was about oil. World War I was the first mechanized war, a war fought with planes, trucks, and tanks. Horses and cavalry were now obsolete. At the turn of the century, it was clear that the country that controlled oil would win wars.

Many of the names, events, and battlegrounds he cited in that class on World War I are still in the news today. I remember him mentioning Mosul, in Northern Iraq, stating that Churchill wanted Mosul for Great Britain, once World War I was over. Today, Mosul is still in the news as a stronghold for ISIS and a major battleground.

In 1914 we were fighting for Mosul. A hundred years later, in 2014 we are still fighting for Mosul.

World War II was about oil. Hitler invaded oil-rich countries, like Libya. We are still fighting in Libya.

Pearl Harbor was about oil. America cut Japan off from oil and the war in the Pacific began.

I was growing up—and waking up. My mind drifted back to my Naval Science class at the academy and I realized the United States was not in Vietnam to protect the Vietnamese people from communism. We were fighting for oil.

Vietnam was about oil. The United States did not want China to have access to Vietnam's oil and American oil companies wanted the profits from oil.

September 11, 2001 was about oil.

Although Osama Bin Laden, and most of the crew that flew into the World Trade Center and the Pentagon, were from Saudi Arabia, that country remains our ally because of oil.

Today, the United States is embroiled in America's longest war, reportedly a war on terror. The United States spends trillions of dollars and puts thousands of lives at risk to fight terrorism, but they're really fighting for oil, oil companies, their shareholders, Wall Street, and the military-industrial complex.

Growing Up—and Wising Up

So, what does oil and war have to do with pensions? They are reminders that we need to wake up. The idea of job security, Social Security, company pensions, government pensions, or someone else taking care of us is, today, a very risky idea.

Vietnam was a turning point in my life because I began to wise up. Just as my brother and I naively believed two brothers would not serve in the war zone at the same time, I had actually believed we were fighting for freedom for the Vietnamese people. In reality we were murdering hundreds of thousands of Vietnamese for their oil. If Vietnam did not have oil, we would not have been there killing innocent people.

Rose-Colored Glasses

I took off my rose-colored glasses in Vietnam. I had many youthful, preconceived notions about life, patriotism, democracy, and the goodness in people.

It is important to me that I say that I was not bitter or angry. I was actually grateful for my time in the Marines and my time in Vietnam. If anything, I was disillusioned and saddened by the greed and fellow human beings' inhumanity to one another. As a result of my time in

Vietnam my vision was clearer. I was less naïve, a bit more cynical, and less gullible.

In January 1973, my year in Vietnam was up and I rotated home.

Our plane was greeted at Norton Air Force Base in California by hundreds of war protestors who were spitting, throwing eggs, and calling us "baby killers."

As soon as we were off the plane and had collected our bags, we were instructed to change out of our uniforms and into civilian clothes, then do our best to disappear into America.

Welcome home.

Why My Poor Dad Was Poor

I spent about a week in California, collecting my things and shipping them to Hawaii. I was fortunate to have been assigned to the Marine Corps Air Station in Hawaii for my next duty station.

When I got to Hawaii, I found my poor dad sitting at home alone in the middle of the day, watching TV game shows. He was only in his early fifties. Although he was a highly educated and extremely successful man—at one time the Superintendent of Education for the State of Hawaii and Republican Party candidate for Lt. Governor of the State of Hawaii—he was unemployed and broke.

My rich dad, my best friend's father, often said, "Social Security is not a good thing." Rich dad thought the Social Security Act, passed in 1935, would make people weak, needy, dependent, and lazy. He would say, "Social Security is Socialism infiltrating the capitalist democracy of America." He also said, "Never take handouts from the government. Every dollar you accept costs you a piece of your soul."

In 1973, I could hear my rich dad's words as I observed my poor dad, dependent upon Social Security for the rest of his life. If not for Social Security and a small teacher's pension, poor dad might have been on the streets.

The reason he was unemployed was because he ran for Lt. Governor of the State of Hawaii, against his boss, the Governor. My dad, an honest man, could not stomach the corruption, greed, and crime he witnessed as a member of the Governor's cabinet.

In his book *Sunny Skies Shady Characters: Cops, Killers, and Corruption in the Aloha State,* published in 2015, investigative reporter James Dooley recounts in detail the reason my father resigned from the governor's staff to run against him. If you read this fascinating book of real crime, you will never watch *Hawaii Five-O* or listen to Don Ho in quite the same light again.

Sunny Skies Shady Characters names names, including Supreme Court Justices, directors of Kamehameha Schools, a richly endowed school for children of Hawaiian descent, Italian and Japanese crime leaders, and hired killers… all people my dad would not work with or for.

Poor dad would have been a rich man if he had cooperated and collaborated. Instead, my poor dad found out how poor he was once the governor took away his job, his paycheck, and his pension.

My dad cashed in his savings and bought a cannot-fail, national ice cream franchise that failed in less than a year. Having been an employee all his life, and trapped in the mental, maximum security prison known as job security, he did not know how to recover from his failures or learn from his mistakes, much less how to start over to replace his paycheck and his pension.

After returning from Vietnam, I would often sit with him, listening as he vented his bitterness, frustration, sadness, and disappointment at friends and co-workers who continued their collaboration with government, the courts, and an education system that was intertwined with organized crime and high level corporate greed, bribery, and pay offs.

On occasion, I would ask him for suggestions, asking him what he thought I should do once my contract with the Marine Corps was over. His reply was robotic, a mantra he was taught by his parents, then repeated countless times as a highly educated teacher to his adoring students, words we have all heard:

"Go back to school, get your master's degree, possibly your PhD, then get a high paying job with benefits and a pension for life."

It was then that I realized why my poor dad was poor. Just as I had drunk the Marine Corps Kool-Aid about the Vietnam War, my dad had been drinking from the Fountain of Deception that was bubbling with the ideas about the value of a good education, job security, and a pension for life. Those words kept him poor.

My dad was a poor man because he believed in words like *job security*, *paycheck*, and *pension*. My dad would always be a poor man unless he changed his vocabulary.

When my dad lost the safety net those words represented—lost his job security, his paycheck, and his pension—he found out how poor he was. That was a bitter pill for a straight-A student, class valedictorian who completed graduate studies at Stanford, Northwestern, and the University of Chicago.

I realized that a good education had got him his job, paycheck, and pension. The problem was his education did not teach him how to survive without them.

Seeing the Future

While sitting with him, I would do my best to keep his spirits up, encouraging him to look toward a brighter future. After all, he was still a young man and in good health. Unfortunately, his spirit was broken and I watched helplessly as life slowly seeped from his soul.

I had seen this kind of lifelessness before, in Vietnam. I had friends, fellow pilots who had lost their nerve, their spirit, their will to fight and to live. One, a CH-53 pilot we called Jolly Green Giant, panicked and lost his nerve over the battlefield. He floated high in the sky and a hand-held heat-seeking rocket found him. The subsonic rocket flew up one of his engines and exploded. Immediately the giant helicopter rolled to the right, crashing to the ground and bursting into flames, killing all 62 South Vietnamese Marines trapped inside. Fortunately or unfortunately, this pilot lived. But would never fly again. He was finally sent home after he was found, repeatedly, walking around aimlessly talking to himself and attempting to justify his actions and handle his guilt and sadness as he relived the screams of dying men.

We had a name for this type of man. We called them, *Corpse-man*. Someone who was alive in body, but had lost their soul.

My poor dad was much the same, living a lifeless existence, reliving the past and justifying his actions while living in fear of the future… a future without a job, paycheck or a pension.

One day, while listening to my dad go over those same life stories of his past glory days—being the class valedictorian, a graduate student at Stanford, a very young school principle, a Superintendent of Education, then a member of the Governor's cabinet—I had a premonition, a glimpse of the future. The vision was not of my father's generation, but of mine, the Baby Boom generation.

The Eve of Destruction

In 2002, I wrote *Rich Dad's Prophecy*, a book forecasting the biggest stock market crash in the history of the world that was anticipated sometime after 2016. As I write this book, in 2019, anyone who has been paying attention to the world economy can see that 2016 crash crumbling in slow motion.

Rich Dad's Prophecy is about the demise of the pension system, specifically the Defined Contribution (DC) pension plans, more popularly known as the 401(k), IRA, Superannuation in Australia, or RRSP in Canada.

Rich Dad's Prophecy is a forecast about the Baby Boomers, the most affluent and luckiest generation in world history, and their ascent into great wealth only to end their lives much like my poor dad, living in poverty or just above poverty, without jobs, paychecks, and pensions.

In Ernest Hemingway's novel *The Sun Also Rises,* one of the characters is asked, "How did you go bankrupt?" His answer, "Two ways. Gradually and then suddenly."

When you see the spread of homelessness in many of the richest cities of the world, you see *Rich Dad's Prophecy,* coming true... gradually.

After my experiences in Vietnam and watching my father slowly lose his spirit, I knew it was time for me to grow up and wise up. I began to wake up to the realities of life when my commanding officer said:

"Grow up. You don't really believe everything our government says, do you?"

When my poor dad recommended that I return to school get my master's degree (and possibly my PhD), work as an employee, and climb the corporate ladder for job security, a steady paycheck, and a pension, I took off my rose-colored glasses.

The next day, I called my rich dad and had lunch with him. I did not want to follow in my poor dad's footsteps. It was time for me to man up, as they say, and find my own path.

In *Rich Dad Poor Dad* I quoted from Robert Frost's poem *The Road Not Taken*.

For those of you looking for a new road to the future, I offer this great poem by a great poet.

The Road Not Taken

Two roads diverged in a yellow wood,
And sorry I could not travel both
And be one traveler, long I stood
And looked down one as far as I could
To where it bent in the undergrowth;

Then took the other, as just as fair,
And having perhaps the better claim,
Because it was grassy and wanted wear;
Though as for that the passing there
Had worn them really about the same,

And both that morning equally lay
In leaves no step had trodden black.
Oh, I kept the first for another day!
Yet knowing how way leads on to way,
I doubted if I should ever come back.

I shall be telling this with a sigh
Somewhere ages and ages hence:
Two roads diverged in a wood, and I—
I took the one less traveled by,
And that has made all the difference.

Robert Frost (1874-1963)

In this book, Ted Siedle and I will encourage you to take off your rose-colored glasses and shine a light on different paths you can choose.

CHAPTER TWO

Welcome to the Greatest Retirement Crisis
in the History of the World

We are in the early stages of the greatest retirement crisis in the history of our nation and indeed the entire world. In the decades to come, we will witness hundreds of millions of elders globally, including the Baby Boomers in America, slipping into poverty.

Too frail to work, too poor to retire will become the "new normal" for many of our oldest.

Global population demographics, coupled with indisputable glaringly insufficient retirement savings and human physiology, suggest that a catastrophic outcome for at least a significant percentage of the world's elderly population is inevitable.

The good news is that more people—globally—are living longer than ever. In developed countries such as the United Kingdom, Japan, Italy, Germany and the United States, the elder population has skyrocketed.

In Japan, the country with the oldest citizenry, 27% of the population is 65 or older today. That number is steadily rising. It is predicted that by 2030, nearly a third of the Japanese people will be senior citizens.

Next on the list is Italy, with 23%.

Portugal, Germany, Finland, Bulgaria, Sweden, Greece, France, Denmark, Spain, the United Kingdom and, yes, the United States, all either already are or are projected to become around 25% elderly. [1]

---

1   The number of Americans 65 and older is projected to more than double from 46 million today to over 98 million by 2060, and the 65-plus age group's share of the total population will rise to nearly 24% from 15%.

Countries with the Largest Elderly Population in the World

Rank	Country	% of population over 65 years old
1	Japan	27
2	Italy	23
3	Portugal	22
4	Germany	21
5	Finland	21
6	Bulgaria	21
7	Greece	20
8	Sweden	20
9	Latvia	20
10	Croatia	20
11	France	20
12	Denmark	20
13	Estonia	19
14	Spain	19
15	Malta	19
16	Austria	19
17	Slovenia	19
18	Czech Republic	19
19	Lithuania	19
20	Netherlands	19
21	Hungary	19
22	Belgium	19
23	United Kingdom	19
24	Switzerland	18
25	Romania	18

According to the World Health Organization, nearly two billion people across the world are expected to be over 60 years old by 2050, a figure that's more than triple what it was in 2000.

For better or for worse, there simply have never been more elderly people living on planet Earth.

The bad news is that only a very small minority of these folks has enough personal savings to pay for—and to survive—decades of retirement.

Worse still, those who are counting upon the few remaining corporate pensions for their retirement security can be sure that the company sponsoring the plan—their past or present employer—is consulting with experts, plotting how to screw workers out of the benefits they mistakenly think they are entitled to and save the corporation money.

Any so-called "promises" an employer may have made are, at best shaky, or even illusory—worthless.

At this very moment, General Electric—the largest company in the world in 2010, which dropped out of the Dow Jones Industrial Average last year for the first time in 110 years—is trying to clean up its balance sheet by offering 100,000 ex-employees tempting pots of cash to give up their valuable pensions. GE's "lump sum" offers tend to be stingy, shortchanging pensioners but boosting the company's bottom line.[2]

State and local government pensions in the United States hold almost $4 trillion in assets and provide retirement benefits for roughly 21 million current and former state and local employees. These are teachers, firefighters, and police officers who serve their communities. However, more than half of these governments have reduced those benefits since the 2008 recession. In a desperate last-ditch effort to solve severe underfunding, government pensions have shifted over $1 trillion in assets to the costliest, riskiest investments ever devised by Wall Street. Reckless gambling will only accelerate insolvency.

Workers in government pensions around the world can count on politicians and taxpayers running to legislatures and courts to cut benefits workers have been "promised" when these already-struggling government pensions start to run out of money. For example, after Croatia's parliament recently approved a government proposal to raise the retirement age from 65 to 67 and trim pensions for people who retire early, three top trade unions revolted and the government backed down—for now.[3]

2 https://www.forbes.com/sites/baldwin/2019/10/20/how-much-is-ge-shortchanging-pensioners-taking-lump-sums-use-our-calculator/#478688ce691c
3 https://www.reuters.com/article/us-croatia-pensions/croatia-revokes-retirement-age-rise-after-trade-union-revolt-idUSKBN1WX1GL

Even millions of participants in the Dutch pension system—widely regarded as the "world's best"—are facing benefit cuts and fearing there may be worse to come.[4]

So much for so-called "retirement security."

Now is the time to take action to stop the looting and protect pensions by ensuring promises made are, in fact, kept.

Doing nothing, sitting back, confident your pension check is "in the mail" is not an option. That's a risk you can't afford to take.

---

4 https://www.reuters.com/article/us-netherlands-pensions-analysis/going-dutch-low-interest-rates-rattle-worlds-best-pension-system-idUSKBN1WX0IU?utm_source=applenews

Old Guys Getting Older

Most of us have heard the adage "You can't teach an old dog new tricks." There is a lot of truth in those words.

Personally, I am an old dog, a dinosaur—a "techno-saurus-rex" when it comes to my cell phone and my computer. My Baby-Boomer brain just does not "get it." I feel handicapped every time I have to do something other than make a phone call or use my computer for anything more than a "typewriter." I'm thankful that I have a team of young people who grew up with technology working at my company.

In 1973, I was a 26-year-old young man who was charting his future. My poor dad was an old dog at 54 years old. And when the franchise business he had purchased failed, it was a lesson for both of us. That business failed not because the franchise was bad, but because my dad could not shift his mindset from *employee* to *entrepreneur.*

His thoughts, actions, experiences, and decisions related to that business venture were those of an employee, not an entrepreneur. He made really foolish decisions that cost him his franchise, his savings, and his early retirement. One foolish decision was to find a location in a strip small because it was cheap. He and his advisors, fellow schoolteachers all, naively thought that location did not matter. They believed a national franchise brand would draw people in. The location was cheap for one reason: there was almost no foot traffic. It was in the back of the strip-center mall. It would have been a great location for an accountant's office, but not an ice cream franchise.

I am not a brain surgeon or a psychiatrist, so take everything I am about to say with a grain of salt and cynicism. It's my understanding that the human brain is like soft cheese, with neural pathways running throughout the brain matter. The problem is, as we age, the neural pathways become ridged, well-worn gullies. A young person appears to learn more quickly because their neural pathways are like shallow streams after a light spring rain, making it easier to learn and to change. There is a lot of truth to the words, "I am in a rut." They may be stuck, deep in a neural pathway. Their rut, their neural pathways, have become a raging river, running through the steep walls of the Grand Canyon.

My poor dad entered school at the age of five and finally left school at the age of 54, after he lost the election and his job. His neural pathways were well worn and deep. He was not able to change.

The good news is, today, people are living longer. The bad news is, they may outlive their money. Today, tens of millions of Baby Boomers are in the same rut my poor dad was in. The question is, can they change in time… before their money runs out?

How Does a Person Change?

In 1994, my wife Kim and I retired. She was 37 and I was 47. What made our retirement unique was we achieved our financial freedom in only 10 years and without jobs, without government support, and without pension plans. We did it with financial education. The kind of financial education that is not taught in our schools.

When people asked us how we retired early and young, we found ourselves unable to explain our path and process to early retirement with words alone. In response to these questions, Kim and I created our CASHFLOW® board game in 1996.

Why a board game? My financial education began with a boardgame. When rich dad's son and I were nine years old, rich dad used the game of *Monopoly*® as an educational tool. The *Monopoly* game was the start of my financial neural pathways. At the age of nine, I knew I wanted to be a professional investor like my rich dad, not a professor like my poor dad.

Kim and I played *Monopoly* in real life. And we did it simply by following the formula taught in *Monopoly*—4 green houses, 1 red hotel. After getting married, while most newlyweds were dreaming of buying their first home, Kim and I were dreaming of buying our first rental property.

Today we own thousands of rental properties, commercial properties, "red" hotels, golf courses, oil wells, licenses, and businesses. We retired by playing *Monopoly* in real life.

It was a slow start. Like most newlyweds, we had very little money. In our spare time, we attended real estate investment seminars and looked at properties every chance we had. We made a lot of mistakes, but kept learning from our mistakes. It took us 10 years to create $10,000 in passive income per month against $3,000 in personal expenses. We were not Bill-Gates rich by any means, yet we were financially free.

I'm often asked if real estate investing is the only road to financial freedom—and retiring young and rich. That's definitely not true. Rich dad used to say, "There are a million paths to financial heaven. Unfortunately, there are billions of paths to financial hell." Your door to financial heaven is only limited by your imagination, which is why Albert Einstein said, "Imagination is more important than knowledge."

Lessons Learned:
Money does not make you rich. What made us rich were the classes we attended, the mistakes we made, the people we met, and the wisdom we gained playing *Monopoly* in real life. We were proactive investors—not passive investors with jobs and pension plans.

Some people take this to mean that knowledge isn't important. Not so. You still need knowledge to support your imagination. Without basic financial knowledge, most people's financial imagination, their dreams, turn into financial nightmares. Without basic financial knowledge, imagination alone can turn into delusional thinking. In 2000, the dot-com bust turned delusional when billions of dollars were bet on dot-com companies—"businesses" without an actual business, profits, or management.

The same thing happened in 2008, when millions of people became "real estate investors." I still remember when tenants in our apartment complexes were leaving to buy their $350,000 "dream home" and become real estate flippers. Many of them could barely afford their rent, yet they roared out into the real world with dreams of becoming Donald Trump.

On May 17, 2007 Federal Reserve Chairman Ben Bernanke stated:

> *"We believe the effect of the troubles in the subprime sector on the broader housing market will likely be limited, and **we do not expect significant spillovers from the subprime market to the rest of the economy or to the financial system**."* [Emphasis added.]

In January of 2008, I was on CNN with Wolf Blitzer and predicted that Lehman Brothers was on the verge of bankruptcy. Wolf did not believe me.

On September 15, 2008 Lehman Brothers declared bankruptcy.

On that day, the Great Recession—which was really, by definition, a depression—began. It was a waste of human capital on a scale most Americans had never seen before. It left 15 million people out of work with over $7 trillion in housing losses and $11 trillion in stock market declines.

Fortune magazine stated:

> *"Ben Bernanke and other officials have claimed that they did not have the necessary tools to save Lehman."*

It was later revealed that Fed Chairman Bernanke secretly sent billions over to Europe to save European banks, but zero went to Lehmann.

Yet the Fed knowingly allowed Wall Street to package subprime debt and sell those toxic assets to the world, and the world economy collapsed. My rich dad would have called that "intelligent insanity."

Many people could see the 2008 crash coming. I could see it by observing the tenants from my apartment buildings borrowing hundreds of thousands of dollars to buy homes they could not afford. The banks were offering "Liar Loans" and "NINJA" (No Income, No Job) loans, which were later packaged as derivatives known as CDO (Collateralized Debt Obligations) and MBS (Mortgaged Backed Securities).

It was easy to forecast a crash. You did not need a PhD in economics to predict Lehman's collapse. All you had to do was observe renters, who could barely afford a $500-a-month rent attempt to turn into—*Do I dare mention his name a third time in this chapter?*—Donald Trump.

Lehmann Brothers was the oldest bank, the fourth largest bank, and the largest bankruptcy filing in United States history.

My poor dad was much like Ben Bernanke, a PhD without real world experience. My poor dad, and his fellow teachers, naively thought a national ice cream franchise would disguise their lack of basic financial knowledge. It is people like Bernanke and my poor dad who teach our kids today.

The 2008 subprime disaster was caused by the geniuses on Wall Street—with the blessing of the geniuses at Federal Reserve Bank—selling toxic subprime assets to subprime investors.

The 2008 disaster was good for Kim and me as investors, because we were prepared to act on opportunities it created. Real estate prices fell, interest rates kept falling, and we kept buying. As rich dad taught his son and me, "You don't need to be right 51% of the time. All you need to do is be right once."

If you would like to see a clip of my interview with Wolf Blitzer on CNN's The Situation Room go to: https://vimeo.com/ 166886842/721f0c0738

These quotes from Warren Buffett say this best:

> *"Opportunities come infrequently. When it rains gold, put out the bucket, not the thimble."*

> *"Widespread fear is your friend, as an investor, because it serves up bargain purchases."*

> *"Whether we're talking about socks or stocks, I like buying quality merchandise when it is marked down."*

> *"We simply attempt to be fearful when others are greedy and to be greedy only when others are fearful."*

The good news is that when the next crash comes, it will be a great time for people, young and old, who have real financial education. Many will find nirvana and financial heaven. Unfortunately, after the next crash, there is likely to be billions of people who will enter financial hell.

Rich dad often said:

> *"When Walmart has a sale, the poor and middleclass rush in."*

He also said:

> *"When the real estate, stock, or bond market has a sale, rich people rush in and the poor and middleclass rush out... and miss out."*

There is more good news: In my opinion, the next crash will be a big one and a long one. The last Great Depression lasted 25 years, from 1929 to 1954. In 1929, the Dow peaked at 380. It took 25 years, until 1954, to reach 380 again. This next depression may last longer because the Fed and Central Banks throughout the world are out of ammunition (at sub-zero interest rates and Quantitative Easing, ie: printing money) and cannot save the world again.

Unfortunately, the coming crash and possible depression will wipe out the pensions of millions of people, many of whom are Baby Boomers who are out of time. On the flip side: it will be the "sale of the century" for those who are prepared.

Louis Pasteur (1822-1895), known for his research in microbiology, pasteurization, and vaccinations said:

> *"Fortune rewards the prepared mind."*

How to Prepare for the Future

So… how do you teach an old dog new tricks? It's not really that hard—if the 'dog' wants to learn.

If you wanted to learn the game of golf, how would you do it? Read a book? Watch pros like Tiger Woods on TV? Play miniature golf at an amusement park? Or, instead of learning to play yourself. Would you have someone play golf for you?

When it comes to professional investing, the approaches cited above are what most passive investors do. They read investment books, watch Warren Buffett on TV, or place a few bucks on a "hot stock tip" that's floating around the office. Most people are counting on "professionally managed funds," such as mutual funds and ETFs, for their retirement. I estimate that 90% of all employees assume their retirement nest egg will be there when they retire. I estimate 90% of all employees have no idea what is going on inside their retirement account.

The Wall Street Kool-Aid

When it comes to investing, most people drink from Wall Street's Kool-Aid.

The flavor: Efficient Market Theory (EMT)… based upon the assumption that "you can't beat the market."

Efficient Market Theory, or EMT, *is a belief that markets are efficient because the prices of stocks have been adjusted for all known information and that price changes instantly as the information is updated.*

This is Wall Street Kool-Aid. This is how financial planners, stockbrokers, and mutual fund managers get gullible investors to believe they cannot beat the market. Once the passive investor drinks this Kool-Aid—once they blindly turn their pension money over to Wall Street—they are trusting someone else with their financial future. Unfortunately, most financial planners, stockbrokers, and mutual fund managers drink the same Kool-Aid. They all believe that they have all the right answers and strategies. In my experience, very, very few can consistently beat the market. And sometimes it's nothing more than "The blind leading the blind."

> Efficient Market Theory, or EMT, *is a belief that* **markets** *are* **efficient** *because the prices of stocks have been adjusted for all known information and that the price changes instantly as the information is updated.*

Here's more Wall Street Kool-Aid: Insider trading is illegal.

In the simplest terms, investing runs on information. That is why EMT claims that markets are efficient and adjust for all known information and change instantly as information changes.

To protect this premise, Wall Street warns mom and pop investors that insider trading is illegal. The truth is, insider trading is illegal some of the time, especially in the stock and bond markets, the markets most pensions are in.

Yet the facts are that legal insider trading is how professional investors beat EMT, day in and day out. Legal insider trading is how professional investors gain incredible ROI, returns on investments, which will be explained later in this book.

Which begs the question: When is insider trading legal… and when is it illegal?

The answer is: it depends. It depends on the investment, how the information was obtained, and the role of the person who obtained the information. Rich dad taught his son and me this: "It's all insider information. It all depends upon how close to the inside you are." That was one of the lessons rich dad reinforced in his son and me as kids, playing *Monopoly.*

Here's an example: One of many reasons I love real estate and see outstanding returns is because real estate is a private asset, not subject to the security laws of the public stock and bond markets. Real estate runs on insider information. The same is true with smaller, non-public businesses, run by entrepreneurs. The laws, rules, and regulations are vastly different between public and private companies.

As an entrepreneur, I have founded three companies and took them public through IPOs, Initial Public Offerings. As a founding member of a publicly-traded company, I had to be very careful not to cross the line between legal and illegal insider information.

I am grateful for my 15 years building those publicly-traded companies. I learned a lot. My rose-colored glasses came off and I grew up. Today, I am completely out of public markets. I own zero public stocks or bonds. I own zero mutual funds or ETFs, Exchange Traded Funds. I prefer being a private investor who uses legal insider information to beat the returns available in public markets.

For most employees with pensions, Wall Street teaches:

1: You're not smart enough to beat the market.
2: Turn your money over to an expert—who is, most often, a salesperson, not a real investor.
3: Insider trading is illegal.

The education system also dispenses its own Kool-Aid. There are two favorite flavors. Our education system is designed to train people to be employees. That is why parents still advise their children to "Go to school and get a job." That is why teachers teach students that:

1: Mistakes make you stupid.
2: Cooperation is cheating.

The reason most employees with pensions are in trouble is because they fail to make mistakes and do not have access to real financial advice. Most pensions, employees, and corporate Human Resource managers deal primarily with salespeople from Wall Street. That is why many retirees and retirement funds are in serious trouble.

Using the golfing metaphor again, how would a person learn to be a great golfer if they never made mistakes? And how would a person learn to be great golfer if they took golf lessons from someone who sells golf clubs, but has never played golf? Golf is a game played as individuals. Real business is a team sport. An entrepreneur's core team is made up of a bookkeeper, accountant, attorney, system engineers, sales people, and marketing professionals.

Most employees do not have a professional business team, which is why many people, like my poor dad, fail in business. His advisors, fellow teachers and employees just like him, who drink daily from the Kool-Aid fountain, believed that cooperation is cheating. Again, rich dad called that "intelligent insanity."

The average pensioner is like Tiger Woods playing football against the New England Patriots. No matter how strong Tiger is, a team of 15 will always win at the game of football, a team sport—like business. For the average investor to win, they need a team of professionals... not salespeople.

Why Games Are the Best Teachers

Kim and I created our *CASHFLOW* game because games are the best teachers. Just ask most young people. They love video games and sports. I loved football, baseball, and surfing much more than math and science. I also loved learning about business and investing by playing *Monopoly*® with rich dad, hour after hour.

The following diagram explains why games are the best teachers.

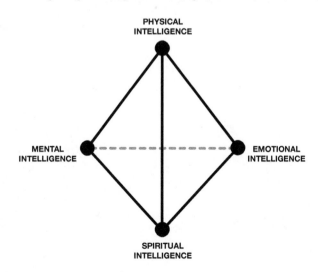

Playing *Monopoly* engages all four intelligences. *The New York Times* called the *CASHFLOW* game, "*Monopoly* on steroids." It is called that because it is the only game that teaches the basics of accounting and encourages the use of debt as leverage. In other words, if you want to win at *CASHFLOW*, you must use debt. That is what capitalists do. They use OPM, Other People's Money. That is what capitalists like Warren Buffett and Donald Trump do. They know that the key to higher returns is OPM. The problem is that most employees with pensions are the OP, the people who provide the money.

Sitting in a classroom listening to lectures engaged nothing for me. Most of the time, my mind was out of the classroom, watching the waves from the window. My body was in the room, but mentally, emotionally, and spiritually I was surfing.

The fun of the *CASHFLOW* game is you are encouraged to take risks, make as many mistakes as possible, learn from your mistakes, and cooperate with your fellow players—without giving them answers so that they, too, can make mistakes and learn from them. And you learn with play money—not your own real money.

So how does an old dog learn new tricks? The same way anyone learns to play golf. Pick up a set of clubs, take lessons from a real golfer… then practice, practice, practice and play, play, play.

In the real world of money, the people who make the most mistakes, have the best teams, and invest from the inside win.

CHAPTER THREE

Who's to Blame for the Retirement Crisis?

There probably are and have always been a few people who have absolutely no interest in preparing for their retirement. Maybe they're carefree souls joyously living fully in the moment without putting anything away for a rainy day they can't envision, or desperate ghouls who have no desire to endure long miserable lives.

But, in my experience, *almost everyone* thinks and cares about how they will survive as they grow old and choose, or are forced, to stop working.

Most people of a certain age, say 50, have made *some* plans for their retirement. Often, these plans are woefully inadequate. Most workers simply do not earn enough to set aside adequate funds for potentially decades of retirement. Others have adequate savings but lack the financial literacy required for prudent planning.

Finally, some have made obviously bad choices and end up with criminal, addiction, or other problems which they are unable to overcome.

So, arguably some of the blame for the impending retirement crisis lies with individuals.

But when you think about it, estimating how long you will live, how healthy you will be, how much you will need to pay for a lifestyle that will be changing year-to-year over decades of retirement, and how to optimally invest your savings, is challenging for even the most financially astute.

Even if you've done everything right—been continuously employed, carry little to no debt, save diligently and live within your means—your carefully conceived plans can prove worthless when disaster, such as an unexpected death, lengthy illness, stock market crash, or pension-plan collapse, strikes.

So, let's not minimize how formidable the task of planning for decades of retirement really is. Whether it is even reasonable to expect the overwhelming majority of workers to be capable of successfully planning for their own retirements is questionable.

When over a billion older workers globally all have the same problem—too little for retirement—it's time to stop blaming individuals for bad investment decisions or not having enough financial resources.

There's a global systemic problem.

The three systemic problems we will address in this book are:

- The elimination or collapse of employer-sponsored pension plans created to pay retirees a monthly lifetime pension.
- The gross mismanagement of pensions.
- The shifting of responsibility onto workers to invest for their retirement using 401(k)-type plans which are structurally flawed and incapable of providing retirement security comparable to a pension.

Workers bear no responsibility for these three systemic causes of the global pension crisis. To the contrary, workers cannot compel an employer to establish or terminate a pension, have no voice in the management of pension investments, and can neither compel nor select investment options for 401(k)-type plans (only select from a menu of costly mutual funds predetermined by the employer).

Time and again, I have been an eyewitness to employers cutting and shutting mismanaged pensions, despite overwhelming opposition from workers.

In April 2011, I stood with over 200 City of Atlanta, Georgia police officers jammed into a crowded Committee Room at City Hall for a workshop held by the Finance Committee of the City Council. By the end of the tense four-and-a-half-hour marathon session, hundreds of other city employees had lined the corridors watching the closed-circuit broadcast on television monitors throughout the building.

The workshop was an opportunity for the police to present their response to a proposal by the Mayor to "freeze" pension benefits and force city workers in a 401(k)-type retirement plan. In other words, city officials had come up with a scheme to reduce the pension benefits promised to employees in response to looming budget deficits.

The police had passed around a hat and collected cash donations amounting to a few thousand dollars to pay for me to fly to Atlanta and speak on their behalf at the Committee meeting—as their expert—specifically about the 401(k) aspect of the proposal.

I explained to the City Council that America was facing a retirement crisis and that corporations closing their mismanaged pensions and forcing their workers into flawed 401(k) defined contribution plans was largely to blame.

"401(k)s cannot and will not provide meaningful retirement security for the overwhelming number of America's workers and certainly not the public employees of the City of Atlanta.

"So if you do vote to force your city's public employees into a 401(k)-type system, at least be honest about it and admit from the get-go that this is no retirement plan."

That same year, I was hired by Rhode Island Council 94, American Federation of State, County and Municipal Employees to conduct a forensic investigation of the Rhode Island state pension. The Rhode Island state legislature had hastily approved a so-called "pension reform" proposal deviously crafted by newly-elected state Treasurer Gina Raimondo to supposedly shore up the pension by "suspending"—in truth, eliminating—the Cost of Living Adjustment (COLA) promised to all state employees, teachers, state police and judges. What the Treasurer hadn't told anyone was that the money saved from the 3% COLA cuts would to be used to pay for a costly $2 billion hedge fund gamble employing some of her wealthiest Wall Street donors—a gamble which would spectacularly fail within five years, costing the pension over $500 million.

In 2013, the findings of my Rhode Island investigation included:

"The projected cost to the Employee Retirement System of Rhode Island (ERSRI) of the Treasurer's $2 billion alternative investments gamble over the next 20 years amounts to in excess of $3 billion and far exceeds the COLA savings the Treasurer has projected—another inconvenient truth that, to date, has been withheld from the public.

"Public pension reform, in Rhode Island, amounts to a transfer of worker's wealth dollar-for-dollar to Wall Street."

To the best of my knowledge, no worker in Atlanta, Rhode Island, or anywhere else ever asked to have his pension cut or eliminated. Rather, workers all over the world are satisfied with—want to keep, indeed strengthen—their pensions.

Nevertheless, corporate employer-sponsored pensions have all but disappeared over the past 40 years. Governments, likewise, are cutting benefits and forcing workers out of their pensions.

According to a 2019 study on global pension systems, only the Netherlands and Denmark have A-graded, first class and robust retirement systems that deliver good benefits, are sustainable, and have a high level of integrity. The United States, United Kingdom, Malaysia, Hong Kong and France received C+ grades, indicating major risks that, unless addressed, will lead to questions about the efficacy and/or long-term sustainability of these pensions.[1]

That's the bad news. The good news?

There really isn't any...

Shifting responsibility for retirement planning onto workers has been disastrous for workers but great for corporate bottom lines.

The 401(k) defined contribution plans which employers and Wall Street sold to workers as providing comparable retirement benefits to pensions have failed dismally. With median 401(k) balances for 65-year-olds at $70,000 or less, it's no secret that the great 401(k) "experiment" has failed in the United States. And, as deeply flawed as they are, approximately a third of America's workers do not have any employer-sponsored retirement plans *at all.*

According to a 2018 study by Northwestern Mutual,[2] 21% of Americans have no retirement savings and an additional 10% have less than $5,000 in savings. A third of Baby Boomers currently in, or approaching, retirement age have between nothing and $25,000 set aside.

The Economic Policy Institute paints an even bleaker picture. Their data from 2013 reports that, "nearly half of families have no retirement account savings at all."[3]

The failure of 401(k) innovation was foreseen decades ago by experts—including me—and was avoidable had legislators and regulators acted in the best interest of investors and had the financial services industry curbed its greed.

Instead, Wall Street firms made money—and were the big winners.

---

1 https://info.mercer.com/rs/521-DEV-513/images/MMGPI%202019%20Full%20Report.pdf
2 https://news.northwesternmutual.com/2018-05-08-1-In-3-Americans-Have-Less-Than-5-000-In-Retirement-Savings
3 https://www.epi.org/publication/retirement-in-america/#charts

Retirement savers who paid higher fees to Wall Street for poor performing mutual fund investments—the big-time losers.

I was involved in the leading class action lawsuits alleging mismanagement of the investments in many of America's largest 401(k) plans, including Walmart, Boeing, Northrop Grumman, Kraft, Edison, Caterpillar, Deere, United Technologies, General Dynamics, ABB and International Paper. Sadly, these cases, challenging 401(k) structures and practices were not brought until 2006—too late for at least two generations of workers.

The solution to the retirement crisis, I assure you, is not costly 401(k)-type defined contribution plans that put all of the responsibility for selection of investments onto individuals.

The solution is simple: better managed pensions.

And that's not going to happen without you.

GRUNCH: Gross Universal Cash Heist

In 1967, I was a student at the U.S. Merchant Marine Academy at Kings Point, New York. That year Expo 67, The World's Fair on the Future was held in Montreal, Canada. My classmate Andy Andreasen and I hitchhiked from New York to Montreal to see the future. We were excited to see the U.S. Pavilion, a giant geodesic dome created by Dr. R. Buckminster Fuller, a "futurist." Expo 67 was a mind-blowing, consciousness-expanding, life-changing event for Andy and me. We did see the future.

"Bucky" was a darling of academics all over the world. My poor dad was one of those academic "groupies." When I was in high school, my poor dad and I would build models that Fuller called "the building blocks of the universe." To say Fuller was controversial, would be an understatement. His views on the mathematics that students were taught were not well received by academics, especially those in math and science. Fuller would say, "How dare we lie to students." One of the lies he was referring to was the concept of "squares" and the mathematical process of "square-rooting." According to Fuller, "squares" did not exist in the real world and he could prove it. The massive geodesic dome, the U.S. Pavilion at Expo 67 was his "proof" that squares do not exist, and that the educational system was lying to students by teaching a mathematical coordinate system based on squares.

The models my dad and I were building out of very thin wood dowels and glue were models of triangles and tetrahedrons, not squares and cubes. The U.S. Pavilion, pictured below, was a colossal extension of his triangles and tetrahedrons.

Riding the monorail into the dome, touring the displays inside, and just standing in the dome and gazing into the "future" was an incredible experience. This dome could not be built with mathematics based on squares and cubes. Today's architecture, modern residences, commercial buildings, and skyscrapers are designed on squares and cube mathematics. That is one reason why modern real estate, both commercial and residential, is prohibitively expensive... making the term "affordable housing" an oxymoron.

One reason why poor dad was excited about Fuller was because, in the 1960s, Fuller was working on a way to provide housing for the world, including plumbing, for $25 a unit. He could do it with mathematics using triangles and tetrahedrons.

When I was a high school student, my rich dad was teaching his son and me about money, playing *Monopoly*. My poor dad was teaching me about being a humanitarian, working for humanity, not money, using sticks and glue to build triangles and tetrahedrons, the building blocks of universe.

When Kim and I designed our CASHFLOW game in 1996, we were influenced by both rich dad and poor dad.

I did not meet Dr. Fuller personally until 1981. In 1981, I was an entrepreneur in the rock and roll industry, developing licensed products for bands like Duran-Duran, Van Halen, The Police, and others. My company was the first business to introduce the nylon and Velcro® wallets for surfers—a business that had morphed into a company that produced products for kids who went to rock concerts. The business was located in Hawaii and our products were manufactured in Korea and Taiwan. We sold our rock products at concerts and through 1600 retailers, including JCPenney and Spencer's gifts, across America.

In the summer of 1981, I was 34 years old and received an invitation to The Future of Business with Bucky Fuller. It was a week-long event, to be held at a ski resort in Lake Tahoe, California. I signed up immediately.

For me, that September in 1981 was more profound and life changing than Expo 67. I returned to Hawaii a changed human being and businessman who had different vision of the future.

In summers of 1982 and 1983, I returned for the same event with Fuller, and again, after each event, my life evolved.

On July 1, 1983, I was driving on the H-1 Freeway in Honolulu when the music was interrupted to announce the passing of Bucky Fuller, a man called the Planet's Friendly Genius and whom John Denver named the Grandfather of the Future. John wrote a song about Fuller entitled *What One Man Can Do.*

When I heard the news of Fuller's death, an immense sadness welled up inside of me and I had to pull over off the freeway, crying as cars whizzed by.

The Cash Heist

In 1983, after Bucky's death, his book *GRUNCH of Giants* was released. GRUNCH stands for **GR**oss **UN**iversal **C**ash **H**eist.

Fuller usually wrote and spoke on math, science, architecture, and generalized principles of universe—all subjects my poor dad loved. *GRUNCH* was about money, a subject my rich dad loved.

GRUNCH is a small book. Most of Fuller's books are tomes requiring superhuman discipline to complete. His book *Critical Path* took me three months to read, and I barely understood it. I finished *GRUNCH* in a few days and it was the first of his books I truly understood.

Buddhists have a word, *satori*, to describe a "cosmic" understanding. Reading *GRUNCH,* I had one of those satori understandings. I understood *GRUNCH* at a level that went beyond Fuller's words.

In *GRUNCH* Fuller describes a level of human beings that manipulate the world via money, government, international inorganizations, big corporations, the stock and bond market, and the economy for their personal agenda. In this book, Fuller describes President Ronald Regan as a "stooge," surrounded by agents of GRUNCH. GRUNCH is invisible—"hiding in plain sight"—to most of us. Some people suspect "secret societies," and other clandestine organizations. I do not have any proof of any such group, yet I do not doubt they exist. Some people suspect the U.S. Federal Reserve Bank and the entire banking system is GRUNCH. I believe GRUNCH is the puppet master and central bankers are its puppets. GRUNCH probably operates through large international organizations such as the United Nations, NATO, the Red Cross, Political Action Committees, labor unions, and the media. GRUNCH uses these "innocent" organizations as "fronts" for running its private agenda and influencing an unsuspecting society.

There is evidence that GRUNCH influences school-age children, entering schools as concerned environmentalists. This does not mean the environmental movement or the United Nations are not important. They are. Anyone who is not concerned about the environment or a world forum is nuts, in my opinion. The real issue is "hidden agendas." One definition of *integrity* is whole. It is especially important today, to be aware of hidden agendas.

Reading *GRUNCH* I could hear my rich dad mumbling, "This is why there is no financial education in our schools."

Today Venezuela, one of the richest oil countries in the world, is on the brink of collapse. How could economic collapse occur in a rich country? Venezuela imported socialist teachers from Cuba to teach their teachers.

In 2019, socialism is rising in popularity on American college campuses. Many of the hippies from the Vietnam War era grew up and became teachers. Columbia University housed the College of Marxist Studies. The 2020 Presidential Campaign is laced with socialist-communist ideals, free education, free health care, free childcare, free food, and UBI, Universal Basic Income.

Another idea on how to pay for the world of free is via MMT, Modern Money Theory. MMT is basically "helicopter money" or a "Magical Money Tree." Rather than the Federal Reserve Bank printing money and giving the money to the banks, many of socialists and the millennial generation want the Fed and the government to print money and give it directly to the people. MMT is expected be a popular campaign theme during the 2020 Presidential election. Of course, when asked how the

U.S. will pay for this world of free, the answer is "Tax the rich"—aka The Robin Hood Theory of business.

If people had a real financial education, they would know that the rich, by and large, pay little if anything in taxes. So, who will pay for the world of free stuff? We will pay for *free with our freedom*. That is the socialist-communist-fascist agenda. This is why, in my opinion, there is no financial education in our schools.

I'll quote Alexis de Tocqueville:

> *"Democracy and socialism have nothing in common but one word, equality. But notice the difference: while democracy seeks equality in liberty, socialism seeks equality in restraint and servitude."*

> *"The American Republic will endure until the day Congress discovers that it can bribe the public with the public's money."*

FAKE

In 2019, my book *FAKE* was released. The subtitle says it all*: Fake Money, Fake Teachers, Fake Assets.*

Simply put, the Universal Cash Heist of our wealth, via our money, could not occur without all three components: *fake money, fake teachers, fake assets.*

Since 1971, the year President Richard Nixon took the U.S. dollar off the gold standard, the world has been running on *fake money*.

For fake money to be accepted as real money, the world needs *fake teachers*. This is why there is no real financial education in our schools. Our teachers know very little, if anything, about money. In 1903, The General Education Board was formed. Many of its founders were infamous Robber Barons such as JP Morgan, JD Rockefeller, and others, who hijacked the education system to fulfill their needs. Their mission was to find the best and brightest minds in America, then train them to run *their* companies. Their mission was not to develop or train entrepreneurs who would compete with them, but employees who would work for them. Today, many of America's best schools are named after or founded by these Robber Barons. A few are Stanford University (Leland Stanford), Vanderbilt University (Cornelius Vanderbilt), University of Chicago (John D. Rockefeller), and Harvard (JP Morgan).

The reason millions of Baby Boomers all over the world have had their retirements stolen is because Wall Street sells the world *fake assets.* After 2008, millions of people are now aware of the toxic financially-engineered fake assets, known as MBS (Mortgage Backed Securities) CDS (Credit Default Swaps), that nearly brought down the world economy. In a few years, more people will wake up and realize their retirement and their wealth was stolen via their innocent mutual funds and ETFs,

These financially-engineered products have but one purpose: to make Wall Street bankers richer.

The Money Games

Reading GRUNCH in 1983 was disturbing. The words that disturbed me most were Fuller's words about "playing games with money." Fuller did not specify or give examples of "the games" being played... so I began looking for them.

For those who are not interested in investing in their financial education, putting money in savings, stocks, bonds, and mutual funds are better than doing nothing.

That said, one of the reasons that Wall Street gets away with selling these fake assets is because many people—those who prefer to turn their money over to financial planners rather than learn to take an active role in their investments— have been lulled into believing Efficient Market Theory: you cannot beat the markets. And that is true. Most fund managers can't either. GRUNCH controls the game and the game is rigged against "the average person" and passive investors.

In 1983, I became a student searching for the different games GRUNCH was playing on you and me via our money. There are many, many, many games. Every time I turned over a rock, I uncovered a new "game"—like a snake, slithering out and heading for cover.

Rich Dad's Lesson #1 is The rich don't work for money. I'm often asked to explain what I mean by that. *Why* don't the rich work for money? Because after 1971, the year President Nixon took the U.S. dollar off the gold standard, all money became fake money. Why work hard for fake money and pay higher and higher taxes the more fake money you earn?

Another lesson from rich dad: *Savers are losers.* Why are savers losers? Ask yourself this question: Why save money when governments and banks are printing money? Rich dad taught his son and me how to print our own money. More on that later in this book.

When *Rich Dad Poor Dad* was first released in 1997, the book drew howls of protest when I explained that *your house is not an asset.* It's a fake asset.

Pensions are in trouble because millions of people are investing in fake assets. They can't tell the difference between fake assets and real assets.

Rich dad's simple definitions of assets and liabilities are:

Assets put money in your pocket.

Liabilities take money from your pocket.

Millions of workers are in trouble because their pensions are assets for Wall Street, but liabilities for them.

One reason Kim and I were able to retire young is that we invested in our own assets, not Wall Street's financially-engineered, fake assets.

Since reading *GRUNCH* in 1983, I have been a student of how many games people can play with fake money. One day, I finally realized the number of games they can play is unlimited—as long as there is fake money, fake teachers, fake assets, and no financial education in our schools.

We often hear people talking about the gold standard. "Why don't we go back on the gold standard?" they ask.

My answer: "Then the games GRUNCH plays with money would have to stop." Why would GRUNCH want to make less money? As long as mom and pop do not know real from fake, let the games continue.

In 1987, I had living proof of GRUNCH in operation... hiding in plain sight. In 1986, Alan Greenspan, became the new chairman of the U.S. Federal Reserve Bank. Alan Greenspan is from the Austrian School of Economics. The Austrian School follows the philosophy of "sound money" and values the gold standard. When Greenspan became the Chairman of the Fed, he had to sell his soul and become a Keynesian economist. Alan Greenspan went from a hard-money economist to a fake-money economist. Oh, the price of fame and power...

John Maynard Keynes said:

"I work for a Government I despise for ends I think criminal."

Alan Greenspan said:

"In the absence of the gold standard, there is no way to protect savings from confiscation through inflation. There is no safe store of value."

The Heist

On October 19, 1987, the stock market fell a record 22%. It was clear to me that GRUNCH was the puppet master and Greenspan was the puppet. Rather than follow his values, as an Austrian economist, The Maestro, as he was affectionately called, implemented the first *Greenspan put.*

What is the Greenspan put?

A *put* is an insurance policy, a guarantee that investors will not lose money. The Greenspan put was the assurance that the Federal Reserve Bank would ride to the rescue of Wall Street and stop the markets from crashing.

What is wrong with the Greenspan put?

I saw several things that concerned me:

1. The Fed saved the rich at the expense of the poor and middle class.

2. Investors became complacent. Every time the market crashed, they would just "buy the dip." The Fed and the PPT, the Plunge Protection Team—officially known as the President's Working Committee on Markets—would print money and magically the market would recover. So why worry?

3. The dips got bigger. After 2008, the Greenspan put was followed by the Bernanke put, the Yellen put, and today the Powell put.

4. In the name of saving the economy (in reality, saving GRUNCH) the Fed, U.S. Treasury, and the "too-big-to-fail" banks destroyed the lives of the mom and pops, their kids, grandkids, and possibly even their great-grandkids... all over the world.

In 2019, the question is: Has GRUNCH put the world at the brink… on the Eve of Destruction?

Can the Fed save the market again? Will the *put* work? I doubt it. Many believe that the "Fed is out of bullets."

What will happen if the Fed cannot save the market? I see more than a few possibilities:

1: The world may enter a depression greater than the 1929 depression.

2: The world may reconvene and create a new world monetary system, possibly built around an IMF-sponsored currency known as the SDR (Special Drawing Rights.)

3: No matter what happens, the odds are that millions of the Baby-Boom generation will lose their retirement.

4: GRUNCH bailed out the rich in 2008… but will GRUNCH bail out the Baby Boomers?

5: Will Socialism take over America?

Two Types of Retirement Plans

Who Stole My Pension? is about two types of retirements.

Ted Siedle is the expert on the heist of DB, Defined Benefit pension plans.

In 1974, ERISA, Employee Retirement Income Security Act was passed. ERISA led to the DC, Defined Contribution pensions, like the 401(k) in America.

In 2002, my book *Rich Dad's Prophecy* was published and it explained how DCs, Defined Contribution Pension plans, like the 401(k), are being ripped off and doomed to fail. In *Prophecy,* I predicted GRUNCH's heist of DC pensions would be exposed around the year 2016.

Bucky Fuller's 1983 book *GRUNCH of Giants* is about the invisible world of GRUNCH. GRUNCH is becoming visible today as workers wake up to find their pensions looted… by GRUNCH and its puppets.

The looting of workers' pensions is only one game. GRUNCH has many more games still in play.

CHAPTER FOUR

When Pensions Break Their Promises to Workers

When Mark Greene, a 30-year UPS truck driver from upstate New York, contacted me in late 2016, he was on an impossible mission and time was running out. Mark was President of the Teamsters Alliance for Pension Protection, a non-profit organization with hundreds of members all of whom participated in the $1.2 billion New York State Teamsters Conference Pension and Retirement Fund. The pension he and his organization's members were counting on for their retirement security was in acute financial crisis.

His membership desperately needed an expert in pensions—a Wall Street expert not beholden to Wall Street—who could help them understand what had caused their retirement plan's collapse. The folks running the pension had spent millions—millions paid from workers' retirement savings—for bad advice from so-called experts who had run the pension into the ground. An online petition for a full forensic investigation of the pension by an independent expert had 1,388 supporters.[1]

And the New York Teamsters pensioners knew they were not alone—they were simply at the forefront of a developing national crisis, a "pension time bomb" according to *The New York Times*.[2] As many as 300 other "multi-employer" pension plans—in which employers and labor unions band together to provide retirement benefits to 1.5 million retirees and active employees—were hurtling toward collapse.

As the U.S. Chamber of Commerce noted in a 2018 report on the subject, "the sheer number and size of plans headed toward insolvency during the next decade present the system with challenges of a size and scope never before seen."[3]

---

1 https://www.change.org/p/u-s-senate-teamster-s-of-upstate-new-york-central-states-pension-crisis?utm_source=embedded_petition_view
2 https://www.nytimes.com/2018/02/18/business/multiemployer-pension-crisis.html
3 The Multiemployer Pension Plan Crisis: Businesses and Jobs At Risk.

A notice sent months earlier in 2016 to New York Teamsters pensioners explained that the plan did not have enough money to pay all the benefits that had been promised and was headed toward insolvency unless action was taken. The notice also stated that benefit suspensions, i.e. benefit cuts, "are almost certainly necessary in the near future."

As the U.S. Chamber of Commerce noted in a 2018 report on the subject, "the sheer number and size of plans headed toward insolvency during the next decade present the system with challenges of a size and scope never before seen."

Cutting benefits to "save" the pension was the plan.

With a funded percentage of 45.8 percent and liabilities exceeding its assets by approximately $1.7 billion, the Fund was projected to become insolvent and require financial assistance from Pension Benefit Guaranty Corporation (PBGC), the federal agency that backstops corporate pensions, by 2027.

How could this have happened to a pension that was nearly fully funded in 1999?

Until 2015, the Board of Trustees of the pension had assured participants that their pension was secure. A summer 2013 and fall 2014 Fund Newsletters stated the following in response to the question "whether there will be sufficient money to pay pension benefits that have been earned and promised": *The simple answer remains: Yes!"*

The pension's overseers seemed unconcerned that the pension was running out of money. Through March 2014, the Trustees, investment advisors, counsel, and actuaries continued to incur annual travel expenses for January and March four-day meetings held in Florida because, according to the Executive Administrator of the pension, "It is too difficult to have meetings at this time in Syracuse due to snow."

Only after the U.S. Department of Labor investigated and concluded the travel expenses were improper for a plan in crisis was the Florida travel curtailed—to a single week-long meeting a year outside of the Syracuse area.

None of this flagrant waste and poor judgment was particularly startling to me. Over the course of my career I've witnessed countless pension boards squander workers' retirement savings on travel and entertainment, most notably to attend lavish conferences held from beaches in Hawaii to golf courses in Scotland, lounging at high-end hotels such as Caesars Palace, Hotel Frontenac, Four Seasons, and Trump Tower, often underwritten by Wall Street money managers looking to get hired by pensions.[4] Luxurious boondoggling by pension overseers has always been highly controversial.[5]

But usually pension overseers are savvy enough to realize that, at a minimum, *the optics* of taking money from a pension that's near collapse to bask in the Florida sun while workers are toiling through a harsh winter are terrible.

Perhaps not surprisingly, the Teamsters pension overseers were not interested in an investigation into the causes of the impending insolvency of the $1.2 billion fund, fearing they might be found culpable. PBGC and the DOL (Department of Labor) didn't want any forensic examination either, for reasons we'll get to in a moment.

Those 34,000 New York Teamsters truckers who had driven decades to earn pension benefits were supposed to accept—without explanation—that their annual payments would be cut 30%-50%. Their retirement plans would have to be dramatically downsized.

Was I willing to forensically investigate the failing pension when no one else would? Could I identify potential wrongdoing and make credible recommendations for further action to the U.S. Department of Treasury which was currently reviewing the pension?

I'd been down this road before—twice.

---

4 For a particularly egregious example of overseer travel related to a struggling local government pension, take a look at my 2015 forensic investigation of the Jacksonville, Florida Police and Fire Pension. https://www.forbes.com/sites/edwardsiedle/2015/10/27/long-awaited-forensic-investigation-of-city-of-jacksonville-police-and-fire-pension-fund/#218633f81e6a

5 So controversial are these Wall Street funded pension conferences that the website for the 2013 National Conference on Public Employee Retirement Systems, an association of publicly-funded pensions, held on the famed beaches of Waikiki, supplied board members hoping to shore up support for their expenses-paid trip a "2013 Attendance Justification Tool Kit."

WHO STOLE MY PENSION?

August 21, 2019

The Honorable Chuck Grassley
Chairman of the Committee on Finance
United States Senate Office Building
Washington DC 20510-1501

Dear Senator Grassley,

My name is Paul Ollivett, I'm a former 30-year employee at United Parcel Service (UPS), and currently a retiree (since 2009) covered under The New York State Teamsters Conference Pension & Retirement Fund.

On October 1. of 2017 my world and life changed dramatically. That is the day my wife and I lost approximately 30 percent of our income. That was the last day we had the ability to pay all our bills. That was the day our credit scores began the spiral down from the mid 700's to the low 500's.

Benefit cuts made by the trustees of our plan on Oct 1st, 2017, carried out under the Multiemployer Pension Reform Act of (MPRA), signaled the beginning of harassing phone calls and letters from the bank and soon to follow the collection agency. I immediately reached out to the bank when the cut happened and after filling out 18 pages of forms and questions the answer the bank came up with was to lower our monthly payment by 200 dollars, Obviously, that would not help. So, in order to continue paying all of our other bills we stopped paying the mortgage. So now the worry of not knowing how much longer we have in our home began.

I worked at UPS, a Fortune 500 company that continues to post record profits, for thirty years knowing that a good retirement plan was waiting for me. I had a woodworking shop in our basement, was an avid hunter and target shooter with a 400-yard gun range on the five-and one-half acres we owned. Everything associated with the woodworking, hunting and shooting is gone. The house we raised our three children in and the spare rooms for when they came to visit so we could see our grandchildren is gone. In our current apartment the space is limited. The free time I use to have is now filled because I took a job 30 hours a week at a grocery store deli for minimum wage, so now our ability to visit them in South Carolina is curtailed. Pictures and facetime just are not the same as a real hug.

My wife is a teaching assistant and was planning on retiring at the end of the 2020 school year after twenty years of service, but now that is in doubt. The process of selling our home in a short sale manner was also very stressful. The house was listed for 15 months and during that time we had several offers to buy, but the bank now holding the mortgage refused them. It's not easy having your real estate agent call saying "we have an offer ", and then two weeks later calls back saying the bank refused it. Also process servers at the door 8:30 at night are no fun either, to which leads us to gather together all the paperwork that is needed at the foreclosure hearing, another file that's half an inch thick.

In closing Senator Grassley, I say that I worked very hard for 30 years for my pension. A pension that was promised from day one, a pension that drove me forward as a package delivery driver on 100-degree summer days and bone chilling winter evenings. We struggled and sacrificed so our three kids could have a better life than we did, don't all parents want that?

Having approximately thirty percent of your income taken from you is not right and definitely hurts. We pensioners paid into our plans for all our working careers, planned our lives to enjoy retirement and now it's not happening. Please Sir help us get back what was taken from us.

Sincerely,

Paul and Susan Ollivett

Hungry Dogs

When I was 16 years old, rich dad's son Mike called and asked if I could come to their hotel and restaurant. "At this hour?" I asked. "It's nearly midnight."

"Yes, it's important," said Mike.

I had to wake up my mom and dad who asked similar questions. "Tomorrow is a school day," my mom said with concern in her voice. "What are you and Mike up to?" asked my dad. He knew 16-year-old boys were not up to much good after midnight.

"Mike said his father needs our help. His employees are taking a vote to form a union," I explained. "If they do, they walk out at midnight. And if they do walk out, Mike's dad wants us to take their places."

With their approval, I went to the hotel and waited as the votes were being counted. The union lost by only five votes, and there was no midnight walkout. I hung around for a while listening to rich dad address his key staff, discussing what they had learned, and thanking them for standing by him.

Needless to say, I learned a lot that night. I was gaining real-life experience about employer-employee relationships; experience I would use later in my life as an entrepreneur with employees of my own.

The next day, my poor dad, wanted to know what the "midnight emergency" was all about. My dad was disturbed when I told him about the employees' vote to form a union, and the possible midnight walk out.

"You would have filled in, if an employee had walked out?" asked my poor dad.

"Yes, I would have," I replied sheepishly. I could tell by my father's tone of voice that he did not like what I had witnessed.

"You would have been a scab," my dad said.

"A scab? What's a scab?" I asked.

"Someone who works despite an on-going strike," said my dad with a smirk.

"Why would I be a scab?" I asked.

"Don't you work for Mike's dad?"

"Yes, I do," I replied. "But I don't get paid. I am an apprentice, an intern, learning about business."

"You still crossed the line," my dad replied in a low tone of voice. "That makes you a scab."

It was only then I realized that my dad had been a union member. Before becoming Superintendent of Education, he had been the leader of the local teachers' union when he was a young teacher. It took a while, but memories came flowing back, memories of the teachers' union meetings held at our home. I distinctly remember not liking the vibes I got from the "delegates." I remembered that the union meetings I had overheard were not about improving education for students, but about more money, less work, and more power for the teachers and their union.

Rather than challenge or question my dad, I just let him refer to me as a scab. I learned a new word at 16.

A few days later, I was working in rich dad's office, after school, doing odd jobs in exchange for real-life entrepreneurial education. Rich dad emerged from his office and motioned for his son and me in to come into his office for a meeting. He then called in Bobby, a desk clerk at his hotel, to join our meeting.

Bobby, a young man in his thirties, walked in silently. Taking a seat, he said, "I guess you're going to fire me, aren't you?"

"I've thought about it," rich dad told him. "You're the organizer, aren't you? The leader of the employees… aren't you?"

"Well, I am not the leader of the employees. Joe in maintenance is," Bobby said. "But I did bring the employees together to vote to form a union."

"And you would have walked out, and shut me down?" asked rich dad, "If you had won?"

"I guess I'm fired," said Bobby. "I understand."

"Hell, no. I'm not going to fire you, Bobby," said rich dad as he smiled at his employee. "But now I can see that you're more than just a punk kid. I had never seen you as a leader… until now."

Rich Dad continued, "From now on you are going to be my employee relations manager. If you accept, you will receive a promotion and raise in pay. Your job is to keep my workers happy and be their representative to me." Then he asked: "Do you accept?"

"What about Joe?" asked Bobby.

"Joe is fine," said rich dad, smiling again. "He, too, is a good leader, but he is not a great communicator between the employees and me. He only brings grievances, but not much two-way communication. He only listens to the complainers. And he will be retiring in two years. I'll make sure he's happy." His words to Bobby: "Treat Joe with respect, let him keep his power, and I will create a new position, title, and job description for you. If you accept, I will make a company-wide announcement next week."

A wide smile crossed Bobby's face as he stood, shook rich dad's hand, smiled at Mike and me, and left the room a very happy man.

Turning to Mike and me rich dad said, "Learn something boys?"

Both of us were stunned. We had expected a lot of yelling and screaming, blame, and acrimony. Instead, rich dad had turned a bad situation into a great situation. The profits from his business and the profit-sharing for his employees soared.

There are words of age-old wisdom that were part of this lesson for me:

"Money follows management."

The opposite of the same coin is also true:

"Money disappears when there is mismanagement."

Speaking of mismanagement, this is a powerful statement from Ted from his section of this chapter:

"None of this flagrant waste and poor judgment was particularly startling to me. Over the course of my career I've witnessed countless pension boards squander workers' retirement savings on travel and entertainment, most notably to attend lavish conferences from beaches in Hawaii to golf courses in Scotland, lounging at high-end hotels such as Caesars Palace, Hotel Frontenac, Four Seasons, and Trump Tower, often underwritten by Wall Street money managers looking to get business from pensions. Luxurious boondoggling by pension overseers has always been highly controversial." [Emphasis added]

Betrayal After Trust

A therapist friend of mine says, "One of the most devasting blows to a person's spirit is betrayal after trust.'" In marriage, it is a spouse having an affair. In business, it's a trusted employee stealing money. Betrayal after trust often leaves a scar on a person's soul.

Repeating these words from Ted's section of this chapter:

> "Perhaps not surprisingly, the pension overseers were not interested in an investigation into the causes of the impending insolvency of the $1.2 billion fund, fearing they might be found culpable. PBGC and the DOL (Department of Labor) didn't want any forensic examination either, for reasons we'll get to in a moment."

If pensions cannot trust their own leaders, Wall Street, the PBGC (the Pension Benefit Guarantee Corporation), or the DOL who can they trust?

Who was the pension money stolen from? Who will pay the price for betrayal after trust? Whose souls will be scarred? As Ted states:

> "Those 34,000 New York Teamster truckers who had driven decades to earn pension benefits were supposed to accept—without explanation—that their annual payments would be cut 30%-50%. Their retirement plans would have to be dramatically downsized."

Fake Money Management

GRUNCH requires all three "fakes" to do its job: fake money, fake teachers, and fake assets. They are powerful tools.

As Ted states:

> *"None of this flagrant waste and poor judgment was particularly startling to me."*

Rich dad would say:

"Never let a hungry dog guard your smoke house."

Pensions are giant smoke houses, guarded by hungry dogs on the inside, outside, and on the government's side.

The same is true for DC pension plans such as 401(k)s. One reason why Kim and I were able to retire young is that we did not have DB or DC pension plans with hungry dogs guarding them.

In his next chapter, Ted describes in excruciating detail how ravenously hungry the dogs are.

CHAPTER FIVE

Why Governments Do Not Want
Pension Failures Investigated

In 2005, a federal bankruptcy judge ruled that United Airlines could default on its pension obligations and turn over control of its pension funds to PBGC. The judge approved the airline management's request to terminate four pension plans—for pilots, flight attendants, mechanics, and other ground service workers. United insisted that it could not emerge from bankruptcy protection with its pension plans in place, i.e. if it was forced to keep its promises to workers. The $9.8 billion pension plan default was the largest in U.S. history.

United Airlines workers asked me to get involved and at the request of Representatives George Miller, a California Democrat, and Edward J. Markey, a Democrat from Massachusetts, I met with the Executive Director and senior staff of PBGC.

I made the PBGC an offer it couldn't refuse—or so I thought.

I offered to conduct forensic reviews for the agency of failed pensions for which it had assumed responsibility. These reviews would focus upon conflicts of interest, hidden and excessive fees, and wrongdoing involving Wall Street firms that had provided investment services to failed pensions. The cost? I indicated that I would undertake these forensic investigations "for free," i.e. on a contingency basis.

Absent a recovery for pensions from the looters, there would be no cost to the agency—I would not get paid a cent.

I explained to PBGC staff that a review of failed pensions was merited for several reasons. First, uncovering wrongdoing would improve the morality of the marketplace, as pension advisers learned they would be held accountable if they contributed to the demise of a retirement plan. Also, these investigations would aid regulators and law enforcement in recovering money from, as well as punishing, the wrongdoers. Finally, fiscal responsibility demanded that prior to a federal bailout a review be undertaken of the causes of the loss.

In the meeting, PBGC staff acknowledged that while the agency had become responsible for nearly 3,500 failed plans since 1974, it had never undertaken *a single* forensic investigation, had no internal capacity to do so, and did not even have access to, or custody of, relevant plan documents necessary for a review.

PBGC couldn't do a forensic investigation if it wanted to and—senior executives admitted—the agency DID NOT WANT TO!

A free forensic investigation of every failed pension by the nation's leading expert, billions potentially recovered from Wall Street wrongdoers and returned to pensioners, fiscal responsibility at a federal agency that was supposed to be self-financing but already has a $34 billion deficit—surely the agency would run, not walk, to accept my proposal!

PBGC rejected my offer claiming—remarkably—that the agency "could not afford the expense." This response was, of course, preposterous. There was *no expense*.

Why couldn't PBGC "afford" free forensic audits? The answer was simple.

While PBGC publicly states its mission is to ensure that corporations sponsoring defined benefit pensions are prepared to honor their obligations to workers, its private agenda is to assist corporations in abandoning their pension obligations. The U.S. government's belief is that if American corporations are to compete globally in the future, they must be freed from promises they made to their employees over the past 60 years or so. Unfortunately, several generations of America workers must be stripped of their retirement security if this effort to boost corporate profitability is to be successful.

Furthermore, the past 60 years of prosperity enjoyed by American corporations would not have been possible without the hard work of millions who are relying upon these pensions.

Forensic audits of failed pensions will not expedite the wholesale abandonment of America's defined benefit pensions. Uncovering malfeasance, assigning blame, and recovering from looters is a dirty job and takes time—but will save pensions.

Based upon my decades of experience I can assure you that investigations, more often than not, will uncover mismanagement and wrongdoing by corporate sponsors and firms providing services to faltering pensions.

This rampant looting of workers' pensions is a "can of worms" PBGC cannot afford to open. It will delay pension dumping.

Unfortunately, no one wanted forensic investigations of United Airlines' four failed pensions badly enough to make it happen in 2005. United's 134,000 workers and retirees were forced to accept drastic benefit cuts without explanation. No one has ever been held responsible for their ruined retirements.

Six years later, in 2011, I was retained by the US Airways Pilots Association (USAPA) to conduct a forensic investigation of the US Airways Pilots' Pension Plan.

This review represented the first-ever comprehensive investigation undertaken of any of the thousands of terminated pensions (including mega-plans such as United Airlines, Delphi, Delta Air Lines, Bethlehem Steel, and Delphi) trusteed by PBGC. Never before had a terminated pension trusteed by PBGC been thoroughly examined for potential abuses.

Note: PBGC did not hire me—the pilot's union hired me to do what PBGC was supposed, but was unwilling, to do.

At that time, USAPA represented more than 5,000 active US Airways pilots who had participated in the pension until 2003 when a bankruptcy court found that the plan was underfunded, terminated it, and appointed PBGC as the terminated pension's statutory trustee.

Pilots' pensions were slashed dramatically—up to 50 percent—when the federal agency took over and, eight years later, the pilots were still tenaciously searching for answers.

Remarkably, PBGC officials told the pilots that the agency had no obligation under ERISA and other federal law to investigate potential pension wrongdoing—unless someone provided "sufficient information to determine the basis for allegations that earlier misconduct has occurred."

The agency would not investigate potential wrongdoing, it said, unless the pilots could prove *actual wrongdoing*. How's that for a Catch 22?

The pilots weren't backing down. In September of 2009, USAPA filed a lawsuit against PBGC demanding that the agency investigate allegations of apparent wrongdoing related to the failed pilots' pension plan.

My 2011 forensic investigation of the bankrupt US Airways pilot's pension revealed profound omissions, errors, conflicts of interest, hidden and excessive fees, and potential violations of law regarding dozens of firms that provided key services to the plan, such as audit, actuarial, custodial, investment consulting, foreign exchange, securities trading, and money management.[1]

There was *ample evidence* that the failure of the US Airways Pilots' Pension Plan was due to mismanagement and wrongdoing, not lack of funding.

PBGC may not have wanted a forensic investigation that uncovered the truth about the causes of pension failures but—like it or not—it got one funded by USAPA.

Thanks to PBGC's continued unwillingness to investigate wrongdoing, firms that kill, as opposed to merely injure, pensions need not worry about ever being held accountable.

The records will be buried along with the pension and there will be no autopsy.

---

1   https://www.forbes.com/sites/edwardsiedle/2012/12/03/us-airways-pilots-investigate-pbgc-trusteed-pension/#7e8f0d1474d1

Pilots and Pensions

I graduated from Kings Point, the U.S. Merchant Marine Academy, in 1969. Most of my classmates were joining the MM&P, the Masters, Mates & Pilots union. After my experience with my rich dad employees' attempt to unionize and my poor dad's teachers' union meetings, I chose to sail for a non-union company, which was Standard Oil of California's tanker operations. Sailing non-union meant a cut in pay. While many of my classmates were earning over $120,000 a year carrying war materials to Vietnam, I was earning $47,000 a year, which was still pretty good for a 22-year-old in the late 1960s.

Today, many of my classmates who joined unions like the MM&P are out of work because their wages got too high and many U.S. shipping companies have gone out of business.

Today, most of the ships in U.S. ports, ships such as the giant cruise liners, are not U.S. ships. They sail under foreign flags with foreign officers and crew.

In 1974, once again, I was faced with the option of joining a union. I was leaving the Marine Corps and was faced with the prospect of joining a union… this time as an airline pilot. Many of my fellow Marine Corps pilots got jobs flying for the major airlines and did join the pilots' unions.

One friend got a job flying for Trans World Airways, which went out of business, and today that friend teaches flying in St. Louis, Missouri. Another flew for Braniff and another for Eastern Airlines, before they too went out business. I have lost touch with those friends.

My roommate flew for Northwest Airlines, did very well flying as a Captain before retiring. He also attained the rank of Lt. General, (three stars) in the Marine Corps Reserves, before retiring. Today he is a U.S. Congressman (R) from Michigan.

Two other friends were hired by United Airlines. They felt very blessed—until they lost their pensions via a program known as an ESOP, Employee Stock Option Plan.

The April 17, 2017 issue of *Forbes* magazine, reflected on United Airlines' ESOP failure:

"United's employee stock ownership plan, or ESOP, began in 1995 with a grand bargain. The airline's pilots and machinists gave up nearly $5 billion in prospective wages and benefits. In return they got 55% of the company's shares. That year, the stock outperformed the S&P 500 index by 67%. Shareholder value increased by more than $4 billion.

"Some of the outstanding performance could be traced to a new attitude among employees. Grievances fell 74%, sick time 17%. 'Everyone from gate agents to mechanics gained new authority to address customer complaints without consulting their supervisors,' the *Chicago Tribune* reported in a comprehensive retrospective published in 2003.

"But the ESOP was born amidst conflict. The flight attendants' union never supported it, saying that its members couldn't afford the wage givebacks. Factions in the other two unions also opposed it, as did many in the executive suites. After a brief first-year honeymoon period, management did virtually nothing to help employees understand the business of which they were now owners, or to encourage a culture of ownership. A newly installed chief HR officer declared that he was 'not enthusiastic' about the whole idea.

"Unsurprisingly, the company soon reverted to the toxic us-against-them labor environment that had plagued it for years. The struggle culminated in a ferocious slowdown staged by United's pilots in the summer of 2000. They taxied at a crawl. They refused to work overtime. On-time performance, which hit 81% during the first ESOP year, dropped to 40%. Passenger traffic fell off a cliff. The pilots as a group still owned some 25 percent of the airline, but never mind: as one reporter wrote, 'they were sabotaging their own company.' The tragedies of September 11, 2001 drove the nails into United's coffin: the company filed for bankruptcy in 2002, wiping out the value of the equity and ending the ESOP. Though United has recently been profitable, it has never overcome its reputation as the worst of the legacy airlines, to be avoided by passengers whenever possible."

Bye-Bye Pensions

As reported in *The New York Times* on May 11, 2005:

"United Airlines, which is operating in bankruptcy protection, received court permission yesterday to terminate its four employee pension plans, setting off the largest pension default in the three decades that the government has guaranteed pensions.

"The ruling by Judge Eugene R. Wedoff of Federal Bankruptcy Court came after a lengthy hearing in a crowded Chicago courtroom, near where United is based.

"Despite pleas by union lawyers, Judge Wedoff sided with United, which had insisted that it could not emerge from bankruptcy protection with its pension plans in place.

"The ruling releases United, a unit of the UAL Corporation, from $3.2 billion in pension obligations over the next five years. The federal agency that guarantees pensions, the Pension Benefit Guaranty Corporation, will assume responsibility for the plans, which cover about 134,000 people."

That is one way of getting employees to work for less and get rid of their pensions.

Whenever I get together with my fellow pilots who flew for United, most are not happy about their decision to leave the Marine Corps.

Flying the Unfriendly Skies

April 9, 2017, Dr. David Dao, a Vietnamese-American passenger aboard United Express Flight 3411 was forcibly removed from the plane when he refused to give up his seat for United Airlines employees on an over-booked flight. He refused to give up his seat because he was a doctor and needed to attend to a patient in need. The United Employees did not care and the horrific video of Dr. David Dao's forcible removal from the flight went viral.

According to ABC News, the doctor suffered a concussion, a broken nose, and had two teeth knocked out. It is reported, but not verified, that Dr. Dao settled for $140 million.

One sure way to make employees unhappy is asking them to take a cut in pay and then stealing their retirement.

As Ted states:

> *"None of this flagrant waste and poor judgment was particularly startling to me."*

And as Ted explained, the reason the PBGC did not want his free investigation is because the real purpose of the PBGC, the Pension Benefit Guarantee Corporation, is to eliminate DB, defined benefit, company-funded pensions. The government is not on the side of the workers.

As I've stated a few times already, when Nixon took the U.S. dollar off the gold standard, it became fake money. In 1974, ERISA, Employee Retirement Income Security Act, was passed and employees went from DB pension plans to DC plans.

Eliminating employee pensions has made many corporations more profitable. As Ted points out, even the PBGC and the DOL so-called benevolent worker advocate organizations are complicit in GRUNCH's cash heist. That is why they, the PBGC and DOL, turned down Ted's offer for a free investigation. GRUNCH's infiltration runs deep.

Every Dead Pension Deserves an Autopsy

When a pension collapses and the retirement benefits promised to thousands, or even hundreds of thousands, of workers are slashed or eliminated, a postmortem examination to discover the cause of death should be demanded. Lives have been traumatized—retirement dreams shattered.

When a pension dies, experts who opined over its lifetime that it never would, have some explaining to do.

Every pension death I've witnessed employed multiple costly experts responsible for monitoring the deceased's "vital signs" i.e. soundness of the plan, including the calculation of future liabilities and assumed rates of return, allocation of assets, selection of investment managers, and investment advisory fees paid.

The judgments of these so-called experts are rightfully called into question by the unexpected death. To the extent they may have contributed to the demise of the plan, they should be held accountable.

Pensions don't just implode overnight. There are always warning signs or "red flags" that have been disregarded for decades. Why?

Pension deaths are almost always foreseeable. Likewise, pension deaths are almost always preventable. If not foreseen and prevented, someone was not doing his or her job. However, autopsies almost never follow pension deaths. Indeed, the possibility of a forensic investigation into the causes of a pension death is rarely even discussed. The scope of such an investigation, as well as probable minimal cost, is rarely researched.

Generally, all parties responsible—including the PBGC—agree there is no need to investigate the causes.

Wall Street firms charging excessive fees for managing pension assets, conflicted investment consultants recommending reckless asset allocations, money managers

> *Pension deaths are almost always foreseeable. Likewise, pension deaths are almost always preventable.*
>
> *If not foreseen and prevented, someone was not doing his or her job. However, autopsies almost never follow pension deaths.*

paying gatekeepers to be recommended, brokers charging inflated commissions to execute trades, and custodian banks, actuaries, and corrupt pension boards—all view an inquiry into potential wrongdoing as ill-advised, even dangerous.

Thankfully, in the case of the New York Teamsters pension, members of the Teamsters Alliance for Pension Protection successfully pooled their small donations to fund a forensic investigation of their dying billion-plus pension. My report entitled, *Trifecta of Imprudence: Forensic Investigation of "Critical and Declining" New York State Teamsters Pension Fund*, was released to the public and submitted to the Treasury Department on December 21, 2016.[1]

Pulitzer Prize-winning financial investigative journalist Gretchen Morgenson of *The New York Times* observed in her article, *New York's Teamsters May Have Their Pensions Cut. What Went Wrong?* that learning what went wrong at the pension could be instructive not only for other imperiled retirement funds but also for taxpayers who may have to cover the shortfalls.

Mark Greene of the Teamsters Alliance for Pension Protection was quoted as saying the investigation was a first step in understanding what went wrong at the pension.

"The plan has a terminal illness... Was it the result of natural causes or was it self-inflicted? Let's look at the role Wall Street played. That's why we're doing a forensic study."[2]

A key finding of the report was that a massive $767 million gamble on high-cost, high-risk, illiquid and opaque "alternative" investments—a losing wager that had already cost $400 million-plus in investment underperformance and $500 million in excessive fees—was inappropriate for a struggling pension that was only 45 percent funded, in critical status, and poised to suspend benefits to workers dependent upon the Fund for their retirement security.

In other words, the New York State Teamsters Conference Pension and Retirement Fund pension did not have to collapse—gross mismanagement caused the crisis.

As detailed in the report, (a) opacity; (b) fees and expenses; and (c) illiquidity, conflicts of interest, and related risks all *dramatically*

---

1 https://www.forbes.com/sites/edwardsiedle/2017/01/03/trifecta-of-imprudence-forensic-investigation-of-critical-and-declining-new-york-teamsters-pension/#6ed7701faa30
2 https://www.nytimes.com/2016/12/30/business/01gret-morgenson-pensions-teamsters.html

increased as the Fund's financial condition worsened—all contrary to prudent fiduciary practice.

Such a *trifecta of imprudence* is all too common among failing pensions, I noted. (We'll talk more about this later when I explain "gross malpractice generally practiced" in the management of pensions.)

The bottom line is if you are a participant in a pension that is ill, dying, or dead—and the benefits you will receive in your decades of retirement have been, or may be, cut—you deserve an explanation.

A Second Opinion

Under no circumstances should you rely upon the explanations and opinions of so-called experts hired (unfortunately, with your money) by the folks managing your fund—the very culprits who may have caused or contributed to its demise. While these "defense" experts are supposed to be acting solely in your best interest, they aren't.

They are not your friends.

At the outset, a deep-dive forensic investigation by an independent expert—an expert of your own—will be required. However, as discussed later, the cost of such a review is minimal when paid through crowdfunding.

Is it worth the cost of a dinner out—say $100—to learn why your pension benefits have been cut hundreds or thousands of dollars a month for the rest of your life?

Depending upon the results of your independent expert investigation, it may be possible to recover money for the pension and its participants through negotiation or litigation. But you and your co-workers would be fools to negotiate or litigate before you knew who stole how much from the pension. A common mistake made with respect to government pensions is that legislation to "fix" pensions is generally crafted, debated, and approved without any investigation into what caused the crisis.

The corollary to my earlier stated rule that **every pension deserves an autopsy** is, when fixing pension in crisis:

1. Investigate, before you
2. Negotiate,
3. Litigate, or
4. Legislate.

Worst case, an investigation by an expert of your own will give you the satisfaction of knowing what went wrong and who, if anyone, is to blame.

Best case, you may recover money from the looters and save the pension.

Thieves with College Degrees

In 1996, when we launched our *CASHFLOW* board game, it was not due to "popular demand." We created, patented, and produced our financial education game because we had a hard time explaining how we were able to retire young—without jobs, pensions, or government support.

We did our first test of the game in Las Vegas with a group of real estate investors and a second test in Singapore, with a group of young adults who were learning to become entrepreneurs.

Both tests were successful. Participants loved the game, and we could almost *see* the lightbulbs flipping on in their brains. The *CASHFLOW* game worked in America and in Singapore. The participants understood how Kim and I retired in 10 years. Our next challenge was how to bring the game to market.

On April 8, 1997, my 50th birthday, we self-published *Rich Dad Poor Dad* and the Rich Dad Company was founded. As you might imagine, it was a great birthday party. We could not have imagined at the time what the next two decades would hold.

Rich Dad Poor Dad was originally written as a brochure, with the intent of educating the reader on the purpose of the game. But it grew into a business dedicated to helping teach financial education to people around the globe.

A Few Words about Experts...

Kim and I were able to retire on passive income from our real estate investments. With the success of *Rich Dad Poor Dad*, the *CASHFLOW* game, and seminars, our income was increasing, along with the complexity of the business. We were advised that we should consider stepping it up... and hire a higher level of accounting firm.

On a Tuesday morning, Kim and I entered the local offices of a national and well-regarded accounting firm. They were expensive and came highly recommended. Rather than one accountant, there was now a team of "expert" accountants, all graduates of top-tier universities. My ego was flattered just having these A students from great schools focused on our little business.

The meeting started off well with the usual pleasantries and the "getting to know each other" progressed. Finally, we got down to the business at hand: the "What we can do for you" part of the presentation. At that point, the "expert" from Washington DC entered the meeting room. He looked the part in his blue Brooks Brothers blazer, button down shirt, striped tie, khaki slacks, and flashy alligator loafers.

Smiling confidently at Kim and me, the Washington DC expert started his presentation by saying: "I have reviewed your financial status and have the following recommendations…"

In a confident and authoritative tone, the preppy accountant said, "I recommend that you sell all your real estate investments and invest in a well-diversified portfolio of stocks, bonds, mutual funds, and ETFs."

Needless to say, I burst out laughing.

The accountants (and a few attorneys) around the conference table were not laughing.

"You're kidding me, right?" I asked. "Who put you up to this?" I was sure it was a practical joke. But no one was laughing.

It took me a moment to realize this was not a joke. These experts were serious.

Surely, I told myself, they had read my book *Rich Dad Poor Dad* before the meeting.

Surely, they knew that in the book I wrote about Ray Kroc, the founder of McDonald's, formula for investing.

Surely, they understood what Ray Kroc meant when he said, "McDonald's is not a hamburger company. McDonald's is a real estate company."

And *surely*, they knew that Kim and I used debt for leverage and that we paid zero in taxes, in large part because we followed the McDonald's formula of business.

It took Kim and me a while to realize that while these accountants and attorneys were really smart, highly-educated experts from great schools, they knew very little about the real world of business, entrepreneurship, and "insider" investing—much less about debt and taxes. They were school smart, text-book smart, and corporate smart... but not smart outside their tiny expert world.

This is the perfect spot to repeat Ted's comments on "experts" on pensions:

"Every pension death I've witnessed involved multiple experts responsible for monitoring the deceased's 'vital signs' i.e. soundness of the plan, including the calculation of future liabilities and assumed rates of return, allocation of assets, and fees paid to investment managers.

"The judgments of these so-called experts are rightfully called into question by the unexpected death. To the extent they may have contributed to the demise of the plan, they should be held accountable.

"Pensions don't just implode overnight. There are always warning signs or 'red flags' that have been disregarded for decades. Why?

"Pension deaths are almost always foreseeable. Likewise, pension deaths are almost always preventable. If not foreseen and prevented, then someone was not doing their job."

Kim and I managed to get through that meeting and were reminded, yet again, that what we've done to build assets, create wealth, and become financially free was not taught to students—even at the very best schools.

Later that week, I realized my poor dad, an academic and a teachers' union executive, would have loved the expert's presentation. Their offices were plush, each expert was a graduate of big-name school, many of them Ivy League, and each had an alphabet-soup after their names... Masters of something, Doctorate of this, and PhD of that.

Poor dad would have swallowed the presentation, hook, line, and sinker.

If not for the education from my rich dad, Kim and I might have been robbed blind by "experts."

When I returned from Vietnam, it was my poor dad who recommended I go back to school to get advanced degrees.

Rich dad suggested I find seminars taught by real teachers. One night while I was watching TV, an infomercial came on promoting a free seminar on how to invest in real estate with "nothing down." I took the bait, showed up at the free seminar, paid the $385 for the 3-day course, and changed the future of my life. If not for that seminar, Kim and I would never have been able to retire in 10 years and we might have been sucked into the Washington DC expert's recommendation—that we sell everything that had made us rich and, more importantly, financially free.

It took a little bit of research to find out why the "expert" recommended we sell all our real estate. It was so obvious I could not see it. The reason he recommended we sell our real estate is simply because he does not make any money from real estate. He would only have made money if Kim and I purchased "fake assets"—stocks, bonds, mutual funds, and ETFs.

Conflicts of Interest

I remember a discussion I had with rich dad many years ago. Our discussion was on the subject of conflicts of interest. My question was, "Why are there conflicts of interest?"

Rich dad's answer: "If there was no interest... there would be no conflict."

As Ted states in Chapter 8, many professionals are really in the business of "malpractice." Interestingly, the word *mal* in French means *ill*.

Life Lesson
Beware of highly-educated experts who want you to believe they are smarter than you are. Just because someone is a graduate of a great school or a well-educated professional such as a lawyer, doctor, accountant, stockbroker, financial planner, or real estate broker does not mean they know anything about money.

CHAPTER SEVEN

Simple Truths: Understanding Pensions

I have spent virtually a lifetime studying pensions and with every new forensic investigation I undertake, I learn more. Pensions are extraordinarily complex and understandably most people are intimidated when the subject arises.

You don't want to spend your life learning about pensions and we don't want you to. The goal of this book is to teach all you need to know to protect your retirement security.

Fortunately, the fundamentals of pensions are easy to understand.

There are three components to the health of a pension:

1. **Money In:** How much money goes into the pension "pot" (contributions)
2. **Money Invested:** How the money in the pot is managed or invested over, say, a worker's 30 years of employment
3. **Money Out:** How much money is paid out of the pot (benefits)

COMPONENTS OF PENSION HEALTH

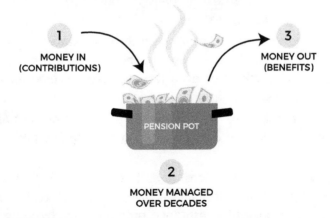

If any one of the above three drivers of pension health is amiss, then the pension may falter or fail.

Likewise, simply put, there are three ways to fix a failing pension.

1. Put more money in the pot
2. Invest the money in the pot better
3. Pay less out of the pot

Why Putting More Money In the Pot Usually Won't Work

When pensions are running out of money, or have already collapsed, there is often debate about whether enough money was put into the pot annually over the prior decades and whether to put more money in the pot immediately to fix the problem.

In other words, people assume the cause of the pension crisis is that not enough money went into the pot.

That makes some sense because often, over the decades, money that was *supposed* to be put into the pot to pay for retirement benefits, wasn't. The country, corporation, state, county, or city failed—for one reason or another—to make the annual required contributions.

So workers or retirees who participate in an imperiled pension have a legitimate complaint where the record indicates required contributions to the pension were not made.

On the other hand, while not putting money in the pot can lead to pension shortfalls, in my experience it is never the sole, or even primary, cause of a collapse.

Pouring more money into a grossly mismanaged pension—a leaky pot—will not result in a healthy pension, only ever-greater amounts squandered, i.e. swelling leakage.

Further, chances are the country, corporation, state, county, or city that chose not to put more money into the pot when the pension was healthy—alive and kicking—is even *less inclined* to come up with the cash when the pension is gasping near-death.

Rather than put more money into the pot, thousands of American private corporations have chosen to dump their failing pensions onto the PBGC.

Who pays when corporations dump their pensions? PBGC claims it receives no funds from American taxpayers. Supposedly, the agency's operations are financed by insurance premiums set by Congress and paid by sponsors of defined benefit plans, investment income, and, for the Single-Employer Program, assets from pension plans trusteed by

PBGC and recoveries from the companies formerly responsible for the plans.

However, since the PBGC has a projected deficit of $30 billion in 2019, the notion that the agency is self-financing is laughable.

Truth be known, U.S. taxpayers pay the price when private corporations dump their pensions. That's precisely why corporations would rather *dump than pump* money into their failing pensions.

Putting more money into the pot when it comes to failing government pensions rarely works for two reasons. First, since most taxpayers today generally lack adequate retirement savings of their own, the last thing they'll vote for is to put more of their money into failing government workers' pensions. Some call it "pension envy."

Second, in light of "pension envy," it's political suicide to campaign for greater taxpayer contributions to shore up government pensions.

So, take the more money "fix" to the pension crisis off the table.

Why Cutting Benefits to Workers Rarely Works

The money paid out to workers is also commonly focused upon when pensions falter because many critics believe pensioners receive lavish benefits that should be cut.

To be sure, there are sickening examples of government workers who have received outrageous pensions.

These abuses should be addressed.

For example, according to *Forbes*:

> No one has hit the pension jackpot quite like the sworn officers of the California Highway Patrol (CHP). Of the 1,066 six-figure retirees, their average pension is $10,192 per month or $122,304 annually. On top of that, there are the 6,350 active employees at CHP averaging $115,000 in pay with taxpayers chipping in another $48,300 in pension contributions. Therefore, each officer costs $163,000 in pay and pension costs alone.
>
> Meanwhile, Riverside County has 461 six-figure retirees and the top 12 retirements each exceed $200,000 per year. Last year, the assistant sheriff made $653,025 by cashing in banks of unused benefits, i.e. leave.[1]

1 https://www.forbes.com/sites/adamandrzejewski/2016/11/26/mapping-the-100000-california-public-employee-pensions-at-calpers-costing-taxpayers-3-0b/#1ada34be3945

But, cases of lavish pensions for government workers are rare, in my experience.

For example, the American Federation of State, County, and Municipal Employees, America's largest trade union of public employees which represents 1.3 million public sector employees and retirees including healthcare workers, corrections officers, sanitation workers, police officers, firefighters, and childcare providers, states that public pensions are "modest." AFSCME notes that its average member "receives a pension of approximately $19,000 per year after a career of public service." The average pension paid to a retiree from the public sector in the United Kingdom is significantly less, approximately $6,800.

Even if you believe government workers' benefits should be cut, this approach is rarely feasible.

For example, in the United States, state constitutions generally provide that "promises" made by the state must be kept. So, take cutting benefits that have been promised to state and local workers off the table as an easy way to "fix" underfunded government pensions.

If benefits are cut, public sector workers will sue and there will be years of difficult litigation.

To be sure, as mentioned earlier, with respect to private pensions in America—thanks to an essentially bankrupt federal agency funded by unsuspecting taxpayers—some corporations can claim or manufacture financial distress to cut benefits to workers when they dump their pensions. But even for these corporations, the preferable course would be to avoid financial distress and worker wrath through prudent management of their pensions.

The Best Plan Is Better Management of Money in the Pot

That leaves us the primary focus of this book—the least understood and least discussed cause of, and fix to, the pension crisis: *mismanagement of the investments.*

In every forensic investigation of a dead or dying pension I've undertaken, I have concluded:

> Had the money in the pot been prudently managed, the pension would not have failed.

That is, enough money had been put into the pot to pay out all the benefits promised—had the money been managed properly.

Likewise, in every case I've witnessed where a so-called pension "fix" or "reform" has been undertaken, mismanagement of the investments was neglected and, not surprising, the "fix" flopped. That is, within a few years the pension was no better off than pre-fix. (So-called "reform" of the Rhode Island state pension in 2011 is a prime example of savings generated from slashing workers' benefits, subsequently squandered through speculative hedge fund investing.)

In every forensic investigation of a dead or dying pension I've undertaken, I have concluded:

Had the money in the pot been prudently managed, the pension would not have failed.

That is, enough money had been put into the pot to pay out all the benefits promised—had the money been managed properly.

Management of pension investments globally today can most aptly be described as "gross malpractice generally practiced." Let me tell you about when I first heard this phrase from a leading expert in an altogether different field—medicine.

Boomers: From Boom to Bust

In 2019, *The New York Times* published a small magazine which I purchased from an airport news stand. The special publication was to commemorate the 50 years since the Summer of '69.

SUMMER OF '69

When Everything Happened. And Everything Changed.

"It was the summer of moral uprising and chilling crimes, a summer when music gathered a counterculture and a human left his footprint on the moon.

"The extraordinary events of 1969 defined an era that sill echoes today."

I'm taking the liberty to paraphrase a few highlights reported by *The New York Times*:

Woodstock: From August 15 to 17, 1969, 400,000 rock 'n' lovers descended on Max Yasgur's muddy farm. Woodstock marked the coming of age of the baby-boom generation and was a defining moment for the counter-culture generation.

Black Power: The civil rights movement of the early 1960s evolved into the Black Power movement, with the Black Panthers demonstrating outside a New York City courthouse on April 11, 1969.

Gay Pride: Hundreds of young men went on a rampage in Greenwich Village after plain clothes police officers raided bars known for homosexual clientele. On June 28, 1969, the "the Stonewall Inn" became the flash point of today's LBGT movement. On July 27, 1969, a month after the Stonewall uprising, about 200 people participated in New York City's first gay pride march.

Air Power: In June of 1969, at the Paris Air Show, the world lined up to see the Boeing 747. At 231 feet, the 747 was nearly twice as long as the Wright Brother's first flight and could carry 362 passengers. The 747 ushered in the "international age" and made air travel accessible and more affordable.

Man on the Moon: On July 20, 1969, astronaut Neil Armstrong radioed back to earth, "The Eagle has landed."

Movies: Hollywood reflected the tremors rippling across America in the movies of 1969. A few classics are *Easy Rider, Portnoy's Complaint, The Godfather,* and *Midnight Cowboy.*

Mass Murderer: At the same time, Vietnamese were being killed in Vietnam, cult leader Charles Manson and his gang were killing Hollywood elite. On August 9, 1969 Roman Polanski's wife Sharon Tate was found murdered by Manson's family.

Vietnam War: Thousands of young men were being drafted to fight a war that, in my opinion, we should not have been fighting. On June 8, 1969, President Richard Nixon announced the United States would pull out 25,000 troops within 30 days. A total of approximately 56,000 American servicemen and women and 3 million Vietnamese men, women, and children were killed.

The year 1969, the year when everything happened... and everything changed.

Invisible Changes

Only a few saw the biggest changes yet to come.

While the world was watching Woodstock, the first man on the moon, the Manson family, *Easy Rider*, the Black Panthers, and the first Gay Pride marches, GRUNCH was busy... changing the future of money in ways the Baby Boomers did not see coming.

The Baby-Boom generation will be known as the "transition generation," the last generation of the *Industrial Age* and the first generation of the *Information Age*. In 1989, the year the Berlin Wall came down, the World Wide Web went up, as the Industrial Age ended and Information Age began. The world was changed forever.

Most people could not see the changes GRUNCH was bringing to the world. The invisible changes GRUNCH initiated are the reason the Baby-Boom generation (those born between 1946 and 1964) will be known as the *boom and bust* generation.

GRUNCH Change #1:

1971: PRESIDENT RICHARD NIXON TAKES THE DOLLAR OFF THE GOLD STANDARD.

In 1971, the U.S. dollar became "fake money." Rather than backed by gold, the U.S. dollar became debt, an IOU from the U.S. taxpayer.

In 1971, those who *worked for fake money*, and those who *saved fake money* became losers.

In 1971, boomers who learned to use *debt as money* became winners.

In 1972, I flew behind enemy lines looking for gold. That story is the opening chapter in my last book, FAKE and why, in *Rich Dad Poor Dad,* rich dad's lesson #1 is "The rich don't work for (FAKE) money."

Rich Dad "Savers Become Losers"

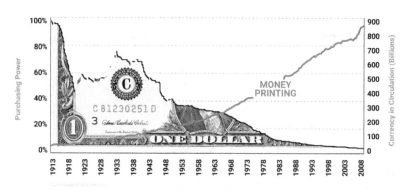

GRUNCH Change #2:

1972: PRESIDENT RICHARD NIXON OPENS DOORS TO CHINA

High-paying jobs begin leaving America. American corporations and investors get richer, American workers become poorer.

In 1974, now that it was legal for Americans to visit China, I traveled to Hong Kong and crossed the border into China to see China before China changed.

Standing on the border, looking at the people on the Hong Kong side, the citizens were "white" and "plump" and lived in tall, modern high rises and many were driving Mercedes.

On the Chinese, side the people were dark and thin, almost emaciated, many living in mud and straw houses, most riding bicycles.

In 1974, the China I saw was a third-world nation. That China no longer exists.

In 1974, the Chinese dragon was tiny and cute. Today, the tiny poor dragon has grown into a rich, armed-and-dangerous dragon. It is obvious the China of today plans on ruling the world.

Boomers are the transition generation, the generation between the Industrial Age and the Information Age. Boomers are also the GAP Generation, the generation where the rich became extremely rich while the poor and middle class grew poorer.

The chart below tells the story growing gap between the haves and have nots.

THE GAP
AFTER INFLATION AND TAXES

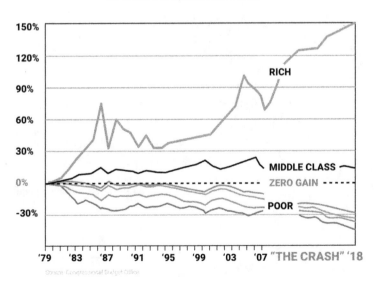

Many Boomers do not believe their children and grandchildren will do as well financially as they did. Today, our education system continues to teach students to look for high-paying jobs, rather than be entrepreneurs who will *create* high-paying jobs.

What did school teach Boomers about money? Little if anything. And today our schools still do not have legitimate financial education.

GRUNCH Change #3:

1974: EMPLOYEES LOSE PAYCHECKS FOR LIFE

> In 1974, ERISA—Employee Retirement Income Security Act— is passed. Defined Benefit (DB) pension plans convert to Defined Contribution (DC) plans. Workers begin losing a guaranteed paycheck for life and a secure retirement.
>
> Today, most DB pension plans are underfunded and many have gone bust.
>
> Today, most Boomers with DC pension plans live in fear of running out of money in retirement. This is why many Boomers are delaying retirement.
>
> And today, Social Security is going broke.

SO-SO SECURITY

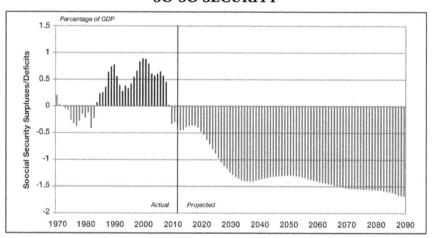

The Boom Turns to Bust

These three changes by GRUNCH set the stage for the biggest financial boom in history. The story of that boom is best told in the chart of the Dow Jones Industrial Average pictured below.

1971 – THE BIGGEST BOOM IN HISTORY BEGINS

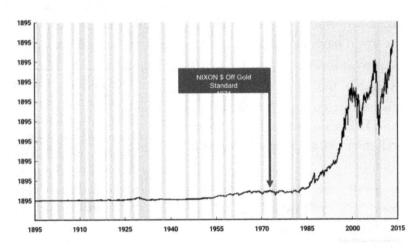

The Bust Begins in 1987

Here's a chronology…

GRUNCH 1987:

The Maestro Changes His Tune

In 1971, GRUNCH began printing "fake money."
In 1987, GRUNCH started producing "fake assets."
You cannot create "fake assets" without "fake money."

October 19, 1987 has become known as Black Monday. The Dow lost 22.6 percent of its value, or $500 billion dollars. Rather than let the stock market correct naturally, newly-elected Fed Chairman Alan Green initiated the "Greenspan put."

Up until then, the "Maestro" was an Austrian Economist. Some say that on October 19, 1987 GRUNCH started pulling the strings and nudged Greenspan to change his economic beliefs.

In 1987, GRUNCH, with the help of the Maestro, began producing "fake assets."

In 2019, my book *FAKE* explained why today most assets that mom and pop invest in are "fake assets." Fake assets make the rich richer, but mom and pop poorer.

Ted does an excellent job explaining in excruciating detail how these fake assets—toxic assets—produced by Wall Street and exported to the world have been a death knell for pensions around the world.

In 1997, I was in Thailand, a first-hand witness to the Asian Financial crisis. It was not pretty, and I watched the crisis spread from Thailand to Singapore and then on to South Korea and the Philippines.

In 1998, the financial crisis spread from Asia to Russia. The collapse of the Russian ruble crushed Greenwich, Connecticut hedge fund Long-Term Capital Management, LTCM. LTCM was founded by infamous John Meriwether.

> Ted does an excellent job explaining in excruciating detail, how these fake assets—toxic assets—produced by Wall Street and exported to the world have been a death knell for pensions around the world.

On LTCM's board were 1997 Nobel Prize recipients in Economic Sciences, Myron Scholes and Robert Merton, who were recognized for their "new method to determine the value of derivatives," aka "fake assets"—and what Warren Buffett calls "financial weapons of mass destruction."

The Maestro, Alan Greenspan, stepped in to bail out a hedge fund. The first of many, non-bank bailouts.

GRUNCH 1999:

U.S. Banks Become Casinos for the Rich and Powerful

In 1933, the Glass-Steagall Act was passed. Glass-Steagall separated "mom and pop" savings banks from investment banks.

In 1999, President Clinton, Larry Summers, and Robert Rubin repealed the Glass-Stegall Act. Mom and pop saving banks become investment banks.

The U.S. banks became hedge funds, casinos for the rich and powerful.

The rich and powerful kept their winnings, even when they lost.

And it's mom and pop who ended up covering the losses.

GRUNCH 2000:

Dot-coms Become Dot Bombs

In 2000, the world was preparing for the Y2K—the millennium bug.

Ravens… Birds of Prophecy
In 2020, corporate counsel to the founder of LTCM, James Rickards—who went on from LTCM to work with the Defense Department on currency warfare and then the CIA on investments as weapons—and I will be co-authoring our book *The Ravens*, a book on financial prophecies.

The *millennium* bug did not bring the world down, but Pets.com did.

People were betting billions on anything with dot-com after its name.

The dotcom bust should have died a natural death, as did Pets.com.

But not one to let a great crash go to waste, the Maestro Mr. Greenspan used the dot-com crash as an excuse to keep the printing presses running and dropping interest rates.

The Maestro's party in the casino roared on. At the same time his free money low-interest-rate policies were killing the pensions of the middle class and driving the poor deeper into poverty.

What are the PhDs at the Fed really up to? That's a great question. There are those who believe this crisis was just an honest mistake. Others believe that they were intentionally setting up the world for the biggest crash and cash heist in world history.

Is it a conspiracy? Some say yes. Others see it as just a normal economic cycle.

And as we all know, there are those among us who say: "What are you talking about? I have a job. I'm doing just fine. Leave me alone."

In 1969, though the magic of television, the world could see the first humans walking on the moon. They could not see the Gross Universal Cash Heist going on in plain sight.

The Boomers will see the heist when they start asking, "Who stole my pension?"

CHAPTER EIGHT

Your Pension Is Being Mismanaged: Gross Malpractice Generally Practiced

Dr. John Sarno, who recently died in his nineties, was the most brilliant doctor I ever met.

He cured hundreds of thousands of sufferers of chronic pain that the medical community had misdiagnosed and was unable to relieve. His groundbreaking life's work focusing upon the "mind-body connection" put him millennia ahead of the medical establishment. His second book, *Healing Back Pain: The Mind-Body Connection*, a New York Times bestseller, is an easy read for anyone willing to entertain his uniquely effective approach.

I first met Dr. Sarno in 1993. I was in my early thirties, single, living in New York City and the owner of an investment firm on Wall Street that traded tens of millions of dollars in stocks daily. My professional life was going great. A few years after graduating from law school and working as a regulatory attorney with the U.S. Securities and Exchange Commission, I had secured the corporate funding I needed to pursue my entrepreneurial dreams. The three-piece, pinstriped suits I used to wear "working for the man" had given way to blue jeans and cowboy boots. The good news was I was now the boss; the bad news was my employees and investors were depending upon me to keep this boat afloat.

Like many of the traders on Wall Street, I was suffering from severe and inexplicable lower-back pain. The doctors and chiropractors I saw provided me with all sorts of implausible explanations for the pain—years of jogging, my swiveling high-back executive desk chair, or how I cradled the telephone were all to blame. The back is very delicate, I was told, and had to be treated gingerly. The slightest wrong movement could cause frightening damage. Imagine living with a back made of fragile glass.

Every day at lunchtime I would hobble a few blocks to the chiropractor's office to undergo electrical stimulation of my lower back muscles (which was supposed to aid relaxation). It seemed the more "treatments" I got, the worse I felt. I was spiraling downhill, growing increasingly debilitated.

A friend recommended I read Dr. Sarno's book *Healing Back Pain* which was already a bestseller. My back pain scared me to death, as did the prospect of giving up physical exercise—which my conventional doctors suggested.

Sarno's message was that in the overwhelming majority of cases, back pain is a symptom created by the unconscious mind as a distraction to aid in the repression of strong unconscious emotional issues. The hopeful message I took from his book was that there was nothing structurally wrong with my back and that I should resume normal activity as soon as possible.

Since he and I were both in New York, I wanted to learn more by meeting with him in person, if I could. I imagined that as the leading expert in his field and best-selling author, getting an appointment with him would be difficult. To the contrary, his secretary said he could see me immediately. In brief, he examined me, confirmed that there was nothing wrong with my back, and explained his "mind-body" theory to me. I attended one or two of his group lectures and the pain went away—completely. There was and is to this day (30 years later) nothing wrong with my back. I have jogged 30 miles a week for 40 years.

From time to time I experience other pains which can be frightening but turn out to be transient and benign. When they arise, I know my unconscious mind is telling me to pay attention to something important. I turn to Sarno's book for answers.

Sarno believed that most people are incapable of accepting the notion that the cause of their pain is not a structural abnormality or an injury, rather their unconscious minds at work. Radical, costly, and ineffectual procedures recommended by the medical establishment, such as fusing of the vertebrae of the spine, are, remarkably, preferred by the majority of patients over an approach that requires the patient to examine his unconscious rage.

It always puzzled me that a doctor who produced dramatic beneficial results for his patients at little or no cost could be considered *controversial* whereas practitioners of costly, ineffectual so-called mainstream medicine, such as back surgeries, are somehow regarded as more *legitimate*.

When I asked him, Dr. Sarno's blunt explanation was that "gross malpractice, generally practiced" was the medical community's standard response to pain symptoms.

Gross malpractice was the rule and "best" practice was rarely administered.

Like Dr. Sarno, I am an, or even the leading, expert in my field of pension forensics.

Like Dr. Sarno, based upon 35-plus years of experience, I have concluded that "gross malpractice generally practiced" pervades pension management as well.

If you are depending upon a pension for your retirement security, you need to fully understand what "gross malpractice, generally practiced" means.

It means that the people responsible for overseeing your pension—who, without your consent, have been entrusted with your retirement savings— are utterly lacking relevant financial experience. They either don't know or don't care about what's best for your pension.

Worse still, they have hired well-known Wall Street firms—household names—who are grossly mismanaging your money. You should presume that these firms are solely interested in profiting from your pension.

If you are depending upon a pension for your retirement security, you need to fully understand what "gross malpractice, generally practiced" means.

It means that the people responsible for overseeing your pension—who, without your consent, have been entrusted with your retirement savings—are utterly lacking relevant financial experience. They either don't know or don't care about what's best for your pension.

Finally, I am not alone in concluding that gross mismanagement is a widespread problem globally.

For example, in Australia, the $2 trillion pension industry is under pressure to improve its performance after a series of government reviews found persistently underperforming funds, excessive fees, and zombie accounts.

The Australian Prudential Regulation Authority recently warned the nation's worst performing pensions that they need to improve or shut down. Some 15 plans had issues with net cash flow or growth that jeopardized their future survival, 28 funds were found to be charging excessive fees, and nine had net returns significantly below a reference portfolio of passive, low-cost, and liquid investments.[1]

Looting pensions is general practice.

Wall Street looting has already, or will, cause your pension to falter, i.e. underperform or fail—unless you do something about it.

---

1 https://www.apra.gov.au/mysuper-product-heatmap

Central Planning vs. Central Banking

In 1972, I was in the Marine Corps and flying in Vietnam furthering the U.S. agenda to kill communists. One day, I came face to face with "the enemy." The problem was that it was a little boy, probably 10 or 12 years old. As we all know, in this age of terrorist warfare, men, women, and children can be our enemies... and many do not wear uniforms.

We were a flight of three aircraft, two gunships, and one VIP aircraft. We landed in a remote field, waiting for our VIP, a Marine General, to complete his meeting for an upcoming battle.

A group of young boys appeared and began climbing in and out of the aircraft. My fear was that they might plant satchel charges in our parked helicopters. The boys were not responding to my demands they get out the aircraft, so I grabbed one of the boys, doing my best to get him out from the pilot's cockpit. He put up a fight as I dragged him out of the aircraft. He tried to get away, biting and kicking me as our struggle escalated, turning more violent. For a kid, he was very strong. Unable to control him, I lost my temper and decided it was time to shoot him. In my mind he was now the enemy, a communist we were there to kill. I pulled my pistol from my shoulder holster and pointed it at him.

The problem was that once he realized I was prepared to kill him, he started to cry. I then made the mistake of looking him in the eye... after which I could not shoot him. He was just a little boy.

As he cried, begging for his life, I could hear my mom's voice pleading, "Stop. Please stop." I paused, becoming human being again. My mother's voice continued, pleading. "I did not give you life to take another mother's child." My mom had passed away about two years earlier, and I understood what she was saying. She had always been concerned about the mean streak in me, and often pleaded with me to be kinder to others.

Deciding to think before doing something I might regret all my life, I put down the hammer of my pistol. He and his friends had a soccer ball, so I holstered my pistol and kicked the ball around... like boys do, trying to diffuse the situation.

I knew that young boy was the enemy. I knew that he saw our VIP passenger, a one-star Marine general, board the aircraft. As soon as he saw the general, he and his friends disappeared. We came under intense enemy fire as soon as we lifted off. Fortunately, all three aircraft made it back to the carrier without casualties.

A few days later, I woke up in the middle of the night—realizing what I had almost done. Commit murder. I also realized that I did not really know what a communist was. I had studied economics at the academy but not the differences between capitalism, socialism, fascism, and communism. I realized I was in Vietnam, brainwashed to believe that Americans were good and communists were evil. Brainwashed into labeling people "communist" and blinded by patriotism, we had been trained to kill our fellow human beings.

Patriotism: A Family Tradition

On December 7, 1941, the Japanese bombed Pearl Harbor. President Franklin D. Roosevelt declared December 7, 1941 "a date which will live in infamy."

In 1942 the U.S. government arrested and transported Japanese-Americans in the United States to concentration camps. Many of my relatives who lived in California were in this group. My aunts and uncles told me they were forcibly moved, with little notice, and had limits placed on what they could take with them. Their private property, farms, businesses, and homes were seized and sold at great financial loss to them.

In 1945, my relatives were released and given $25 and a train ticket home. They were never reimbursed for the confiscation of their wealth.

When I asked my dad why the Japanese-Americans in Hawaii were not put in concentration camps, he simply said, "There are too many Japanese in Hawaii."

Most Japanese-Americans were embarrassed and shamed by the attack on Pearl Harbor. To prove their loyalty to America, thousands of my parents' generation, from all over the United States, volunteered to fight, forming the 442nd Infantry Battalion, an all Japanese-American Battalion that went on to become the highest decorated combat unit in the European theater.

In total, I had five uncles who served in World War II. All returned alive, one severely wounded. One uncle fought against the Japanese. After he was captured, he was accused of being a spy and severely tortured. He finally escaped and spent the rest of the war hiding in the jungle of the

Philippines. He was not found until after the war in the Pacific was over. His problems began after he surrendered to American soldiers. He had to prove he was American, or risk being put into another POW camp. Another uncle was part of the occupation army, stationed in Japan.

My father's youngest brother, who was fluent in Chinese, served as an American Air Force officer, translating Chinese transmissions, during the Korean war.

Years later, I found myself in Vietnam as a result of blind unquestioning patriotism… until I woke up. Vietnam was not World War II. We all knew why we fought World War II. I did not know why we were in Vietnam… and I realized that I did not know what a communist was.

I began to study communism, while on a carrier in the South China Sea.

What Is a Communist?

The first thing I wanted to understand was what a **communist government** was. The definition I found most useful was: *"A government operating around **Central Planning.** "*

What is a **capitalist government**? Again, there are many definitions. One I found interesting was:

> *"A government operating around **Central Banking.** "*

Is there much of a difference between *Communist Central Planning* and *Capitalist Central Banking?*

No, not really.

GRUNCH is not communist or capitalist, Republican or Democrat, Liberal or Conservative. GRUNCH is not about politics. GRUNCH is about control.

As Mayer M. Rothshild said:

> *"Give me control of a nation's money and I care not who makes the laws."*

Rothschild (1744 -1812), godfather of the Rothschild Banking Cartel of Europe, had five sons and they went about controlling the world via central banks. Today, almost every country in the world has a central bank.

In 1815, Mayer's son Nathan Mayer made the following statement:

"I care not what puppet is placed upon the throne of England to rule the Empire on which the sun never sets. The man who controls Britain's money supply controls the British Empire, and I control the British money supply."

An interesting sidebar, in my opinion, are the words of Guttle Schnapper, the wife of Mayer Amschel, in 1849:

"If my sons did not want wars, there would be none."

Central Banks of the World

The first central bank in the world was the Bank of England, founded in 1694. King William and Queen Mary were at war with France. War is expensive. To pay for the war, the first central bank was founded, by bankers, to lend money to England to fight the war. King William and Queen Mary, the first shareholders in this new type of bank, explained that the bank was founded "to promote the public Good and Benefit of our People."

The U.S. Federal Reserve Bank is not U.S. and it is not Federal; it has no reserves, and it is not a bank. The Fed is a banking cartel. Not all members of the Fed cartel are American.

In 1983, Bucky Fuller didn't name names in his book GRUNCH. I had to do my own digging. My research, prior to Google and search engines, led to the Rothschild Banking Dynasty, the Morgans, and the Rockefellers.

There have been three central banks in America. The first two central banks were: The First Bank of the United States (1791-1811) and the Second Bank of the United States (1816-1836).

In **1816** – Rothschilds secured license to begin a central bank called the **Second bank** in America. They now controlled the money supply in America.

In **1832** – President Andrew Jackson ran for presidency with the slogan "Jackson and no bank"—a campaign against the Rothschilds banking dynasty. A year later he started removing the government deposits from the second bank. In retaliation, the

Rothschilds started contracting the money supply in America. This caused a depression.

Controversy swirled around the first two central banks and controversy continues to surround central banks today.

The third Central Bank—the infamous "Fed"—had to be formed secretly at a meeting on Jekyll Island. In November 1910, six men—Nelson Aldrich, A. Piatt Andrew, Henry Davison, Arthur Shelton, Frank Vanderlip, and Paul Warburg—met at the Jekyll Island Club.

Due to past controversy about central banks, this powerful group of men had to meet in secrecy, pretending to be duck hunters who did not know each other. Rather than name the new bank the Third Bank of the United States, the six leaders decided to give is third bank a more prestigious name. This is what they came up with: The Federal Reserve Bank of the United States.

Today, the Federal Reserve is the central bank for the United States. Its decisions affect the U.S. economy, and therefore the world. This position makes it the most powerful force in the global economy. It is not a company or a government agency. Its leader is not an elected official. This makes it seem highly suspicious to many people because it is not subject to either voters or shareholders.

What do central banks do? In simplest terms, they create money out of nothing. They create "fake money" and loan it to governments. Taxpayers pay the central bank for this fake money, via taxes paid to the government treasuries. Taxpayers cannot pay taxes in gold, silver, bitcoin, or chickens… only "fake money." Taxes are one of the primary methods via which GRUNCH controls the people of a country with a central bank.

I've wondered why there has been so much controversy around Central Banks. It's because Central Banks control a nation's money supply and determine the quantity of money in circulation by buying and selling debt. Hence, they have more power than governments and the people. That is why the three Rothschilds' statements I quoted earlier in this chapter are so prescient.

And that is why I say there is little difference between *communist central planning* and *capitalist central banking*. Central banks look capitalist on the surface but have their roots in communist literature. And that is why I say there is little difference between *communist central planning* and *capitalist central banking*. Central banks look capitalist on the surface but have their roots in communist literature.

Advocates of centrally planned economies believe central authorities and economic planning is consistent with socialist and communist systems. Capitalism is a market-driven economy in which market forces shape society and life. Socialism is characterized by state ownership of businesses and services. Central planning is used to attempt to make society more equitable.

The Fed is nothing but a puppet show. Which is why I do not get worked up every time the Fed makes announcements, aka Fedspeak. To keep my sanity, I remind myself that Fedspeak is really "Puppet-speak."

The Creation of the Creature

Today's Federal Reserve Bank was created on December 23, 1913, by President Woodrow Wilson, America's first President with a PhD. From the official date of its creation, the bank was shrouded in controversy. The December 23rd date meant many Congressmen and Senators had already left Washington for the Christmas holidays, and, hence, did not vote for the Fed.

G. Edward Griffin, a documentary film maker with a genius for deep research wrote a classic—*The Creature from Jekyll Island*—in 1994 and that book filled in many of the blanks that I was left with after reading Fuller's 1983 book, *GRUNCH of Giants*.

I read *GRUNCH* in 1983 and The *Creature from Jekyll Island* 13 years later in 1996.

As I read Griffin's book, more pieces of the puzzle of "Who is GRUNCH?" fell into place.

Reading and studying *The Creature from Jekyll Island* made my blood boil and my skin crawl. I wanted to cry. Ed Griffin is a genius at deep-dive research. It was easy to see why there has always been wars and controversy surrounding central banks.

In *The Creature from Jekyll Island*, Griffin boldly states that the purpose of the "Creature" is Marxist communism. He writes, "the spirit of the American people is too strong. Before Marxist communism can take over Americans, the American spirit must be broke. The way to break the American spirit is to make Americans poor."

These words ring true for me, which is why today's gap between the rich and everyone else is troubling and dangerous. Once Americans are poor, their capitalist spirit can be broken, opening the door for socialism and communism.

People often ask me what I think the ultimate objective is. I prefer you come to your own conclusions. The possible answers are too hot, too diabolical, too controversial.

The Red Pill

G. Edward Griffin has become a trusted friend. As I said, his genius is deep research. Whenever I need to find the "truth," he is my trusted source, my "deep throat." Ed puts on an annual event, The Red Pill Expo, for those who are seekers of the truth.

For those who are fans of the movie *The Matrix* starring Keanu Reeves, the blue pill is for those who prefer life in "Alice's Wonder-in-La-La-land." The red pill is for those who choose to see what is real—and Ed Griffin's Red Pill Expo delivers. If you want your blood to boil and skin to crawl as your eyes are opened, the Red Pill Expo is for you.

Ed Griffin and I have talked at length about this, his view on how to break the American spirit. The more I take the "red pill" the more I can understand what he is saying. By stealing the American spirit via the dollar, the more desperate Americans will become... more accepting of, first, socialism and then communism.

Bucky Fuller's book *GRUNCH* does not name names, save for calling President Ronald Reagan a "stooge" for surrounding himself with advisors like Casper Weinberger and a few others.

Many believe Reagan was a fiscal conservative. Yet, the facts are that Reagan spent fortunes building conventional weapons which were used in the first Gulf War.

GRUNCH and The Creature love wars and weapons, which is why President Dwight D. Eisenhower warned of the "military-industrial complex" taking control of American foreign policy.

Reading *Creature* and *GRUNCH*, I understood why I was in Vietnam, a war that made no sense. The bottom line is that wars are profitable. Wars are about control.

Naming Names

The great thing about *The Creature from Jekyll Island* is that Ed Griffin names names, including Neil Bush, son and brother of two Bush Presidents. Ed often refers to The Council of Foreign Relations, which today, is often in the news as a respected authority on the global economy. According to Ed Griffin, the Council of Foreign Relations is a close relation of the Creature and GRUNCH.

Although the original six who met at the Jekyll Island Club have passed away, their progeny live on. An example is Nelson Rockefeller, a former Vice President of the United States and descendent of John D. Rockefeller, one of the richest men in history. Nelson Rockefeller was named after Nelson Aldridge, one of the six at the Jekyll Island secret meeting.

Paul Warburg, also one of the six at Jekyll Island, was born in Germany to a powerful Jewish banking dynasty, M.M. Warburg & Co, established in 1798, still among the oldest investment banks in the world.

Bailouts: The Name of the Game

In his book, G. Edward Griffin, succinctly explains why bailouts are not accidents. Bailouts are the name of the game. "Bailouts" have been the objective of the Fed since that meeting at Jekyll Island. Bailouts are one of the ways that the Creature and GRUNCH steal our wealth.

In the 1989, it was Neil Bush whose Silverado Savings and Loan was "bailed out."

In 2008, Hank Paulson, as Secretary of the Treasury, insisted on establishing TARP, Troubled Assets Relief Project. TARP was a bailout.

Paulson was a former CEO of Goldman Sachs, the multinational investment bank with more alumni as heads of central banks than any other. Paulson made sure his friends at "too-big-to-fail banks," were bailed out and paid bonuses, via QE–quantitative easing… another name for "bail out."

Remember, "bailouts are the name of the game." Bailouts are but one of the ways, GRUNCH and The Creature steal our wealth. If Quantitative Easing, QE, continues and more fake—fiat—money is printed (coupled with ZIRP, Zero Interest Rate Policy) the world economy will move closer to the brink of collapse and wipe out the middle class and the poor. And the house of cards? It comes crashing down.

Will the next wave of big bailouts be pensions? I think so. Once again, bailing out pensions protects the "too big to fail" banks who get rich selling fake, toxic assets to the world. When the pensions go bust, the big banks will once again be bailed out in the name of saving pensioners' retirements.

It is estimated that the U.S. pension bailouts could be between $7 to $14 trillion.

For a little perspective, the 1989 Savings and Loan bailout was only $124 billion. The 2008 TARP bailout, signed into law by Neil Bush's brother, President George W. Bush, started out at $700 billion and went up from there, going as far as to bail out European banks. To this date, no one really knows how much the 2008 bailout has cost.

The most important fact is that not one banker has been prosecuted for the crime, for the cash heist. These same bankers were paid billions of dollars in bonuses... while billions of people paid the ultimate price—losing jobs, homes, savings, retirements, and the security of their financial future.

Wheelbarrow Money vs. Helicopter Money

Looking at history, that is how fascist dictators such as Hitler' rose in power and, with him, the rise of the Nazi Party, the National Socialist German Workers' Party.

Hitler came to power following the collapse of the German Reichsmark, which led to hyperinflation. Hyperinflation

Q: What is "Wheelbarrow Money?"
Hitler came to power due to "wheelbarrow money." As the story goes, a person went to a store to buy some food, leaving his wheelbarrow—filled with money—outside. When he returned, someone had stolen his wheelbarrow but left the money. There are dozens of photos from that time of people using the worthless Reichmarks to fuel furnaces.

led to "Wheelbarrow Money." And "Wheelbarrow money" brought Hitler to power.

After 2008, "Helicopter Money" made Fed Chairman Ben Bernanke infamous.

Both "wheelbarrow money" and "helicopter money" are terms synonymous with bailout, and quantitative easing and TARP. More ways that GRUNCH has its hand in our pockets…

Take a minute to review the two charts below. Do you see a pattern?

History Repeats: Germany 1918-1923

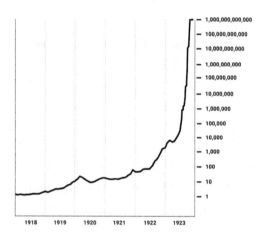

Fed Printing Money

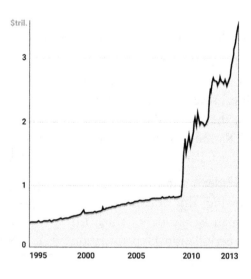

We Were Warned

We should have seen this coming.

President Thomas Jefferson (1801-1809) is quoted as saying:

> *"I believe that banking institutions are more dangerous to our liberties than standing armies. Already they have raised up a monied aristocracy that has set the government at defiance. The issuing power (of money) should be taken away from the banks and restored to the people to whom it properly belongs."*

President Andrew Jackson (1829-1837) had this to say:

> *"Controlling our currency, receiving our public monies, and holding thousands of our citizens in dependence, it would be more formidable and dangerous than a naval and military power of the enemy."*

> *"It is to be regretted that the rich and powerful too often bend the acts of government to their selfish purposes."*

> *"You are a den of vipers and thieves. I have determined to rout you out, and by the Eternal [ringing down his fist on the table] I will rout you out.*

And in the words of President Abraham Lincoln (1861-1865):

> *"I have two great enemies, the Southern Army in front of me and the bankers in the rear. Of the two, the one at my rear is my greatest foe."*

A few more contemporary thoughts... including these from Congressman Ron Paul Republican Presidential Candidate and Republican Congressional representative for Texas from 1997 to 2012. He is also author of *End the Fed.*

> *"It is no coincidence that the century of total war coincided with the century of central banking.*

> *"First reason is, it's not authorized in the Constitution, it's an illegal institution. The second reason, it's an immoral institution, because we have delivered to a secretive body the privilege of creating money out of thin air; if you or I did it, we'd be called counterfeiters, so why have we legalized counterfeiting? But the economic reasons are overwhelming: the Federal Reserve is the creature that destroys value."*

Are We Becoming Socialists?

Today we have new words for Wheelbarrow Money and Helicopter Money. Popular politicians are supporting Socialist economics such as:

MMT: Modern Money Theory
MMT: Magical Money Tree
UBI: Universal Basic Income
Free College Education
Free Healthcare

A few of these politicians are:

Senator Bernie Sanders
Senator Elizabeth Warren
Representative Alexandria Ocasio-Cortez

I know I quote Alexis de Tocqueville (1805-1859) often and am compelled to include his words of warning, yet again, here:

> "Americans are so enamored of equality that they would rather be equal in slavery than unequal in freedom."

More Words of Warning

Words that confirm that we, indeed, have been warned…

> "Democracy and socialism have nothing in common but one word, equality. But notice the difference: while democracy seeks equality in liberty, socialism seeks equality in restraint and servitude."

> "The American Republic will endure until the day Congress discovers that it can bribe the public with the public's money."

In concluding this chapter, I think back to that young Vietnamese boy I nearly killed. I doubt that he was a communist. It's possible that, much like me, he was just a young man blinded by patriotism.

My concern is that, as the global pension crisis worsens, more and more people will turn to socialist and communist ideals—and politicians who embrace them—for salvation.

If and when this happens, GRUNCH and The Creature from Jekyll Island will rule the world. Their ultimate dream of a One World Government and One World Order could prevail.

CHAPTER NINE

The People Overseeing Your Pension Lack Investment Experience

In the United States, the combined value of pension plan assets held by state and local governments in 2018 was over $4 trillion. These pensions are overseen by boards of trustees comprised of lay men and women who generally lack *any* knowledge or expertise in investment matters. There are a few state and local laws which require one or more board members of public pensions to possess some financial experience but such requirements are extremely rare.

Typically, public pension boards include some individuals, such as active or retired teachers, cops, firefighters, and sanitation workers, who are supposed to (and, in my experience, rarely do) represent the interests of workers and pensioners. Other board members are appointed by politicians, such as governors and mayors, who are supposed to (and, in my experience, rarely do) represent the interests of voters, aka taxpayers.

Again, typically none of the worker or political representatives know anything about investing—yet they decide how trillions in public pension assets are invested.

What could possibly go wrong, you might ask?

Far more than you can imagine.

Here's an example. With $354 billion in assets under management, the California Public Employees Retirement System, America's largest state pension, has historically been considered the "gold standard" for public pensions in its investment approach, its integrity, and its management.

How well is the nation's "best of the best" American public pension managed?

In 2016, the former chief executive of the pension was sentenced to a prison term of 4.5 years after pleading guilty to a conspiracy charge for taking more than $250,000 in cash and other bribes from his friend and former CalPERS board member Alfred Villalobos. Prosecutors said Villalobos, who killed himself weeks before he was due to stand trial, reportedly made $50 million as a middleman for investment firms looking to get a piece of CalPERS' business.

Later that same year, a former director of New York's massive public pension was charged with accepting crack cocaine, money for prostitutes, and other lavish bribes to steer more than $2 billion in securities trades.

Preet Bharara, U.S. attorney for the Southern District of New York, said at the time, "The hard-earned pension savings of New Yorkers should never serve as a vehicle for corrupt, personal enrichment. The intersection of public corruption and securities fraud appears to be a busy one, but it's one that we are committed to policing."

A recent study of U.S. public pensions concluded that oversight of these funds is vitally important to government officials, plan participants, and taxpayers. The effectiveness of pension boards depends on their structure, composition, size, and member tenure. Most important, better board composition is associated with a higher 10-year investment return on fund assets.[1] Hardly surprising.

Members of public pension boards and pension staff may be crooked for hustling cash, hookers and blow, but they're Boy Scouts compared to the wolves of Wall Street who make billions selling their latest high-cost, high-risk, complex, and opaque deals to unsophisticated public pensions.

When it comes to stealing from Main Street, no one does it better than Wall Street.

Corporate or private pensions are generally no better off than government pensions. Usually someone from the Human Resources or Finance Department has been assigned responsibility for the neglected pension, but it's not his or her full-time job. (I remember a deposition when the Chief Financial Officer responsible for overseeing a multi-billion-dollar corporate pension sheepishly admitted after repeated

> *A recent study of U.S. public pensions concluded that oversight of these funds is vitally important to government officials, plan participants, and taxpayers. The effectiveness of pension boards depends on their structure, composition, size, and member tenure. Most important, better board composition is associated with a higher 10-year investment return on fund asset. Hardly surprising.*

---

1 https://crr.bc.edu/briefs/does-public-pension-board-composition-impact-returns/

aggressive questioning that he only spent 10 percent of his time on pension matters.)

By the way, Human Resources experience is scarcely relevant to pensions and even corporate finance isn't very helpful. Pensions are unique and complex. I don't think it's too much to ask that the person safeguarding your retirement savings, as well as the savings of thousands or millions of workers, has some special training.

Fortunately, there are globally-recognized experts in pensions and investments who offer sound advice on how pensions should be prudently managed.

You'd think pension overseers, especially financially-illiterate public pension boards, would listen to these experts. You'd be wrong.

Shadow Banking

It is not complicated… it's complex.

For years I have been hearing about "shadow banking." I would hear about China being run by shadow banking, the United States being run by shadow banking, and Europe being run by shadow banking. The problem was, I could never fully understand what that meant. So I started to study… to learn about shadow banking and what it is.

I thank Danielle DiMartino Boothe, and her book *Fed Up*, for bringing shadow banking out of the shadows.

I will do my best to keep the explanation of shadow banking simple—actually KISS… keeping it super simple. If you can grasp the complexity of shadow banking, you may understand why Ted writes:

> *"Typically, public pension boards include some individuals, such as active or retired teachers, cops, firefighters, and sanitation workers, who are supposed to (and, in my experience, rarely do) represent the interests of workers and pensioners. Other board members are appointed by politicians, such as governors and mayors who are supposed to (and, in my experience, rarely do) represent the interests of voters, aka taxpayers."*

Once I understood the complexity of shadow banking, I had more compassion for the boards of public pensions. The retired teachers, cops, and firefighters do not have a prayer in a world run by shadow banking.

Complicated vs. Complexity

Paraphrasing Jim Rickards: there is a difference between *complicated* and *complexity*. Jim uses the example of a fine wristwatch, being an example of something that is complicated. Although a complicated system, a wristwatch is not a complex system.

The problem with the economists at the Fed is they are trained to think of financial markets as watches, complicated but not complex. Hence most classically trained economists use obsolete watch repair—elite Ivy-league, macro-economic models—to guide the economy. Most Fed economists think they can fix the economy like they fix a watch.

That was Danielle DiMartino Boothe's frustration. Danielle and her boss Richard Fisher, President of the Federal Reserve Bank of Dallas, came from the complexity of financial markets. They too, had a lot to learn about shadow banking.

What Is Shadow Banking?

First of all, modern shadow banking could not occur if these events did not take place:

- if Richard Nixon had not taken the dollar off the gold standard in 1971

- if the Greenspan Put had not been initiated, following the 1987 stock market crash

- if the repeal of the Glass-Stegall Act, by President Clinton, President of Harvard Larry Summers, and Secretary of the Treasury, Robert Rubin had not happened in 1999.

Simply put, shadow banking is off-balance-sheet banking, banking in the dark and out of sight of the traditional world of investing. Shadow banking would be like if you had a friend who owed $100,000 to his father but did not disclose that debt on his loan application to his bank.

In her book, Danielle made shadow banking simple, but my simple brain could not totally comprehend shadow banking's complexity. Most people cannot. And the complexity of shadow banking is why the world economy is on the edge of collapse.

Danielle emphatically states:

"Now pay attention, because it was shadow banking that caused the crisis of 2008. Though the subprime housing market was the virus, shadow banking transmitted the virus that nearly killed the patient. The Fed's army of a thousand doctors of economics had no understanding of its enormity and its significance."

In her book *Fed Up*, Danielle made shadow banking simple, but my simple brain could not totally comprehend shadow banking's complexity. Most people cannot. And the complexity of shadow banking is why the world economy is on the edge of collapse.

In other words, it was not the real estate market that nearly caused the world economy to collapse in 2008. It was not derivatives such as MBS, Mortgage Back Securities, CDOs, Credit Default Obligations, and ABS, Asset Backed Securities, that caused the 2008 crash. *It was the complexity of the unregulated shadow banking system that nearly bought down the world economy.*

And there is a new crash on the way.

For years, most people invested in traditional stocks and bonds. Stocks and bonds followed sound economic and business principles.

As greed set in, more and more investors sought higher and higher returns. After the 1987 crash, and saved by Federal Reserve Bank Chairman Alan Greenspan and his Greenspan put, shadow banking emerged in the 1980s and 1990s. It was called *financial engineering* or *structured finance.*

Why was the Greenspan Put so important? Because with that action, the Fed Chairman signaled to Wall Street that the Fed would cover their mistakes. It would be like your rich uncle saying to you, "Go to Las Vegas and bet as much as you want. If you win, you keep all your winnings. If you lose, I will give you your money back."

Desperate for more fake assets to sell, shadow bankers began packaging "fake assets," such as taxi-cab medallions, David Bowie's music royalties, intellectual property royalties, aircraft leases, mobile home sales, and—as we now know all too well— subprime real estate mortgages made to many people without income or jobs.

The problem is, the rules for shadow banking assets are different from the rules of the stock and bond markets. Rules for stocks and bonds are complicated.

Shadow banking rules are opaque, loose, fast and changing, which is why shadow banking is beyond complicated—it's complex.

Shadow banks hide their fake assets in an OBS—Off Balance Sheet. The biggest banks hide these off balance sheets in

> The problem is, the rules for shadow banking assets are different than the rules of the stock and bond markets. Rules for stocks and bonds are complicated. Shadow banking rules are opaque, loose, fast, and changing, which is why shadow banking is beyond complicated—it's complex.

SIVs, Special Investment Vehicles. Many of these assets were sold many times to different investors, who sell them again and again.

No one really wants these fake assets. Once they are packaged, Danielle describes them as "hot potatoes" that needed to be sold as soon as possible to unsuspecting, unsophisticated investors—such as public employee pensions staffed by retired schoolteachers, firefighters, cops, and politicians.

In 2008, these "hot potatoes" blew up... which is why Warren Buffett described them as "financial weapons of mass destruction." Buffett should know. His "hot potato" rating company, Moody's, rated many of these financial weapons of mass destruction as AAA.

It was the shadow banking system, not subprime real estate mortgages, that nearly collapsed the world economy. As Danielle discovered, the subprime debt was the virus, and the shadow banking system was the syringe. The Fed had no idea what was going on right under their noses.

The Fed was watching the stock market. The shadow banking system trades in the *repo market*. In the repo market, it is perfectly OK to "rehypothecate" a fake asset. Rehypothecate means to sell the same asset, over and over again, to different clients... including pension funds managed by retired teachers, cops, and firefighters.

Danielle writes:

> *"The Fed had no data...zilch. The Fed had no official data on the size of the repo market, nothing official on repo haircuts, nothing on rehypothecation. The Fed had allowed this to flourish under their nose and had no clue to its size, structure, or danger."*

I don't believe that I have done a thorough (or crystal clear) job translating Danielle's explanation of the shadow banking system. If you want to better understand what she found out, I suggest you read (and, better yet, *study*) her findings in her book, *Fed Up*.

So... how does an average person like you or me beat the shadow bankers?

One recommendation that both Jim Rickards and I have is: Create your own gold standard. We both keep real gold and silver coins and bars, hidden (legally) and out of reach of the banking system. In other words, we do not save fake money and we do not invest in fake assets.

As I state in *FAKE*, I keep things simple. I invest in god's money, real gold and real silver. I do not invest in fake gold or fake silver, specifically gold and silver ETFs. Many ETFs are in the orbit of shadow banking. When the next market crash arrives, many ETFs will be hard to get out of.

In *FAKE*, I write about how *my* gold standard started in 1972, when my carrier group sailed to Hong Kong and I purchased my first gold coin, a South African Krugerrand. I paid approximately $50 for it and I still have that coin today. Today, in 2019, that same Krugerrand is worth approximately $1,700 US. At that time it was illegal for Americans to own gold, but President Gerald Ford changed that in 1975 making it legal for Americans to own gold.

The chart below tells the story.

Why Workers and Savers are Losers

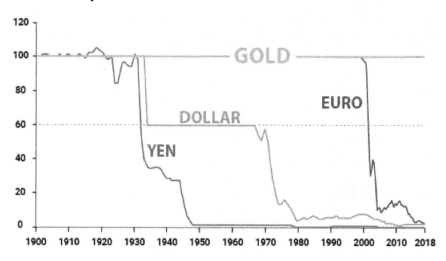

Gold and silver were here when the earth was formed and will still be here long after humans—and our fake money and fake banking systems—are gone.

Your Pension Overseers Think They're Smarter than Warren Buffett—and They're Not

In case you've been living under a rock your entire life, Warren Buffett, the chairman and CEO of Berkshire Hathaway with a net worth of $90 billion (making him the third wealthiest person in the world), is considered one of the most successful investors in the world.

Over the years, Buffett has had a lot to say about how corporate and government pensions should be prudently managed. If pensions ignore Buffett's advice, it would have to be because they believe they are smarter than Buffett. Right?

Well, they're not.

Tragically, corporate shareholders and public pension stakeholders—taxpayers and government workers—pay the price when pensions ignore the best advice and choose instead to follow the herd, i.e. gross malpractice generally practiced.

So, what advice has the Oracle of Omaha had to offer to pensions?

Buffett has been an outspoken critic of pension accounting practices in the United States, and, particularly, the investment returns corporate and government pensions assume they'll earn on their investments. For example, in an oft-cited 2007 annual letter to Berkshire Hathaway shareholders, Buffett noted corporate pensions on average assume they will earn 8% a year, while, says Buffett, 6% would be more realistic.

Buffet also noted that some companies have pension plans in Europe as well as in the United States and, in their accounting, almost all assume that the U.S. plans will earn more than the non-U.S. plans.

"This discrepancy is puzzling: Why should these companies not put their U.S. managers in charge of the non-U.S. pension assets and let them work their magic on these assets as well? I've never seen that this puzzling question explained. But the auditors and actuaries who are charged with vetting the return assumptions seem to have no problem with it.[1]

---

1 Note that Buffett recognizes the role so-called "experts" play in facilitating looting.

"What is no puzzle, however, is why CEOs opt for a high investment assumption: It lets them report higher earnings. And if they are wrong, as I believe they are, the chickens won't come home to roost until long after they retire."

More often than not, America's state and local pensions' projected rates of returns have proven to be overly optimistic. For example, from 2000 to 2018, state pensions collectively returned just 5.87 percent, badly trailing their own 7.75 percent return assumption over that same timeframe.

The historical performance shortfall—with annual returns over the 18-year period falling almost two percentage points below public pension assumptions—contributed greatly to a decline in state and local government pension funding ratios[2] from close to 100 percent (i.e. holding all the funds needed to provide promised retirement benefits) in 2000 to just 73 percent in 2018.

To make matters worse, as public pensions failed to meet their overly optimistic return assumptions over the past two decades and dug themselves into a deepening funding hole, they allocated ever-greater assets to the highest-cost, highest-risk investment ever devised by Wall Street—hedge and private equity funds.

Like Las Vegas gamblers who have lost big, public pensions decided to "double-down" on the riskiest of investments—at the suggestion and to the delight of Wall Street.

Wall Street's solution to every investor problem is and will always be "pay us more in fees."

With respect to hedge funds, over a decade ago the world's greatest investor warned public pensions against these speculative investments. Buffett also very publicly wagered $1 million that hedge funds would not beat the S&P 500 over the next 10 years. His pick, the S&P 500, gained 125.8 percent over ten years. The five hedge funds, picked by a firm called Protégé Partners, added an average of about 36 percent.

John Bogle, Founder of the Vanguard Group, in a 2013 Letter to the Editor of the *Wall Street Journal* also warned public pensions that "hedge funds are hardly a panacea."[3]

---

2 We'll talk more about funding ratios and underfunding later in the book.
3 Wall Street Journal, June 6, 2013.

America's public pensions ignored Buffett and Bogle's expert advice, resulting in hundreds of billions in foreseeable, and indeed foreseen, hedge fund losses. Wall Street, on the other hand, profited handsomely from the exponentially greater fees these funds charge—2 percent of assets under management and 20 percent of profits—fees which Buffett regards as "obscene."

Buffett also warned pensions against investing in private equity. "We have seen a number of proposals from private equity funds where the returns are really not calculated in a manner that I would regard as honest," Buffett said at Berkshire Hathaway Inc.'s annual meeting in May 2019. "If I were running a pension fund, I would be very careful about what was being offered to me."

Again, his advice has been almost universally ignored in America and, as we'll discuss later, foreign pensions are now loading up on private equity and other toxic investments that have failed spectacularly in the USA.

Buffett has a consistent history of blasting Wall Street firms for charging high fees for actively managed investments and has recommended pensions invest in low-cost passively managed index funds.

You might think that underfunded pensions struggling to pay benefits would heed Buffett's advice and seek to cut the fees they pay Wall Street. Embrace austerity. Tighten their belts. Trim the fat.

In fact, every forensic investigation I've ever undertaken has exposed that the nearer a pension is to insolvency, the *higher* the fees and the *greater* the risks the pension takes on.

Desperate measures—Hail Mary passes—are resorted to at desperate times.

In summary, ignoring Buffett's advice and choosing instead gross malpractice generally practiced, translates to pensions as:

- Using overly optimistic investment return assumptions
- Gambling in high-cost, high-risk hedge and private equity investments
- Paying exponentially greater "obscene" fees to Wall Street
- Entrusting assets to firms that Buffett regards as dishonest
- Eschewing the lowest cost, passively managed investments
- Moving further and further away from transparency

What are pensions doing globally? The *exact opposite* of what Warren Buffett has told them to do—with predictably disastrous results.

To protect your retirement security, you need to regularly remind the people managing your pension to follow the expert advice and give up trying to outsmart people like Buffett.

The Parasite Class

The definition of a parasite is an organism that lives on or in a host organism and gets its food from or at the expense of its host.

The story of GRUNCH is a story of human parasites.

In this book, Ted and I are writing about human parasites in our global pension system… *"organisms that live on or in a host organism and get its food at the expense of the host."*

In *FAKE,* I write about fake money, fake teachers, and fake assets. All three organizations and organisms—parasites all—must be in place for GRUNCH and its the global cash heist to work.

The key phrase in the definition of parasite is: *at the expense of the host.*

Billions of human beings, worldwide, are "hosts" to these parasites. Much like a vampire, GRUNCH sucks the life out of these human beings. For years, I have observed basically good, honest human beings turn into blood-sucking vampires, desperate for more money in the hope of saving their retirement dreams.

"It's Our Money, Stupid."

During the 1992 Presidential Campaign, Bill Clinton's campaign strategist James Carville coined the phrase "It's the economy, stupid."

That slogan defeated President George H.W. Bush and his promise, "Read my lips: no new taxes." The first President Bush lost to Clinton when he broke his promise to the American people and raised taxes.

Since 1983, after reading GRUNCH, I have considered saying, "It's our money, stupid."

I was cautioned to tone down calling people stupid by my wife Kim who has been a sure and steady rudder as we have navigated the whirlwind of the past two decades. We then came up with a more socially acceptable—yet just as accurate—slogan, "What did school teach you about money?"

We are also prey to our educational system that teaches us nothing about money as well as our banking system that sells us "fake assets" and encourages us to save "fake money." This is why I see our entire money system as an unsuspecting "host" overrun with "parasites"—human vampires in search of fresh necks from which to suck life blood.

Great Investors

So if great investors like Warren Buffett and John Bogle recommend a 6 percent return, where do the 7.75 to 8 percent numbers come from? There are four somewhat complex answers to this question.

> The definition of a parasite is an organism that lives on or in a host organism and gets its food from or at the expense of its host.
> The story of GRUNCH is a story of human parasites.

One: For years, politicians promised labor leaders and government employees 7.5 to 8 percent returns on their pensions. The problem is, most unions and governments funded their budgets for 5 percent returns. Gains in the stock market were supposed to cover the shortfall. If there was a shortfall, the difference was to be paid for by the taxpayers.

Two: The *politically incorrect* answer (which I will put out here in spite of that…) is that politicians lie and make promises they don't intend to or can't keep just to get elected. Pension leaders lie for the same reason: they need to stay in power. Government bureaucrats lie, budgeting less than politicians promise. Why should government bureaucrats tell the truth? Most are in the same pension, as are most of our Congressmen and Senators.

Three: Union members and government employees don't care who is lying. All they want is to feel safe in the belief that *their* pension is safe. Nor do they care if their fellow citizens, the taxpayers they represent, have to pay for their retirement.

Four: Most taxpayers are sound asleep, as they are robbed blind.

So are Warren Buffett and John Bogle lying? I don't think so. They are, like me, older men who were successful in the past. As the saying goes: "When a paradigm shifts… your past success means nothing."

One of my favorite old television shows is *Married with Children*. Al Bundy plays an aging shoe salesman who lives in (and relives) his past glory …the days when he was a high school football star, scoring four touchdowns and then marrying a cheerleader. Now they are "married with children." The paradigm shift is from football star to shoe salesman.

Another paradigm shift is Eastman Kodak, the company that invented digital photography but did not make the shift into the digital age. They stayed with film and the world of digital photography wiped them out.

Today, we are all in the same boat—in the midst of the biggest paradigm shift in world history. In 1989, the Industrial Age ended and the Information Age began. Buffett and Bogle are very smart men. I have tremendous respect for both of them. Yet, their past success does not assure them of success in the future.

Jim Rickards and I are about the same vintage as Buffett and Bogle. We are co-authoring *The Ravens*, in 2020, because we see a different future. Personally, Jim and I do not do, nor do we recommend doing, what Buffett and Bogle do. This does not mean you should not follow Buffett and Bogle's advice. We agree with them on many, if not most, points. But no expert advice can beat getting your own financial education and evaluating the investment plans that work best for you.

As Ted wrote:

> *"Buffett also very publicly wagered $1 million that hedge funds would not beat the S&P 500 over the next 10 years. His pick, the S&P 500, gained 125.8 percent over ten years. The five hedge funds, picked by a firm called Protégé Partners, added an average of about 36 percent.*
>
> *"John Bogle, Founder of the Vanguard Group, in a 2013 Letter to the Editor of the Wall Street Journal also warned public pensions that 'hedge funds are hardly a panacea.'"*

In the previous chapter, I warned of the Shadow Banking" system. Hedge funds operate within the shadow banking system.

Simply stated, Buffett and Bogle follow the rules of the *stock market*. Hedge funds follow the rules of the *repo market*. This is why Jim Rickards warns of the differences between complicated and complexity. The stock market is complicated. The repo market is complex.

Simply stated, Buffett and Bogle follow the rules of the *stock market*. Hedge funds follow the rules of the *repo market*. This is why Jim Rickards warns of the differences between complicated and complexity. The stock market is complicated. The repo market is complex.

It is easy to understand why retired schoolteachers, police and firefighters would be lured into hedge funds. Most think that hedge funds follow the same rules as mutual funds.

Again, if you want to further understand the shadow banking system, Danielle DiMartino Booth does an admirable job explaining the differences between the stock market and the repo market. I'll reiterate: it is more than complicated. It is easy to lie to people who have no financial education. The economists at the Federal Reserve Bank, with their PhDs from Ivy League Schools, had no idea the shadow banking system was operating right under their noses.

As Ted writes:

> *"America's public pensions ignored Buffett and Bogle's expert resulting in hundreds of billions in foreseeable, and indeed foreseen, hedge fund losses. Wall Street, on the other hand, profited handsomely from the exponentially greater fees these funds charge—2 percent of assets under management and 20 percent of profits—fees which Buffett regards as "obscene.""*

One of the biggest deceptions (aka lies) told to the general public is found in the words *assets under management.* If you watch a network like CNBC or read fake investment news magazines (I could name a few…) you will always hear mutual fund managers or ETF managers touting the words "assets under management." For example, "We have $65 billion under management."

To Mr. and Mrs. John Q. Average, who have relatively little, $65 billion may sound impressive—and it is. But what does it mean to average Americans? Not much. As Buffett states, charging fees of 2 percent for assets under management is obscene.

Even more obscene to Buffet is the 20 percent on profits they reap. In the investment world, the hedge fund collects 20 percent on positive alpha. Positive alpha measures how much that hedge fund beats the average, such as the S&P. Keeping it simple, for example, the S&P has a gain of 10 percent, and the hedge fund has gain of 15 percent. That means the hedge had a "positive alpha" of 5 percent. The hedge fund then takes 20 percent of the 5 percent. Again—to Buffett and Bogle—this is obscene. It would be to most people, I expect, if they knew what was happening.

As I see it, it's old school vs. new school. In old school thinking, business fundamentals counted. In old school thinking, corporate credit rating counting.

After 1987, after Greenspan became Chairman of the Fed, new-school thinking focused on structured finance, financial engineering, and massive leverage. That is why, today, most public corporations are deeply in debt, with their credit rating just above "junk."

Even the United States had its credit rating downgraded from AAA to AA in 2011 after the U.S. Congress agreed to raise the debt ceiling. Some call a downgrade to AA "pre-junk."

The United States retaliated and began an investigation into S&P and Moody's, and Buffett's rating agency.

The real question, I believe, is, *Who is measuring what?* Again, the shadow banking system does not follow the same rules as the stock market. And (again) the stock market is complicated. Shadow banking is complex.

This is why Ted writes:

> *"Buffett also warned pensions against investing in private equity.*
>
> *"'We have seen a number of proposals from private equity funds where the returns are really not calculated in a manner that I would regard as honest,' Buffett said at Berkshire Hathaway Inc.'s annual meeting in May 2019. 'If I were running a pension fund, I would be very careful about what was being offered to me.'"*

Buffett and Bogle are being politically correct. Being a Marine, I would say, "Be careful, they are liars."

Political Correctness in Money

What Buffett and Bogle do not say is that all these con-artists (liars) have done is change the words to sound more PC. In the world of financial pollical correctness, *junk bonds* has been changed to *high-yield bonds*. And LBO—Leveraged Buy Outs—are now referred to as Private Equity.

And Private Credit is a much nicer, more polite, more PC term than *junk bonds* or *highly leveraged loans.*

These efforts at political correctness are a dodge, a play to hide the shadow banking system. The key words here are *private* vs. *public.* Publicly traded investments such as stocks, bonds, mutual funds, and ETFs, by law, operate in the light of day. When the word *private* is used, it means they can operate in the shadows, hence *shadow banking.*

In the interest of full disclosure, I am not in the public markets. I do not own any stocks, bonds, mutual funds, or ETFs. Kim and I are 100 percent private.

If you read *Rich Dad's Cashflow Quadrant,* you're familiar with the CASHFLOW Quadrant pictured below:

Those on the left side of the quadrant—the Es and Ss, *employees* and the *self-employed*—tend to invest in public markets. It is better they do, in most cases, although it is not necessarily safer. For most of them, a 401(k) or an IRA may be the best plan.

The I quadrant, which stands for *Investor,* really stands for *private investor,* or more specifically, *insider investor.* Kim and I only invest as private equity or private credit investors. Although private, we do not operate in the shadow banking system, where the rules are complex and deceptive, and from what I understand, often dishonest.

I'm often asked if those in the E and S quadrants can invest as a private investor. The answer is, *Yes.* Most entrepreneurs who start their own business are private. An S— which can also stand for *small business* or *startup*—may migrate to a B, a *big business*. A B-quadrant business can stay private. A few private B-quadrant businesses are Publix Super Markets, Koch Industries, and Deloitte.

Some small entrepreneurs, such as Jeff Bezos, Steve Jobs, and Mark Zuckerberg, took their businesses public, via an IPO, an Initial Public Offering. These once-small entrepreneurs are among today's most successful and wealthy businessmen. Oh, the magic of capitalism.

I have taken three S businesses public via IPOs. Although only two IPOs were successful, I learned a lot. My silver mine in Argentina has been a great success story.

My gold mine in China was also extremely successful, but the Chinese have been stealing property, intellectual property, and mining assets for years. Our gold mine was "taken" by the Chinese once we discovered a massive ore body of gold and took the company public on the Toronto Stock Exchange. That's another story for another day.

Today, I am 100 percent out of my Argentina and China mines, although I am grateful for the experience. Today I prefer to stay a private investor in the I quadrant.

Another question I'm often asked is: *Do I have to be in business to be in the I quadrant?* The answer to that question is, *No.*

Most real estate investors are in the I quadrant as private investors. My first real estate investment was on the island of Maui, in Hawaii. I was still flying for the Marines and took a 3-day real estate investment course that cost me $385, a fortune for a Marine pilot who was earning about $800 a month. As I've shared many times over the past 25 years, that $385 investment has made me a multi-millionaire over and over again, as a private investor in the I quadrant, the *Insider* quadrant.

The best thing about being a private entrepreneur and private real estate investor is that Kim and I operate outside corporate America's publicly-listed companies. We avoid doing business with public companies, public banks, public stock and bond markets, and the shadow banking system. We prefer doing business with private businesses and private people. And so can you.

Does being private protect us from predators? No, it does not. As any homeowner knows, all homes have roaches, rats, and termites. Wherever there is money, human roaches, rats, and termites can be found.

Buffett and Bogle

There are reasons why I am cautious about Buffett and Bogle's recommendations.

Although both of them are very smart and successful men, their ideal client is a passive investor, most of whom are in the E and S quadrants, and most of whom invest from the outside.

Buffett and Bogle did very well from 1971 to 2019. Today, Jim Rickards and I, and many other professional investors, are concerned about the mantra, "Invest for the long-term in a well-diversified portfolio of stocks, bonds, mutual funds, and ETFs." What concerns us is what 2020 and beyond will hold.

As the statement about paradigms goes:

"When the paradigm shifts...your past success means nothing."

When you look at the 125-year history of the Dow, pictured below, you may understand why we are concerned. We believe the paradigm is about to shift. What do you think?

MONEY PRINTING STARTS

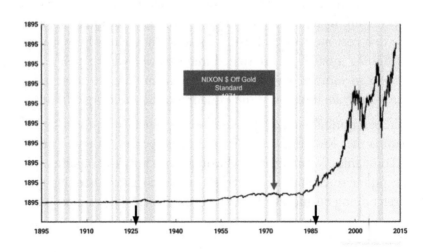

CHAPTER ELEVEN

Why Foreigners Come to America to Learn About Their Pensions

One bright sunny morning four years ago, two tall thin men with sandy hair approached a landscaper busily trimming a green ficus hedge surrounding my beachfront home in Florida. One of the two men was carrying a large professional television video camera.

"Does Edward Siedle live here?" the other man asked with a heavy foreign accent.

"Yes," said the landscaper, totally unconcerned that foreigners toting a television camera were asking about his employer.

Thankfully, it wasn't an investigative team from CBS' *60 Minutes* showing up on my doorstep unannounced.

Instead, it was a scheduled interview with Dutch documentary filmmaker Cees Grimbergen who is best known for his 7-part *Black Swans*[1] series about the lack of transparency, perverse incentives, excessive risk-taking, and outlandish compensation related to the Dutch pension system.

The Dutch pension system consists of three "pillars"—state pensions, private employee pensions, and individual private pensions—and covers everyone who has lived or worked in the Netherlands. Thus, it is far better designed to provide meaningful retirement security for the aging Dutch population and is considered one of the best, if not the best, in the world.

But even the world's "best" pension systems can be dramatically improved by input from participants. So, you should always get involved with improving your pension's transparency, lowering the fees it pays to money managers, and exposing gambling and illegalities. Doing so will improve your pension's investment performance, as well as increase the likelihood that you will receive the full retirement benefits you have been promised.

---

1 https://www.youtube.com/watch?v=qm-9RsyORHc

Cess came to America for his film because most of the highly-secretive alternative investments held in the Dutch pension were created in the United States and are registered with, and regulated by, our federal regulator—the Securities and Exchange Commission. Also, America's pensions provide greater transparency regarding their investments—including alternative investments—than foreign pensions.

As illogical as it seems, he could learn more in America about secretive pension investments in the Netherlands.

Before stepping onto the sands of my beach in Florida, Grimbergen had tried to interview JP Morgan and Blackstone, both managers of Dutch pension assets, and had interviewed Dutch pension board members. He was getting nowhere; he had hit a wall of silence. The Wall Street money managers handling Dutch pensions were unwilling to talk to him, or any Dutch pensioners about their retirement assets, and Dutch pension overseers claimed they were prevented by Wall Street secrecy agreements from disclosing any information to him.

Cees needed to talk to an expert who was knowledgeable about Wall Street secrets but not bound to keep those secrets.

That led him to me. I told him on camera:

"Today the velvet-throated hucksters on Wall Street are saying, 'Give us your money, let us manage it in secret, and this will be the best thing that ever happened to you.'

You should never have blind trust in Wall Street money managers. The secrecy breeds corruption and corruption results in lower investment returns. So the argument that more secrecy increases investment returns ultimately will fail.

Documentary filmmaker Cees Grimbergen needed to talk to an expert who was knowledgeable about Wall Street secrets but not bound to keep those secrets. That led him to me. I told him on camera: "Today the velvet-throated hucksters on Wall Street are saying, 'Give us your money, let us manage it in secret, and this will be the best thing that ever happened to you.' You should never have blind trust in Wall Street money managers. The secrecy breeds corruption and corruption results in lower investment returns. So the argument that more secrecy increases investment returns ultimately will fail. The Dutch workers should wake up and realize that their retirement safety is at risk."

The Dutch workers should wake up and realize that their retirement safety is at risk."

If the people running the pension fund tell workers, "we can't tell you what's happened with your money," then the workers have no idea if the people running the pension even know. Through transparency the workers can evaluate whether the people running the pension know what they're doing.

The workers should tell the pension fund board to refuse any secrecy agreements with investment firms. There is no justification ever for secrecy agreements.[2]

---

2   https://www.youtube.com/watch?v=qm-9RsyORHc&t=318s

For Cees Grimbergen, traveling to America for his documentary project was well worth the effort. He learned more in New York and Florida about how Dutch pension monies are handled than he could learn in his native country.

If you are a participant in a foreign pension, you can learn a lot about your pension's investments from American sources, including media reports, regulatory filings, pension websites, databases and, finally, experts familiar with Wall Street scheming.

America is a leader in financial innovation, including the creation of Financial Weapons of Mass Destruction sold to pensions globally. These toxic products, made in America, are typically sold here first and by the time they are marketed abroad—perhaps a decade later—the damage they cause to investors and pensions has already begun to surface. For example, as mentioned below, while pensions in Japan and Australia are just beginning to invest in private equity, serious questions regarding private equity practices and performance have already surfaced in the United States.

In scrutinizing and protecting your pension, do not assume that you are limited to the paltry information your pension and its overseers are willing to provide to you. If you are denied important information, look abroad and do not be discouraged. (Likewise, if you are an American pensioner and your pension is not forthcoming, look to other pensions in other cities, states, or countries—anywhere—for the information you need.)

The truth is, through accessing information from any and all sources—globally related to your pension's investments, including experts unaffiliated with your pension—you can probably become *more knowledgeable* about the secret investments in your pension's portfolio than your pension's overseers themselves.

When pensions give in to Wall Street secrecy demands, they agree to be kept in the dark and stop asking important questions.

You don't have to.

Liars, Cheaters, and Thieves

In 1973, while stationed in Hawaii and flying for the Marine Corps, I asked my rich dad what he would suggest that I learn next. His answer: *"Become a student of how people lie, cheat, and steal."*

"How do I do that?" I asked.

"Just become a student," he said. "Once you are aware that all people have the potential to lie, cheat, and steal you will see it everywhere."

"People do it intentionally?" I asked.

"Some do, many don't... " rich dad said. "Many people lie, cheat, and steal unconsciously. Or they do it and don't think it matters. I've seen you do it."

"What! You have?" I stammered. "When?"

"Every time you go into the restaurant's refrigerator, I've seen you help yourself to a snack, a slice of roast beef or a piece of cold pizza. I know you don't think it matters, but it does." He continued: "The people you need to be most aware of are people who believe they are saints. They are delusional in believing they are perfect. Always remember, it is easy to find fault with others. It takes a very aware and big human being to look critically into a mirror."

Working the Night Shift

Since I was considering opening a bar or nightclub after leaving the Marine Corps, rich dad suggested I get a part-time job managing a bar. "You will earn a PhD in employee theft," said rich dad. "Bars and restaurants are tough to manage."

I finally got that part-time job, managing a bar and nightclub at a large hotel in Waikiki. The hours were perfect and fit around my flying schedule in the Marine Corps. And it wasn't long before I understood the lesson rich dad wanted to teach me.

One of my primary duties as manager was the bar's PC—or pour count. PC measured the amount of liquor sold compared to cash register receipts.

I was fortunate in that the hotel's general manager, Steve, was a great teacher. I learned about real business management, people management, and money management managing the bar's nightly PC.

Unfortunately, Steve and I could never figure out how the six bartenders or the 20 cocktail waitresses stole. All the bartenders and waitresses were great people, with great personalities. But one or more of them were stealing—right in front of our eyes.

And we were never able to figure it out. The lesson in awareness that I learned was priceless.

The Biggest Loser

I have been the biggest loser many times in my life. I have lost millions to friends, business partners, accountants, attorneys, and advisors who stole from me.

I am not saying everyone steals. I'm saying we all have the *potential* to lie, cheat, and steal.

There is a saying that goes like this:

> *"If you steal something small you are a petty thief, but if you steal millions you are a gentleman of society."*

GRUNCH of Giants and *The Creature from Jekyll Island* are the "gentlemen of society."

Ted says this about those gentlemen and women.

> *"You should never have blind trust in Wall Street money managers. The secrecy breeds corruption and corruption results in lower investment returns. So, the argument that more secrecy increases investment returns ultimately will fail. The Dutch workers should wake up and realize that their retirement safety is at risk.*
>
> *"If the people running the pension fund tell workers 'we can't tell you what's happened with your money,' then the workers have no idea if the people running the pension even know. Through transparency the workers can evaluate whether the people running the pension know what they're doing."*

The Value of Money

High school economics teaches that money is:

1. A medium of exchange
2. A unit of account
3. A store of value

Most major currencies, such as the U.S. dollar, Japanese Yen, Euro, and British pound do a pretty good job as mediums of *exchange* and units of *account*.

When I am in an international airport, currencies are easy to exchange at any money changer. For example, I can go to the foreign exchange window and easily exchange U.S. dollars for British pounds.

Bitcoin does not fit the definition of unit of exchange. I cannot go to the same foreign exchange kiosk and exchange U.S. dollars for Bitcoin. I may be able to someday, but not in 2020.

When we talk about currency being a unit of account it means that the currency is stable. Value can be exchanged easily or readily. During the 1980s, the period of hyper-inflation in America, prices were changing daily. I remember going to restaurants, and the prices for food had Wite Out® covering the old price with the new price handwritten in place of the old.

In countries like Zimbabwe, hyperinflation caused panics. People would get their paychecks and run to the store to spend their Zimbabwe dollars before prices went up.

Money as a store of value means that the currency is trusted, backed by something more than paper. Since 1971, the store of value of all currencies has been systematically stolen from people who work for money.

Bonfire of the Currencies

In 1971, the year Nixon took the dollar off the gold standard, the *Bonfire of the Currencies* began. What I mean by that is that a person without knowledge and without financial education was having their wealth, their life, and their future stolen via their money.

Which brings me to Fedspeak. Fedspeak is the language the Fed speaks to lie, cheat, and steal from the world. Mom and pop—the fast majority among us—have no idea how the Fed is lying, cheating, and stealing their money via words. For example:

1. Rather than say to mom, pop, and kids, "We at the Fed are going to rip you off by printing money," the Fedspeak says, "Quantitative Easing."

   Unable to understand the words "quantitative easing," mom, pop, and kids continue to "work hard, pay taxes, and save money" as the Fed prints trillions in new "fake money" out of thin air.

2. Rather than tell mom, pop, and kids, the truth that, "We at the Fed are going to loot the value of your savings by lowering the interest rates to zero," Fedspeak lies, saying "ZIRP," which is code for Zero Interest Rate Policy.

Fedspeak is how leaders of the Federal Reserve Bank communicate to world markets.

Fedspeak is how Fed Chairman delivers Forward Guidance, a cryptic language about the Fed's intentions and future moves. And because so few people have even basic financial education, they blindly listen to this Fedspeak and hand their money over to criminals.

This is the "Bonfire of the Currencies"—Fedspeak for "Your hard-earned money and after-tax savings are going up in smoke."

Pension Poaching

In 1974, when U.S. corporations switched employee pension plans from DB pensions to DC pensions, the poaching of our wealth via our pensions began. **Banks** steal our wealth via printing money and interest rates. **Wall Street** steals our wealth via financially engineered assets.

As Ted writes:

"America is a leader in financial innovation, including the creation of Weapons of Mass Financial Destruction sold to pensions globally. These toxic products, made in America, are typically sold here first and by the time they are marketed abroad—perhaps a decade later—the damage they cause to pensions has already begun to surface. For example, as mentioned earlier, while pensions in Japan and Australia are just beginning to invest in private equity, serious

questions regarding private equity practices and performance have already surfaced here."

Warren Buffett warned:

"If you've been playing *poker* for half an hour and you still don't know who the *patsy* is, you're the *patsy.*"

Ted writes:

"The truth is, through accessing information from any and all sources—globally related to your pension's investments, including experts unaffiliated with your pension—you can probably become more knowledgeable about the secret investments in your pension's portfolio than your pension's overseers themselves."

Rich dad would say:

"This is why there is no financial education in our schools."

If I could not figure out how bartenders and cocktail waitresses were stealing (either liquor or money) right under my nose, what chance do mom, pop, and kids have against the brains of GRUNCH and the Creature?

Rich dad warned: "The fish rots from the head." He was saying that "lying, cheating, and stealing in an organization starts at the top." The heist starts with the ultra-rich and powerful.

My concern is that, as GRUNCH and the Creature continue their heist, more and more good people will become desperate, ever more tempted to lie, cheat, and steal.

The good news is that with the appropriate information and knowledge, we can always protect ourselves... not from bartenders and cocktail waitresses, but from the gentlemen and gentlewomen of society.

CHAPTER TWELVE

Getting Information About Your Pension

To ensure pension promises are kept—to be an effective pension watchdog—you will need access to information regarding management of your pension and its investments.

On the one hand, thanks to the internet, state and local access to public records laws (often referred to as "Freedom of Information Act" or "FOIA" laws), as well as legal/regulatory requirements, participants in America's pensions have more immediate access to more pension information than ever before. On the other hand, Wall Street investment firms have in recent years devised the most secretive investments in history—schemes designed to conceal outrageous fees, risks, unethical and even illegal practices—specifically to thwart pension transparency.

Worse still, pensions have loaded-up—as much as nearly 60 percent—on these opaque investments which promise to outperform the stock market and cure any pension underfunding woes.

Two opposing forces are at work: technology facilitating transparency versus finance industry legal machinations thwarting transparency.

Perhaps the best example of pension transparency is in the United States where virtually all state and local government pensions today have websites that disclose key information relating to the investments, such as the asset allocation, performance, investment managers and fees—i.e. information generally required under state access to public records laws. All pension stakeholders should visit these websites and learn as much from them as you can.[1]

---

1 See, for example: https://www.calpers.ca.gov/
   https://www.state.nj.us/treasury/pensions/
   http://www.ersri.org/#gsc.tab=0

129

Likewise, in the United States regular (monthly) meetings of state and local pension boards are generally open to the public. You should make a point of attending these meetings whenever you can—if for no other reason than to remind these boards that they are being watched by the very people whose money they supposedly oversee. In my experience, public pension boards hate it when participants or taxpayers attend meetings. Particularly annoying to boards are members of the public who regularly attend meetings, familiarize themselves with the issues, and ask probing questions.

For participants in America's private or corporate pensions, the federal statute, Employee Retirement Income Security Act (ERISA), requires plan administrators—the people who run plans—to give plan participants in writing the most important facts they need to know about their retirement plans, including plan rules, financial information, and documents on the operation and management of the plan. Some of these facts must be provided to participants regularly and automatically by the plan administrator. Others are available upon request, free of charge, or for the cost of copies. The request should be made in writing.[2]

One of the most important documents participants are entitled to receive automatically when becoming a participant of an ERISA-covered retirement plan or a beneficiary receiving benefits under such a plan is a summary of the plan, called the summary plan description or SPD. The plan administrator is legally obligated to provide the SPD to participants, free of charge. The summary plan description tells participants what the plan provides and how it operates. It provides information on when an employee can begin to participate in the plan, how service and benefits are calculated, when benefits become vested, when and in what form benefits are paid, and how to file a claim for benefits. If a plan is changed, participants must be informed either through a revised summary plan description or in a separate document called a summary of material modifications, which also must be given to participants free of charge.

In the United States, regular (monthly) meetings of state and local pension boards are generally open to the public. You should make a point of attending these meetings whenever you can—if for no other reason than to remind these boards that they are being watched by the very people whose money they supposedly oversee.

In my experience, public pension boards hate it when participants or taxpayers attend meetings. Particularly annoying to boards are members of the public who regularly attend meetings, familiarize themselves with the issues, and ask probing questions.

In addition to the summary plan description, the plan administrator must automatically give participants a copy of the plan's summary annual report each year. This is a summary of the annual financial report that most plans must file with the Department of Labor. These reports are filed on government forms called the Form 5500. The summary annual report is available at no cost. To learn more about the plan assets, participants can ask the plan administrator for a copy of the annual report in its entirety.[3]

---

2 https://www.dol.gov/general/topic/retirement/planinformation
3 If participants are unable to get the annual report from the plan administrator, they may be able to obtain a copy by writing to the U.S. Department of Labor, EBSA, Public Disclosure Room, Room N-1513, 200 Constitution Avenue, N.W., Washington, D.C. 20210, for a nominal copying charge.

While America possibly leads the world in pension transparency, transparency is far from complete even in the United States and more under attack today than perhaps ever in history.

In the past, transparency was largely limited to what was technologically feasible. Today, in the Information Age, legions of lawyers employed by the finance industry are tasked with thwarting transparency requirements globally. That is, while delivery of information to investors is easier than ever—and transparency is lauded by industry regulators, politicians, and investors—investment firms with the most to hide are busy opposing transparency.

The only way to counter Wall Street's well-funded concerted efforts to increase secrecy is for pension participants to organize in opposition. When exposed, secrecy is difficult to defend—particularly withholding information from the very people whose retirement savings is at risk. After all, it's their—and your—money.

Demand full transparency from your pension and whenever you are stonewalled, make your voice heard.

Rail Against Secrecy!

While foreign pensions are generally not required to provide participants as much information regarding their management and investments as American pensions, foreign pensioners would be well-advised to initially ask for comparable disclosure.

For openers you need to know the assets (e.g. stocks, bonds, mutual funds, hedge funds, private equity, etc.) in which your pension is invested, the names of firms managing the assets, how much these firms get paid, and how well these firms have performed, i.e. investment performance of the managers as well as the pension as a whole.

As I've mentioned earlier, if you are a participant in a foreign pension, you can learn a lot about your pension's investments from American sources.

Beat the Fed—at Its Own Game

The more I learned about GRUNCH and then The Creature, aka the Fed, I decided I would just beat the Fed.

Two books I highly recommend are *End the Fed* by Congressman Ron Paul and *Fed Up* by Fed insider Danielle DiMartino Booth. Both are great books, and I recommend that those with DB and DC pensions read them thoroughly.

How to Beat the Fed

As Ted states:

> *"For openers you need to know the assets (i.e. stocks, bonds, mutual funds, hedge funds, private equity etc.) in which your pension is invested; the names of the firm's managing the assets; how much these firms get paid; and how well have these firms have performed, i.e. investment performance of the managers as well as the pension as a whole."*

Ted also acknowledges the power of the internet related to access to information:

> *"… thanks to the internet, state and local access to public records laws (often referred to as 'Freedom of Information Act' or 'FOIA' laws), as well as legal/regulatory requirements, participants in America's pensions have more immediate access to more pension information than ever before."*

And the importance of making your presence—and vested interests—known:

> *"You should make a point of attending these meetings whenever you can—if for no other reason than to remind these boards that they are being watched by the people whose money they supposedly watch over."*

Best of all, perhaps, in Ted's words:

> *"In my experience, public pension boards hate it when participants or taxpayers attend meetings."*

I agree with Ted: When it comes to their pensions, most people are sound asleep... while their pockets are being picked. Being proactive is the best way to keep your pension and the board honest.

But there's always two sides to a coin, as Ted has pointed out:

> *"On the other hand, Wall Street investment firms have in recent years devised the most secretive investments in history—schemes designed to conceal outrageous fees, risks, unethical and even illegal practices— specifically to thwart pension transparency."*

My personal experience has been that many of the people who work for GRUNCH and The Creature are like roaches in your kitchen. When you turn on the light, they run for cover.

Earlier in this book, I wrote about the former Big 8 accountants and their financial expert who recommended that I sell all my real estate, the vehicles that made us financially free. Had they taken the time to understand my investment strategies and our business, they probably would not have offered this old and formulaic advice—*"Invest in a well-diversified portfolio of stocks, bonds, mutual funds, and ETFs."* After I realized that they were all serious... I knew I was in a boardroom filled with roaches.

Kim and I invest outside Wall Street. We retired in 10 years because we did not have to deal with the academic elite... employed by GRUNCH and the Creature.

Kim and I "beat the Fed" by not buying into their snooty academic elite, corporate elite attitude.

I've written a lot over the years about why *Rich Dad Poor Dad* was originally self-published—because it was rejected by the academic elite employed by the major book publishing houses in New York. The academic-elite editors objected three of the book's main points:

1. The Rich Do Not Work for Money
2. Your House is not an Asset
3. Savers are losers.

These lessons from my rich dad—taught decades ago and time-tested by Kim and I over the past several decades—are how we beat the Fed.

In 2019, when I was writing *FAKE,* we were able to capture the entire essence of the book in the subtitle: Fake Money, Fake Teachers, Fake Assets. And today, as I revisit the machinations of GRUNCH and the Creature, I'm reminded, yet again, that control of all three of these components—money, teachers, and assets—are required for GRUNCH and company to work its magic with money.

In my teaching and presentations, I talk a lot about teachers; teachers in the school systems but also those we look to for information and guidance and mentoring throughout life. I talk about understanding the difference between a teacher and a salesperson. Many of the academic-elite experts on Wall Street have little real-world financial education or actual experience. They live in ivory towers and, in most cases, are salespeople, more interested in getting you to buy what they're selling than they are in mentoring and guiding you through the complex financial world.

In his book *Tailspin,* Steven Brill—a Yale undergraduate and Yale Law School graduate—writes a damming account of how these "elite" graduates from our best schools have actively destroyed the global economy. And they did it by producing toxic, financially engineered assets (financial Frankensteins) and exporting them to a naïve and unsuspecting world.

Education is our best weapon in fighting—beating—the Fed. And it can start with simply changing the words you use and how you think about money.

At the same time that Fedspeak provides "forward guidance" warnings for the rich, that same Fedspeak blinds the poor and middle class, as their lives and wealth are looted. The poor and middle class continue to be encouraged—advised, even—to "save money," while the Fed is warning the rich on QE and ZIRP.

For generations, parents (who probably learned little if anything about money in school) have told their children to:

> *"Go to school, get a job, work hard, pay taxes, save money, buy a house, your house is an asset, get out of debt, and invest for the long term in a well-diversified portfolio of stocks, bonds, mutual funds, and ETFs."*

Words have power. And that's why changing the words—those in your head as well as those you speak—is a first step if you, too, want to beat the Fed.

There is a passage from the Bible that I often refer to... and I relate it to how we *become* our words. It's from John 1:14: "*And the word became flesh and dwelt amongst us.*" I've been told that I'm taking a bit of license here in how I'm interpreting and applying John's words, but for me the thought that words could have physical manifestations was both unsettling and powerful. If, in fact, the words we speak determine who we become... why not take a serious look at the words you use every day and whether they are moving you toward your goals and dreams... or holding you back.

When we were kids, rich dad forbade his son and me from saying "I can't afford it." Rich dad would say to us, "*Poor people say 'I can't afford it' more than rich people. That's why they are poor.*"

My poor dad said "I can't afford it" habitually. Rich dad trained his son and me to frame the thought differently, to challenge ourselves and our thinking by saying, "How *can* I afford it."

Asking yourself *how you can afford something* opens your mind and makes you richer as you look to a world of possibilities.

Parents' Advice

Let's take each phrase, from every parent's advice, individually.

1: **"Go to school."**

Education is very important, but what does school teach students about money? Nothing.

My financial education began at the age of nine, having fun playing *Monopoly*. It wasn't school, but the lessons I learned taught me more about money than my teachers ever did.

2: **"Get a job."**

Book #2 in the Rich Dad Series is *The Cashflow Quadrant*, based upon the icon pictured.

E stands for employee

S stands for self-employed, small business, specialist

B stands for big business – with 500 employees or more

I stands for investor – who invests from the inside

Poor dad advised me to become an employee.

Rich dad advised me to become an entrepreneur and an investor.

When a parent advises "get a job" the child is being programmed for the E or S quadrants. Rich dad taught his son and me to focus on and operate in the B and I quadrants. That is why our financial education with rich dad began with the game of *Monopoly*. Rich dad was teaching us to be entrepreneurs and professional investors.

3: "Work hard."

In *Rich Dad Poor Dad*, rich dad's lesson #1 is the rich don't work for money.

These words make more sense if you're looking at a financial statement. Poor dad, an employee, worked very hard for money in the Income column.

Rich dad worked hard to build cash-flowing assets, in the Asset column.

Poor dad

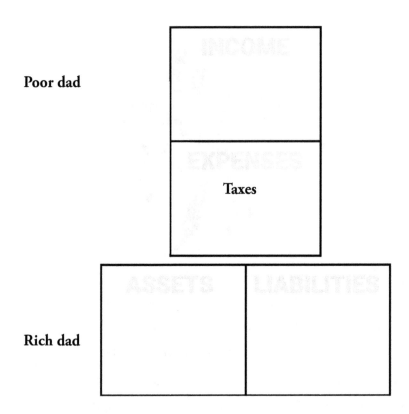

Rich dad

4: "**Pay taxes**."

Notice that the first line item expense in the income column is taxes. Remember, in 1913, both The Fed and the 16th Amendment, were created. The 16th Amendment authorized the creation of IRS... aka the taxman. This is important because the Fed needs taxes from taxpayers via the Treasury to make "fake money" work.

Also remember, you can only pay taxes with fiat currency, fake government money.

TAX PERCENTAGES PAID PER QUADRANT

The people who pay the most taxes are Es and Ss, the people who work for money. They went to school and got a job. The people who pay the least in taxes are Bs and Is, people who have other people and money work for them.

5: "Save money."

You already know why this is bad advice today. Why save money when the government is printing money and reducing the interest rates to zero or below? Decades ago, it was a different story… but today saving money is an obsolete idea because savers *are* losers. A better plan is to focus on ways to make your money work for you. One option: put yourself on your own gold or silver standard. Rather than save fake money, I save real gold and silver, and keep it somewhere safe.

If you're looking for more on tax strategies and the quadrants, Rich Dad Advisor Tom Wheelwright's book *Tax-Free Wealth*, is your book.

Rich Dad "Savers Become Losers"

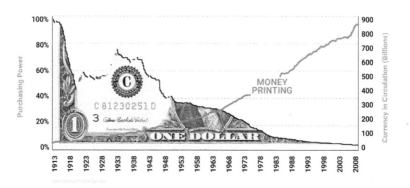

Since 1971, the U.S. dollar has lost 95 percent of its purchasing power.

Every time the Fed makes its moves—related to QE and ZIRP—my gold and silver go up in value.

Here's a sobering thought: Never, in the history of the world, has fake, paper money, ever survived. And neither, many believe, will the U.S. dollar. In a few years, I expect there will be another global meeting and money will change. And all those dollars you've been saving up may be worthless.

6: "Buy a house."

This advice was based upon your house being an asset. Your house *is* an asset, but it is not *your* asset. If your house has a mortgage, your house is the asset of your bank and the government via property taxes. They are the ones earning money on your house.

Look at the financial statement below:

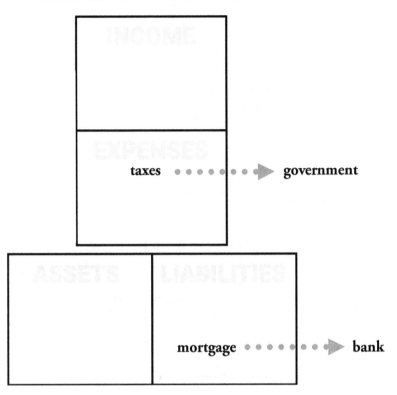

7: "Get out of debt."

In 1971, the U.S. dollar and all currencies became debt. Debt became money.

And *debt is making the poor and middle class poorer.* Your credit cards, car loan, and home mortgage are your liabilities and the bank's assets.

Rich dad's definitions of asset and liability: Assets put money in your pocket. Liabilities take money from your pocket.

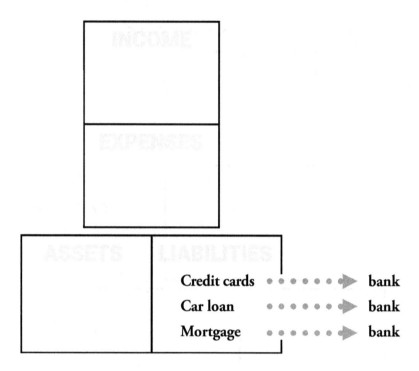

On the flip side of that coin: *debt is making the rich richer.*

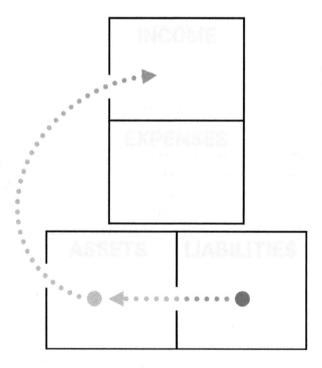

Remember that debt is tax-free money. Using debt is better than using your own, after-tax dollars to acquire assets.

For example: Let's say I borrow $100,000 to buy a rental property. That $100,000 is debt free. If I pay cash for the $100,000 property, the property actually costs me $140,000 in pre-tax dollars.

Keep in mind that using debt, or OPM (Other People's Money) is extremely risky. If you do use debt, please study, start small and practice, practice, practice before using debt or OPM.

My point is that the ultra-rich—people like Warren Buffett or Mark Zuckerberg or Walt Disney—did not get rich using their own money. They used debt or OPM.

Most people, the mom and pops and children, are the Other People who provide the money that banks lend.

8: "Invest for the long-term in a well-diversified portfolio of stocks, bonds, mutual funds, and ETFs."

For most people, their pension is Wall Street's asset. To repeat and reinforce this point: most people—and their pensions—are the Other People's Money.

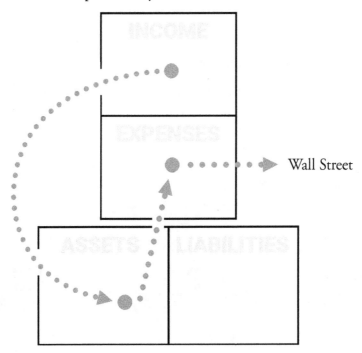

Change the World

If everyone refrained from saying "I can't afford it" and began asking "How can I afford it?" the world would change.

If everyone did this, we the people, would be smarter, richer, and happier.

Change your words and you will change your life.

Words have the power to make you rich... as well as keep you, or make you, poor.

The best news: words are free.

CHAPTER THIRTEEN

Your Pension Is Becoming Less Transparent

Wall Street cockroaches prosper—thrive—in the dark.

U. S. Supreme Court Justice Louis Dembitz Brandeis once famously said, "Sunshine is the best disinfectant." In other words, transparency ensures that public officials, civil servants, Wall Street money managers, pension board members, and companies act visibly and understandably, and report on their activities.

Despite global support for greater transparency in all fields of endeavor, pensions are actually becoming less transparent. Why is there less pension transparency today in the Information Age?

In recent decades, pensions globally, in hopes of boosting investment returns, have shifted assets away from highly-transparent traditional investments, such as publicly-traded stocks and bonds. Today, many pensions hold a quarter or more of their assets in "alternative" investments such as private equity, venture capital, real estate, and hedge funds.

To protect your retirement security, you need to pay particularly close attention to your pension's investments in these risky "alternatives" because these deals are riddled with abusive provisions amounting to a license to steal—from you.

America's state and local government, pensions' investments in "alternatives" have more than doubled in recent years from 11 percent to 26 percent, amounting to an estimated $1 trillion.

For example, the City of Nashville, Tennessee's pension has the nation's largest share of risky, high-priced investments among its peers—a staggering 57 percent of its $2.8 billion fund.[1] The pension has allocated ever-greater taxpayer money into junk bonds, hedge funds, troubled mortgages, private equity funds, and other "alternatives" to highly-transparent conservative stocks and bonds.

---

1 https://www.tennessean.com/story/money/2016/10/12/nashville-pension-fund-leads-us-risky-investments/91736216/

State and local pensions gambling on alternative investments that demand high fees and carry the risk of heavy losses is bad enough. These highly complex funds lack virtually all of the hallmarks of prudent, sound investments—more on that in the next chapter.

More damning is the fact that when taxpayer-funded (and supposedly subject to public scrutiny) pensions invest in these funds, the pension overseers routinely and sheepishly submit to draconian confidentiality agreements which preclude public disclosure of key information.

It bears repeating: Wall Street cockroaches prosper—thrive—in the dark.

So, legions of high-priced lawyers representing the cockroaches, aka alternative investment firms, have crafted seemingly iron-clad agreements demanding secrecy.

There are two sinister levels of secrecy you should be concerned with:

1. The pension agrees to keep secret (from you and the general public) certain key information it receives from the alternative investment manager handling pension assets.

2. Pension overseers agree the alternative money manager may keep secret—withhold—certain key information from them. As illogical and perverse as it sounds, there are officials at even the largest multi-billion pensions who are subject to a legal—fiduciary—duty to watch over the investments yet agree to be kept in the dark with respect to certain investments.

What this means is that these pension assets simply disappear off the radar—no one knows what's happening to this money. Any pension that agrees to such secrecy schemes becomes complicit in—aids and abets—the looting, in my opinion.

Here's the shocking disclosure from one well-known private equity firm regarding the secrecy scheme it foists onto pension clients that invest in its funds:

> *So, legions of high-priced lawyers representing the cockroaches, aka alternative investment firms, have crafted seemingly iron-clad agreements demanding secrecy.*
>
> *What this means is that these pension assets simply disappear off the radar—no one knows what's happening to this money. Any pension that agrees to such secrecy schemes becomes complicit in—aids and abets— the looting, in my opinion.*

"The organizational documents of certain Funds permit the Adviser and/or each such Fund's General Partner to **withhold information** from certain limited partners or investors in such Fund in certain circumstances. For instance, information may be withheld from limited partners that are subject to **Freedom of Information Act** or similar requirements. The Adviser and/or General Partner may elect to **withhold** certain information from such limited partners for reasons relating to the Adviser's and/or General Partner's **public reputation** or overall business strategy, **despite the potential benefits to such limited partners of receiving such information.** In addition, due to the fact that potential investors in a Fund may ask different questions and request different information, the Adviser may provide certain information to one or more prospective investors that it does not provide to all prospective investors." [Emphasis added.]

In other words, if the investment manager engages in criminal activity which, if disclosed to the pension might later be disclosed by the pension (in response to a valid request for information from the public), and such disclosure would negatively impact the crooked manager's public reputation, then the crooked manager may withhold the information regarding its crimes from the pension overseers.

Uncovering the Secrets

I have been sounding the alarm about growing pension secrecy for over a decade now.

In Tennessee in 2006, I warned the Shelby County pension that due to secrecy provisions the fund had $135 million or approximately 15 percent of its assets invested with over 120 largely unregulated high-risk money managers scattered throughout the world whose identities, securities holdings, trading costs, and custodians were unknown.

My 2013 forensic investigation of the Rhode Island state pension noted:

"Transparency and accountability have suffered as the pension has increased its allocation to hedge, venture capital, and private equity funds to almost $2 billion or 25 percent and the Treasurer has withheld most information about these high-risk, high-cost investments from both the State Investment

Commission, a 10-member volunteer body that is chaired by the General Treasurer and oversees the investments of the state pension, and the general public. Ironically, in Rhode Island, limitations on public access to records have grown in the Information Age."

During my investigation, four open-government groups—Common Cause Rhode Island, the state's chapter of the American Civil Liberties Union, the Rhode Island Press Association, and the League of Women Voters of Rhode Island—sent a letter to the state Treasurer voicing their concerns regarding the Treasurer's strategy of withholding hedge fund records. These groups believed that since the financial reports were paid for with public funds and detailed how the state was investing the public's money, they should be made public in their entirety; further they found "troubling" the Treasurer's decision to allow the hedge funds to decide what information to release.

A year later, my forensic investigation of the North Carolina state pension concluded that, without precedent, the pension had entered into agreements with Wall Street to keep secret 35 percent or $30 billion of pension assets.

"Today the assets of the pension are directly invested in approximately 300 funds and indirectly in hundreds more underlying funds (through funds of funds), the names, investment practices, portfolio holdings, investment performances, fees, expenses, regulation, trading, and custodian banking arrangements of which are largely unknown to stakeholders, the State Auditor, and, indeed, to even the Treasurer and her staff.

"As a result of the lack of transparency and accountability at the pension, it is virtually impossible for stakeholders to know the answers to questions as fundamental as who is managing the money, what is it invested in, and where it's gone.

"Worse still, the Treasurer has betrayed her fiduciary duty by entering into expansive agreements with Wall Street to keep the very details of their abuse of pension assets secret—including withholding information regarding grave potential violations of law.

"Kickbacks, self-dealing, fraud, tax evasion, and outright theft may be designated as confidential pursuant to the North Carolina Trade Secrets Protection Act, says the Treasurer."

In summary, less transparency in pensions results in less accountability and greater looting. Therefore, to protect your retirement, you should do everything in your power to promote transparency at your pension and pay particular attention to secretive investments.

Wherever transparency is denied, you should presume that someone has something to hide.

In pension matters, there is never any justification for keeping secrets from taxpayers and pensioners whose retirement savings are at risk. After all, it's your money.

What Did School Teach You About Money?

In 1997, nearly 25 years ago, *Rich Dad Poor Dad* was published. The theme of the book is a story of contrast between my poor dad, a highly educated teacher, and my rich dad, a man without any formal education but who had serious street smarts when it came to money and investing.

Rich Dad Poor Dad is simply a book on financial literacy and financial education.

Twenty-five years ago, financial literacy programs in schools were rare. Today, I am happy to hear that more and more educational institutions are offering financial education programs to students. While I do not take the credit for this progress in education, I am happy our schools are doing their best to make financial education available and relevant to the real world.

After all, rich or poor, educated and uneducated, young or old, we all use money.

> Rich or poor, educated and uneducated, young or old... we all use money.

An Educational Disaster

In 2016, Tom Wheelwright, our Rich Dad Advisor on taxes and accounting, and I were in a small town doing a seminar for a group of entrepreneurs. Since we were already in town for other events, we were invited to put on a seminar for a small private high school. The school was excited to show us their financial education program.

When it was all said and done, our financial education program with entrepreneurs was a roaring success; our financial education event in the school was a disaster.

Sparing you the painful details, I will get to the low point. The school's principal had read my books and decided to start a financial literacy program. She asked the school's accounting teacher to head the new program. The accounting teacher hired a local financial planner to assist her with course content. Neither had read my books or Tom's book, much less played the board game *CASHFLOW*.

There were about 100 students, 20 teachers, and 30 parents in the classroom that day. I began by telling the story of my rich dad and poor dad. I shared my story of financial education and the years of playing

Monopoly with rich dad. I emphasized having fun learning about money, playing a game, working in rich dad's businesses, sitting in on his Saturday business meetings with his staff, and visiting his real estate investments.

On a flip chart, I drew the Cashflow Quadrant, explaining that the world of money is made up of four types of people: Es, Ss, Bs, and Is. I explained that Es and Ss were passive investors who invested from the outside, generally in stocks and bonds. Pointing to the I on the flip chart, I stated that the I stood for "Insider," an investor who invests from the inside, with insider information.

Tom began the program by explaining the financial statement— referring to it as "your report card when you leave school." Tom focused on the three financial statements:

1: Income Statement, aka a "P&L" – Profit and Loss Statement

2: Balance Sheet of Assets and Liabilities

3: Statement of Cash Flow

Tom then went into debt and taxes, two subjects essential for real life financial education.

At that point, the accounting teacher raised a loud objection. What she was objecting too, we did not know. Moving on, I started the game play with teachers, students, and parents in groups of five playing the *CASHFLOW* game.

About two hours later, while debriefing the game play, the financial planner went ballistic. He stood up and said, "What you are teaching is not real life. What you are teaching is risky and illegal."

The teachers, students, and parents in the room were mortified. Not wanting to cause further problems, Tom graciously asked him to tell us what he was teaching the students.

The financial planner took the stage and said:

> *"We teach our students to pay taxes, not avoid taxes. You know that's illegal. I teach people to save money and get out of debt. We do not teach people to use debt to invest. And we teach long-term investing in a well-diversified portfolio of stocks, bonds, mutual funds, and ETFs. If a person wants to invest in gold, silver, or real estate, I recommend gold, silver, and real estate ETFs."*

The financial planner took a break, stopping to look at the notes he had jotted down.

> *"And we do not recommend starting your own business. Most businesses fail. Everything you recommend is risky and illegal, especially investing with from the inside, with insider information."*

To say he was hot would be an understatement.

For Tom and me, the seminar was over. The financial planner droned on, explaining the school's financial education program. He did not invite us back on stage. For Tom and me, it was our turn to grin and bear it. Everything the financial planner call *financial education* caused us to squirm and shudder.

At the end of the day, the principal pulled Tom and me aside, thanked us, and apologized in private for how the day unfolded. She is a wonderful and dedicated educator who said, "The accounting teacher teaches economics. We converted her to an accounting teacher. She knows little about accounting. She teaches from a textbook."

"What upset her so much?" Tom asked.

"She hates President Trump," said the principal. "She lost it when you explained how you and the President use debt to invest and pay no taxes."

Tom and I nodded, indicating merely that we understood. Gently, Tom said, "In 1913 the Federal Reserve Bank was formed. And the 16th Amendment was passed, which led to the formation of the IRS. Money could not exist without debt and taxes. That is why debt and taxes are essential to financial education."

The principal nodded, doing her best to understand the relationship that debt and taxes have to money.

"And the financial planner?" I asked.

"I think he was embarrassed. He should have read your books before agreeing to teach our financial literacy program."

"What embarrassed him?"

"We are a private school. Our teachers do not have a public employee pension. I believe he was embarrassed because most of the teachers and many of the parents are his clients." She added: "When you said you achieve infinite returns, and the best his investments return is less than 5 percent, I saw him squirm. When you explained how you use debt and pay no taxes, he lost it."

"We apologize," Tom said.

"No need," said the principal. "I should have thought this through more. I thought all financial education was the same."

"The level of financial education the accounting teacher and financial planner teach is best for most people," I explained. "What we teach only a few people can and should do." We shared with her the positive response we got from the entrepreneurs in the room.

"Your teachers teach what is best for people on the E- and S-side of the quadrant," said Tom. "And we teach financial education for those who want to be on the B- and I-side of life."

I chimed in: "What we teach violates the values of those on the E-and-S side."

The principle nodded and said, "I have learned a lot. Financial education is not the same for everyone. But why does he say what you teach is illegal?"

"What we teach may be illegal for Es and Ss… but it's legal for Bs and Is," Tom clarified.

"And, that is the purpose of financial education," I added. "Knowing the laws is essential to real financial education."

"And is that true about 'insider information'?" asked the principal.

"Yes," I replied, "The investing laws as well as the tax laws are different for Bs and Is than they are for Es and Ss."

"I wish you had had the opportunity to explain that," said the principal.

"So do we," said Tom. And, smiling, he added: "Real financial education can be an exciting subject."

Real — vs. Fake — Financial Education

Most people have no idea what is going on inside their pension, regardless of whether it is a DB pension or a DC pension, such as a 401(k) or IRA.

Schools have taught us little about money and without financial education, how *could* anyone really know? And if they do seek financial education, many drink the Kool-Aid dispensed by financial experts.

Most financial planners are not rich people. Most, I would venture, are good people, but they are salespeople, trained to sing the company song and sell the company's products. Most are Es and Ss. Financial planners are not much different than real estate brokers or stockbrokers. Rich dad often said, "The reason they are called 'brokers' is because most are broker than you." My friend and personal advisor on financial planning matters is John McGregor, a CFP, a Certified Financial Planner, and a trainer of financial planners. He is the author of *The Top 10 Reasons Rich People Go Broke,* a book on financial-planner horror stories, in which he says:

> *"It takes longer for a hairdresser to get a license, than a financial planner to get a license."*

Warren Buffett had thoughts on that subject as well:

> *"Wall Street is the only place that people ride to in a Rolls Royce to get advice from those who take the subway."*

And as Ted states:

> *"In recent decades pensions globally, in hopes of boosting investment returns, have shifted assets away from highly-transparent traditional investments, such as publicly-traded stocks and bonds. Today many pensions hold a quarter or more of their assets in 'alternative' investments such as private equity, venture capital, real estate and hedge funds."*

You may have guessed that I do not invest in publicly traded stocks and bonds. I am 100 percent in "alternative" investments, which is why Tom is my advisor. The laws are different and we must understand and respect them.

Ted also wrote:

> *"To protect your retirement security, you need to pay particularly close attention to your pension's investments in these risky 'alternative' assets because this is an area of serious looting.*
>
> *"America's state and local government pensions' investments in 'alternatives' have more than doubled in recent years from 11 percent to 26 percent, amounting to an estimated $1 trillion.*
>
> *"For example, the City of Nashville, Tennessee's pension has the nation's largest share of risky, high-priced investments among its peers—a staggering 57 percent of its 2.8 billion fund. The pension has allocated ever-greater taxpayer money into junk bonds, hedge funds, troubled mortgages, private equity funds and other 'alternatives' to highly-transparent conservative stocks and bonds."*

As covered in an earlier chapter, there are *public markets* and *private markets,* aka the world of shadow banking. Personally, I invest from the private side, the shadow banking side. I invest via private equity and private credit. Why? Because that is where the money is. That is why the financial planner was embarrassed. He was proud of his 5 percent average returns. I spoke about *infinite returns*. Infinite returns mean I make money without money. Let me be very clear: I would not be investing as I do today were it not for a lifetime of financial education and study—and a team of great advisors who guide me through the maze.

Financial planners invest, with clients' money, on the public side. I invest from the private side, without money. Investing from the private side requires a different level of financial education. Most people do not have access to that level of financial education, which, for me, began by playing *Monopoly* with my rich dad as my teacher.

This is why Ted states:

> *"State and local pensions gambling on 'alternative investments' that demand high fees and carry the risk of heavy losses, is bad enough. These highly complex funds lack virtually all of the hallmarks of prudent, sound investments."*

Wall Street collects the high fees. And the pension pays those fees—and covers the losses when Wall Street's toxic assets collapse.

As an entrepreneur, I put my own private alternative investments together. The high fees are mine and contribute to my own infinite returns.

All Coins Have Three Sides

Rich dad often said:

> "All coins have three sides: heads, tails, and the edge.
>
> There is no such thing as a two-sided coin."

F. Scott Fitzgerald puts it this way:

> "The test of a first-rate intelligence is the ability to hold two opposed ideas in mind at the same, time and still retain the ability to function."

In other words, intelligence is found on the edge of the coin, not on the sides.

Real education is not about memorizing answers or knowing right from wrong. Real education is about being intelligent, standing on the edge where you can see both sides—and then deciding which side is best for you.

CHAPTER FOURTEEN

Your Pension Is Gambling More Than Ever— and Lying About It

In 2015, Japan's $1.2 trillion public pension fund—the largest fund of its kind in the world—apparently decided the time was right to roll the dice.[1]

The pension, which long had a portfolio of conservative domestic government bonds, was ready to take its first step toward investing in high-risk, high-cost private equity funds.

Other historically conservative Japanese pensions cannot resist the allure of these toxic investments and are significantly increasing their investments in hedge, private equity, and other alternative funds. The average Japanese corporate pension fund now has a 17 percent allocation to alternative investments, up from 11 percent in 2013, according to J.P. Morgan Asset Management's annual survey.[2]

As alarming as the reported percentages of pension high-risk alternative holdings are—in Japan and globally—don't believe them.

My investigations regularly reveal that pensions *conceal* and *underreport* their riskiest investment holdings. While certain hedge, private equity, and venture funds may be categorized as alternatives, other alternatives such as real estate, precious metals, distressed debt, infrastructure, inflation-linked bonds, and credit opportunity funds may not be properly categorized.

For example, my second investigation of the Rhode Island state pension—America's first "crowdfunded" forensic investigation of a state pension—revealed that, contrary to the pension's financial reports, **40 percent** of the pension's assets—not the 25 percent disclosed— had been allocated to secretive alternative investments.[3]

---

1 https://www.wsj.com/articles/japans-pension-fund-moves-to-invest-in-private-equity-1442461689
2 https://www.institutionalinvestor.com/article/b1902fj6jzy6k1/Japanese-Pensions-Push-Hard-into-Alternatives
3 https://www.forbes.com/sites/edwardsiedle/2015/06/05/crowdfunded-rhode-island-state-pension-investigation-finds-2-billion-in-preventable-losses/#49e3d9db206d

Australia's largest pension fund recently announced that it "plans a global shopping spree."[4] The fund will invest tens of billions of dollars in overseas assets as part of a diversification strategy that will shift most of its portfolio outside its home market for the first time. The fund will invest more in private equity, its chief executive said.

Australia's third-largest pension fund, First State Super, says it wants to "partner with private equity firms."[5]

When your pension says it wants to "partner" with private equity, hedge or venture firms, watch out.

Wall Street does not "partner" with pensions. Wall Street makes money preying on pensions, win or lose. Regardless of whether the investments they create and peddle soar or fail, Wall Street gets paid big money and the pensions pay.

There is no "partnership" here—no sharing of the pain.

As Warren Buffett recently said about private equity investments:

> "It's a lopsided system whereby 2% of your principal is paid each year to the manager even if he accomplishes nothing—or, for that matter, loses you a bundle—and additionally 20% of your profit is paid to him if he succeeds."

The salesman who sells you a car is not your partner. He's in business to make money for himself—not you.

When pension overseers, i.e. "buyers" of financial products, make statements to the effect that they are on the same team as Wall Street "sellers" of costly investments, that's a huge red flag. They've been duped.

Pension overseers are supposed to be on your side—diligently protecting your interests—not cozying-up to investment firms.

When Japan, Australia, and other government pensions go on a "global shopping spree" for alternative investments, they'll primarily be buying toxic investment products manufactured in the United States, i.e. Wall Street.

Since most alternative funds have a minimum 10-year life, which can be extended for years or even decades and are permitted to manipulate their interim performance results, it will be at least a decade before

---

4   https://www.ft.com/content/78e2d522-7c4f-11e9-81d2-f785092ab560
5   https://www.bloomberg.com/news/articles/2019-06-19/wave-of-retiring-baby-boomers-to-test-australian-pension-funds

the results of gambling by these foreign pensions is exposed/disclosed. (Note: the worse these investments perform, the longer their lives will be extended and a final accounting delayed.)

Chances are the people who made the decision to enrich Wall Street at the expense of the pensions will be long gone when the results of the gamble are disclosed. That's exactly why if you are a participant in these funds, you need to speak up **now**—you can't afford to wait.

In previous chapters we discussed that investment legend Warren Buffett and other experts (including me) have advised pensions *against* investing in alternative investments, such as hedge and private equity funds and that pensions globally have ignored these warnings. Why?

Gross malpractice generally practiced.

We also discussed that alternative investment firms demand secrecy, which has resulted in less pension transparency in the Information Age.

So, by now you may be wondering:

1. What's so dangerous about these investments that Warren Buffett would tell pensions to steer clear of them?

> *By now you may be wondering:*
>
> *• What's so dangerous about these investments that Warren Buffett would tell pensions to steer clear of them?*
>
> *• Why are alternative investment managers so intent on hiding from pensions and their participants through secrecy agreements?*
>
> *Money managers who are delivering superior investment performance to their clients want to shout about it from the rooftops—advertise in the Wall Street Journal, not hide the good news from potential investors. Right?*

2. Why are alternative investment managers so intent on hiding from pensions and their participants through secrecy agreements?

Money managers who are delivering superior investment performance to their clients want to shout about it from the rooftops—advertise in the Wall Street Journal, not hide the good news from potential investors. Right?

So, why the secrecy?

Do You Know a Secret?

Officially, since 1977, the Federal Reserve Bank has a dual mandate that addresses these issues:

    1: Maximum employment
    2: Stable prices
    3: Moderate long-term interest rates

This begs the question, obviously… as a dual mandate would imply two. Why are there three mandates? I could attempt humor—"That might be the heart of the problem: the economists at the Fed can't count!"—but this is serious business. So I started studying the Fed and its dual mandate.

In doing so, I met a young man who had worked at the Fed and asked him that question. His reply:

> *"We never talked about the dual mandates. We were constantly reminded the Fed had but one purpose."*

"And what was that?" I asked.

"To protect the banking system."

Jim Rickards writes:

> *"From its creation in 1913, **the most important Fed mandate** has been to maintain the purchasing power of the dollar; however, since 1913 the dollar has lost over 95 percent of its value. Put differently, it takes twenty dollars today to buy what one dollar would buy in 1913."* [Emphasis added.]

Devaluing the dollar is another way in which GRUNCH and the Creature legally steal your wealth.

As Ted states:

> *"Australia's third-largest pension fund, First State Super, says it wants to 'partner' with private equity firms.*
>
> *"When your pension says it wants to 'partner' with private equity, hedge, or venture firms, watch out. Wall Street does not 'partner' with pensions.*

Wall Street makes money preying on pensions, win or lose. Regardless of whether the investments they create and sell soar or fail, Wall Street gets paid big money and pensions pay.

"There is no 'partnership' here—no sharing of the pain."

So Who Runs GRUNCH?

In his book, *GRUNCH of Giants,* Fuller writes:

"Who runs GRUNCH? Nobody knows. It controls all the world banks. Even the muted Swiss banks. It does what its lawyers tell it to. It maintains technical legality, and is prepared to prove it. Its law firm is named Machiavelli, Machiavelli, Atoms and Oil. Some think the second Mach is a cover for Mafia."

Fuller goes on to say:

"There is no dictionary word for an army of invisible giants, one thousand miles tall, with their arms interlinked, girding the planet Earth."

So Fuller invented *GRUNCH.*

Earlier in his book, Fuller describes the formation of legal entities, today known as *corporations.* Simply put, a corporation was a "corporate human, "a body with a soul."

Who Stole Hawaii?

Hawaii was stolen from the Hawaiians by churches and corporations—the "corporate humans" Bucky describes as "an army of invisible giants." This made more sense to me when I learned that churches and many corporations are international, not national. They have no borders and obey different rules of law.

During the times when I studied with him Fuller explained to our class that "When you see paintings of conquistadors, such as Columbus, Magellan, Cortez, and other 'great pirates' as Fuller called them, right behind the 'great pirate' was another 'great pirate, a priest.'"

As soon as the conquistador came ashore and planted the flag of England—or Spain, or Portugal, France, Holland, or Germany—the 'great pirate' says, "I claim this land in the name of King and Queen so-

and-so." Immediately, the other 'great pirate,' the priest would say, "And God blesses this."

Corpse-O-Rations

This is why rich dad called "The Big Five," the five giant corporations that ran Hawaii's agricultural lands, plantations, mills, hotels, and banks, "Corpse-o-rations."

These "centuries-old international giants," were descendants of the British East India Company.

In school, students are taught Hawaii was discovered by Captain James Cook, on January 18, 1778. What Hawaiian education leaves out is that Captain Cook sailed for the British East India Company... a corpse-o-ration.

Protestant missionaries soon followed. In *GRUNCH*, Fuller calls them "power ordained ministers of god." Many of the ultra-rich, the "old money" of Hawaii are descendants of the Big-Five and Protestant missionaries.

The Great Pirates

In *GRUNCH* Fuller writes.

> *"In 1522 Magellan's ship demonstrated that the world is not a laterally extended plane (not flat) off the edge of which a ship might plunge, nor an ocean extended laterally to infinity, from which there was no return. Magellan's ship circum-voyaging proved the earth was a sphere-a closed system with enormous trade-monopolizing potentials. The laws of the land could not be enforced on the sea. The seagoers, were outlaws, privateers or pirates. The most powerful outlaws became the sovereigns of the ocean sea."*

In 1965, I left the sleepy little sugar plantation town of Hilo, Hawaii, and reported to the U.S. Merchant Marine Academy, at Kings Point, New York... ready for adventure and explorations of my own.

In 1972, my carrier group was sailing to Australia, for R&R, Rest and Recuperation, in the land Down Under. There were thousands of sailors and marines aboard the seven ships of our carrier group.

Suddenly our fleet of ships turned—and we were sailing back to Vietnam. To say we were disappointed is an understatement. The NVA and VC were rolling south at high speed. We knew we could not stop them.

Interestingly, as I look back, this was the point at which my book FAKE begins.

President Nixon had taken the dollar off the gold standard in 1971, and the price of gold was rising on the international markets. My co-pilot and I flew in search of a gold mine we saw on a map. The problem was the gold mine was now behind enemy lines. That didn't deter us and we walked into an "enemy" village unarmed, hoping to buy gold at a discount. A tiny Vietnamese woman, her teeth stained red from chewing beetle nuts, was selling the gold... and she schooled us—two college graduates—with a priceless lesson on the difference between real money and fake money.

We did not buy anything that day, because we were confused. We only knew fake money, the U.S. dollar. The Vietnamese woman knew much more than we did about real money, god's money... gold.

When I say that Vietnam changed my life, it's not the war that I'm referring to. It was flying behind enemy lines in search of gold. I learned that gold and silver are god's money. They were here when the earth was formed and will be here long after we are gone.

The Real Secret

The Fed's dual mandate is not dual. It has a single and focused mandate:

"To protect the banking system"

That is the Fed's real secret.

CHAPTER FIFTEEN

Why You Should Beware of
Alternative Investment Secret Looting

In a nutshell, the alternative investments that are being sold to and bought by pensions today are the costliest, riskiest, most complex, and secretive investments ever devised by Wall Street financial wizards. Every facet of these "financial weapons of mass destruction" has been created to benefit the investment firms that sell them and to disadvantage buyers, like your pension.

If the financially illiterate overseers of your pension are playing poker with these professional card sharks, they're the dumbest players at the table, otherwise known as "losers."

As I ominously stated in my 2014 North Carolina state pension investigation:

"The profound lack of transparency related to these risky so-called 'alternative' investments provides investment managers ample opportunities to charge excessive fees, carry out transactions on behalf of the pension on unfavorable terms, misuse assets, or even steal them outright."

We'll discuss excessive fees in the following chapters. For now, let's focus on other forms of looting common to alternative investments you should be concerned about.

With respect to private equity investments, a 2014 internal review by the U.S. Securities and Exchange Commission found that more than half of approximately 400 private-equity firms the SEC examined charged *unjustified fees and expenses* without notifying investors.[1] In other words, America's premier financial regulator has determined that charging "bogus" fees is commonplace in the private equity industry— in addition to the excessive fees we'll talk about later.

If half of all the bottled water sold was poisoned, would you buy a bottle?

---

1   Bogus Private-Equity Fees Said Found at 200 Firms by SEC, Bloomberg News, April 7, 2014.

The likelihood that your pension overseers have presciently avoided the majority of private equity funds which the SEC found to be crooked and picked only the good guys is nil. Your pension overseers aren't that smart!

So, guess who's paying those bogus fees?

You.

As mentioned earlier, Warren Buffett has found that private equity funds often calculate their investment performance in a manner that's not "honest."

So, in addition to stealing, they lie about—inflate—their poor investment performance.

Don't just take my word for it. Currently, United States presidential contender Senator Elizabeth Warren is proposing new regulations on the private equity industry designed to end what she calls "legalized looting" by "vampire" investment firms that take over troubled companies.[2]

In my forensic investigations I routinely review the offering documents related to alternative investments in order to assess the risks and potential violations of law.

These are the "Top Secret" documents the alternatives firms do not want you to see. In these documents the managers cryptically disclose—admit—to pension overseers the corrupt acts they "may"—i.e. absolutely will—engage in.

However, pension investors must agree, in writing, they will not disclose to participants (like you)—whose money is at stake—the contents of the "Top Secret" documents.

Each Top-Secret offering document is approximately a hundred pages long, consisting half of potentially damning legal boilerplate and half litany of highly unethical and potentially illegal practices.

The thousands of documents I have reviewed typically include some or all of the following disturbing disclosures:

---

2 https://www.cbsnews.com/news/elizabeth-warren-private-equity-firms-are-like-vampires-proposes-curbs-on-wall-street-in-new-bill/

- Alternatives are high-risk, speculative investments. Contrary to what pensions often claim in defending alternatives, these investments do not reduce—but magnify—risk.

- The funds' investments are highly illiquid subject to enormous valuation uncertainty. That means these investments are very difficult to sell and no one really knows what they're worth.

- The offerings involve serious conflicts of interest regarding valuation of portfolios by the managers themselves and calculations of fees, as well as opportunities for self-dealing between the various funds. In other words, since the managers of the funds get to determine on their own what the hard-to-value investments in the fund portfolio are worth and get paid a percentage of any increase in value, they have every reason to inflate values and thereby increase their compensation. That's a serious, I'd say, insurmountable, conflict of interest.

- The managing partners and their affiliates may violate state and federal law. For example, a manager may buy for himself the very same assets in which the fund he manages invests on more favorable terms and at the expense of investors in the fund, including pensions. He personally profits while your pension gets screwed.

- Alternatively, in the event that an investment opportunity is available in only limited amounts, the manager may simply gobble up the entire investment opportunity for himself—robbing pensions invested in the fund he manages, in breach of applicable legal (fiduciary) duties. Again, he profits by keeping the best deals for himself and screws you.

- The offering documents often reveal that pensions are required to consent to managers withholding complete and timely disclosure of information regarding the assets in their funds. Further, investors must agree to permit the investment managers to provide certain "mystery investors," i.e. industry insiders, with greater information than they provide your pension and the managers are not required to disclose such arrangements your pension. As a result, your pension is at risk of other mystery investors in the fund—friends of the manager—profiting at its expense, i.e. stealing from the pension. Why would your pension overseers ever consent to mystery investors being treated better than the pension? Are they more concerned about Wall Street billionaires' retirement security or your own?

- Alternative funds generally disclose a litany of risky strategies they may pursue (all of which are arguably inappropriate for pensions) such as short-selling; investing in restricted or illiquid securities in which valuation uncertainties may exist; unlimited leverage, margin borrowing; options; derivatives; distressed and defaulted securities and structured finance securities.

- Further, alternative investment documents reveal that managers may engage in potentially illegal investment practices, such as investing in loans that may violate the anti-predatory lending laws of "some states" and life settlement policies which give rise to lawsuits alleging fraud, misrepresentation and misconduct in connection with the origination of the loan or policy. Do you believe "potentially illegal investments practices" are suitable for pensions? Do you want them in your pension?

- Unlike traditional investments, the alternative funds may be managed by investment advisers not registered with regulators and the funds themselves generally are not registered. As a result, pension investors lack many meaningful legal protections. Why would you choose to invest your retirement savings in a fund that admittedly lacks meaningful protections?

- Alternative investment funds that are incorporated and regulated under the laws of foreign countries, present additional unique risks which pension fiduciaries must consider. Further, since alternative investment assets are held at different custodian banks located around the world, as opposed to being held by a single master custodian, the custodial risks are heightened. Are your comfortable with your retirement savings being held a secret Cayman Islands account? You shouldn't be, in my opinion.

In short, hedge, private equity, and other alternative funds lack virtually all of the hallmarks of prudent investments including transparency, liquidity, reasonable fees, sound investment practices, and adequate regulatory oversight. They disclose to pensions in their secret offering documents countless unethical dealings, unnecessary risks and illegalities. That's bad enough.

Worse still, to my knowledge, no pension in the world has ever:

1. Understood all the unique risks related to these investments
2. Established procedures to address these risks
3. Disclosed to participants the heightened risks to the pension and safeguards established to protect against them

To the contrary, every pension I ever investigated that invests in alternatives has contractually kowtowed to manager secrecy demands and thereby become complicit in the looting.

Again, secrecy not only precludes you from knowing about the risks related to alternative investments, perhaps most sinister it also makes it impossible for you to know if your pension's overseers are aware themselves of the risks and have taken steps to guard against them.

For the above reasons, Warren Buffett and other experts, including myself, believe the best course is for pensions to simply avoid these financial weapons of mass destruction. If your pension is gambling on alternatives—and many are risking 20 percent or more—the gambling will not end well for the pension and you.

You need to make your voice heard because, at this point in our book, you already know more about the dangers of alternative investments than your pension's overseers.

One final warning to U.K. readers. Private equity firms claim to have found a way for U.K. businesses to keep the promises they made to the 11 million participants in their pension plans, many of which are under-funded. The firms claim to be able to achieve higher returns with lower costs, greater stability and less risk.

Private equity promising to save U.K. pensions?

That's more than a little ironic given that in recent decades the PE industry has been accused of *looting* America's pensions—particularly state and local government pensions—with their uber-costly, high-risk, secretive, underperforming investment funds and breaking pension promises made to employees of companies they bought.

Private equity has lost its luster on this side of the pond, as the "solutions" to America's underfunded pensions the industry touted have failed to materialize. Struggling U.S. pensions that paid handsomely to gamble on PE funds are no better off; on the other hand, PE titans who made tens of billions off of American workers' retirement funds are a whole lot wealthier.

In the U.K., private equity firms are backing so-called "superfunds" that are seeking to enter the business of taking over pension funds from companies struggling to keep them going. To date, insurers have dominated the market.

According to Bloomberg, "U.K. 'superfunds' are awaiting approval of their debut deals from a regulator that's pushing for consolidation." Since they don't face the costly capital requirements imposed on insurers, private equity firms submit they can consolidate and manage pension plans at lower cost and generate better returns.[3]

Will the U.K. government buy PE's disingenuous, self-serving argument that lack of regulation—evading those pesky capital requirements—is a "positive?" I sure hope not. As a former regulator, I can assure you that there are colossal risks related to allowing so-called superfunds without new regulations to protect retirees.

The U.K. government should also be aware that across America PE firms have systematically eviscerated state and local access to public records laws (often referred to as "Freedom of Information Acts"), claiming that lack of transparency regarding these speculative investments is also a "positive." It is well-documented that from sea to shining sea the industry has claimed "trade secret" protection to thwart public accountability.

Whenever PE firms are entrusted with workers' retirement assets, transparency plummets. Count on it.

If you are a participant in a U.K. pension, this expert would advise you to be very concerned. Pension promises made may not be kept.

---

3 https://www.bloomberg.com/news/articles/2019-11-19/private-equity-muscles-into-britain-s-booming-retirement-market

Insider Trading

C-15 INSIDER TRADING

Earlier in this book I wrote about insider trading and when it's legal and when it isn't.

It's an important distinction and worth covering again.

For almost anyone with a DB pension, government pension, or someone with a DC 401(k) or IRA pension, insider trading is illegal. It gets a little trickier when you venture outside these retirement plans. It's important to have a clear understanding of the difference and you personal situation. It's an important distinction:

Inside Trading is:

> *"The illegal practice of trading on the stock exchange to one's own advantage through having access to confidential information."*

Inside Information is:

> *"Insider information is a non-public fact regarding the plans or condition of a publicly-traded company that could provide a financial advantage when used to buy or sell shares of that or another company's securities."*

One of the reasons I attain higher returns with less risk, than with Wall Street's assets, is because I invest from the inside with insider information… legally in private assets. And, in most cases, if a person invests in Wall Street's "assets," trading with insider information is a crime.

Jim Rickards, in his book *Aftermath* does a great job explaining the differences between legal and illegal insider trading. He uses two interesting examples to make his points.

An important distinction:

Inside Trading
"The illegal practice of trading on the stock exchange to one's own advantage through having access to confidential information."

Inside Information
"Insider information is a non-public fact regarding the plans or condition of a publicly-traded company that could provide a financial advantage when used to buy or sell shares of that or another company's securities."

In 2004, famous businesswoman and TV personality Martha Stewart served five months in federal prison at Alderson in West Virginia. After she served her time at the federal prison camp, she was placed on two additional years of supervised release, a portion of which she spent in home confinement.

Her crime: trading on insider information.

Just before September 11, 2001, the volume of *put options* on American Airlines and United Airlines spiked. It appears that friends and families of the hijackers had inside information. And it's reported that many people made millions as the towers of the World Trade Center came down.

Those are both examples of trading with insider information.

A Guy with a Cell Phone

In 1994, after Kim and I "retired." We no longer needed a paycheck or a pension. We were financially free.

Kim bought a small, 18-unit motel and repurposed it into an apartment house. I wanted to continue my financial education, so I took on two projects. The first project was to learn to be a real estate developer. Until 1994, I had purchased only existing properties. My first new project was to take land and build on it. My goal was to achieve an infinite return on that investment—making money without any money. I will write more about infinite returns later in this book.

My second project was to learn to take a start-up business public, via an IPO. I had the good fortune to be asked to join a team that was developing an oil field in Portugal. We raised $6.5 million via an IPO on the Toronto Stock Exchange and started to drill. Every day we would make our required announcements. Every day, as favorable drill results came in, we watched the price of our stock climb from .25 cents, to $1.25 to $1.60 a share. It was exciting—especially since Kim and I had 400,000 founders' shares.

As we got closer to the "pay zone," the stock price spiked at $2.35. We were all jumping around, high-fiving, and congratulating each other in our office in Scottsdale, Arizona.

Suddenly, the price of the stock started to plunge, from $2.00 to .50 cents and then to .15 cents.

My friend, Frank just shook his head. At 83 years of age, Frank had been through this before. He had taken more 30 companies public in his lifetime.

"What happened?" I asked Frank.

"No oil."

"But how would anyone know?" I asked. "We're the owners! We should have known first."

Frank just smiled at me and said, "You have a lot to learn."

"In life," he taught me, "all trading is insider trading. The only question is: How close to the inside are you?"

"But we *are* the insiders," I insisted. "There is no one more inside than us."

Frank smiled again and said, "The insider is probably a guy on the rig in Portugal, with a cell phone. He is closer to the inside than you. He and his friends got out at $2.35."

"Isn't that illegal?" I asked.

Frank just smiled again and said, "Welcome to the real world."

We shut the office down and went to lunch.

Writing Books

Writing a book is a pain in the butt... sitting for long hours and killing many brain cells figuring out how to say what I want to say. But it's all worthwhile when someone comes up to me and says, "Your book changed my life."

My first two books and my game *CASHFLOW* focused on how beat GRUNCH and the Creature.

BOOK #1: *Rich Dad Poor Dad* is a book on accounting. Pictured below is a financial statement, your report card when you leave school.

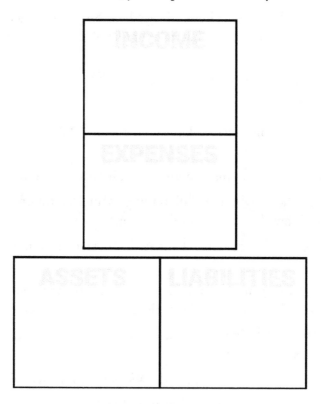

GRUNCH and The Creature want to control your personal financial statement. This is why there is no financial education in school.

Poor dad focused on the **income** and **expense** columns. Rich dad focused on the **asset** and **liability** columns.

GRUNCH and The Creature want to control **your** asset column. This is why we are taught that *our house is an asset*—when it really is, in most cases, a liability. And why they advise *investing for the long term in the stock market.*

BOOK #2: *Rich Dad's CASHFLOW Quadrant* introduced the quadrant pictured below.

Schools teach students to be Es and Ss, employees, self-employed, small business, and specialists, like doctors and lawyers.

The rich focus on the B and I quadrants of big business and inside investors. People on the B and I side are Jeff Bezos, Bill Gates, Walt Disney, Henry Ford, and Steve Jobs.

The most important quadrant is the I-quadrant. GRUNCH and the Creature want to control your I quadrant. Why? So you will invest for the long-term in their toxic assets, which come with fees, fees and more fees.

As Ted states regarding DB public employee pensions:

> *"With respect to private equity investments, a 2014 internal review by the U.S. Securities and Exchange Commission found that more than half of approximately 400 private-equity firms the SEC examined charged unjustified fees and expenses without notifying investors."*

The same is true for DC pensions, such as 401(k)s and IRAs. John Bogle, founder of the Vanguard Fund says:

> *"The miracle of compounding returns is overwhelmed by the tyranny of compounding costs (fees)."*

The *CASHFLOW* Game

Earlier in this book I referenced F. Scott Fitzgerald's words about the ability to hold opposing ideas in your mind at the same time. I like that thought—and his quote—because it underscores the important of being open to multiple points of view.

And rich dad's words carry that same message:

"All coins have three sides, heads, tails, and the edge."

Your intelligence increases when you stand on the edge and see both sides. Tragically, our educational system teaches students that there are only right answers and wrong answers. That is why we have so many highly educated people who live in the world of "I am right" and "You are wrong." Unable to see the other side or other points of view, they are blind to the world on the other side of the coin.

Public and Private

When Kim and I designed the *CASHFLOW* game, we intentionally included publicly traded assets and private assets. In the game, the player rolls the dice, moves his or her game piece, and lands on an Opportunity. Just as in real life, sometimes the opportunity is a stock, a public asset. And sometimes it's real estate, a private asset. It makes little difference if it is a public asset or a private asset. All that counts is how the asset supports your financial goal of financial freedom.

When Kim and I were developing *CASHFLOW*, we sent it to a game expert for evaluation. His report said,

> *"Your game is too difficult. Your game requires people to think. Today, I would have to turn down Monopoly for similar reasons. Today, even Monopoly would be too difficult for most people. People have stopped thinking. They want to be given the answers, and then told what to do."*

Our *CASHFLOW* game was rejected by the game companies we presented it to, as were my books… for similar reasons. When it comes to money, most people just want to be told what to do. I'm sure that's what led to this advice that we hear repeated over and over again:

> *"Go to school, get a good job, save money and invest for the long term in a well-diversified portfolio of stocks, bonds, mutual funds, and ETFs."*

GRUNCH, the Creature, and Wall Street just want you to send your money to them… for the long term.

Personally, I want an infinite return. And I cannot achieve an infinite return if Wall Street keeps my money. I want my money back as soon as possible so I can keep that money moving to acquire more assets for Kim and me—not for Wall Street.

Remember this:

1: If you own a small house to rent out, you are an **insider.**
    If you invest in a REIT, a Real Estate Investment Trust, you are an **outsider.**

2: If you buy gold or silver coins, and keep them in a safe place, you're an **insider.**
    If you buy a gold or silver ETFs you're an **outsider.**

3: If you invest in a friend's family restaurant, you're an **insider.**
    If you invest in shares of McDonald's, you're an **outsider.**

Does GRUNCH and The Creature want us to be insiders or outsiders? That's a question you need to answer for yourself.

Ted keeps it simple:

> *"If the financially illiterate overseers of your pension are playing poker with these professional card sharks, they're the dumbest players at the table, otherwise known as "losers.""*

And in *GRUNCH of Giants* Fuller states:

> *"The 'abstract being' corporation operating within the United States, receives legal authority from state and city governments to sell common shares in 'outright risk' ventures, to which common shareholders they promise only proportional sharing of cash profits from their economically successful operation.*

> *"But corporations also receive legal authority to sell 'preferred stocks' to the owners of which the corporation becomes legally obliged to pay a fixed annual rate of interest, before distributing any part of the profit to those corporation's common stockholders."*

There are insiders even inside the "abstract beings" common shareholders. Think about *that*.

And give some thought to Frank's words about being an insider:

> *"In life, all trading is insider trading. The only question is: How close to the inside are you?"*

CHAPTER SIXTEEN

Why You Need to Know about the Investment Fees Your Pension Pays

Unlike most other industries, the fees money managers charge institutional and retail investors globally for virtually identical investment services vary astronomically.

Passive, or index investment management services, can be purchased by pensions for 1 basis point (one one-hundredth of a percent) or even "for free."[1] Active managers, who attempt to beat the market by stock-picking, may charge pensions fees that are 120 times greater (1.2 percent). Alternative investment managers, including hedge, venture, and private equity, may charge asset-based, performance, and other multiple layers of fees amounting to approximately 9 percent—900 times greater fees than indexing.

Paying higher fees (for active traditional or alternative asset management services) does **not** guarantee and, in fact, **negatively correlates** to superior investment performance. Indeed, the overwhelming majority of active managers fail to outperform market indexes over time net of fees. The higher the fees, the greater the drag on investment returns.

Forget the old adage, "you get what you pay for."

When it comes to investing, almost always the more you pay, the less you get—net.

A 2013 report by the Maryland Public Policy Institute and the Maryland Tax Education Foundation which examined the investment fees and investment performance of U.S. state pension funds concluded:

> "State pension funds, including Maryland, have succumbed for years to a popular Wall Street sales pitch: 'active money management beats the market.' As a result, almost all state pension funds use outside managers to select, buy, and sell investments for the pension funds for a fee. The actual result—a typical Wall Street manager underperforms relative to passive indexing—is costly to both taxpayers and public sector employees.

---

1 Certain index managers will manage large accounts at no cost, in exchange for securities lending income related to the portfolio.

For example, **the top ten states—in terms of Wall Street fees— had a lower pension fund investment performance, over the last five fiscal years, than the bottom ten states.** State pension funds should consider indexing. Indexing fees cost a state pension fund about 3 basis points yearly on invested capital vs. 39 basis points for active management fees (or 92 percent less). By indexing most of their portfolios, we conclude the 46 state funds surveyed could save $6 billion in fees annually, while obtaining similar (or better) returns to those of active managers."[2] [Emphasis added.]

It is well established that sponsors of government and corporate retirement plans have a legal, fiduciary duty to ensure that the fees their plans pay money managers for investment advisory services are reasonable.

Fees paid for investment services have always been an important consideration for corporate retirement plan fiduciaries. Further, in recent years such fees have come under increased scrutiny in the United States because of class action litigation, Department of Labor regulations, and congressional hearings.[3]

> It is well established that sponsors of government and corporate retirement plans have a legal, fiduciary duty to ensure that the fees their plans pay money managers for investment advisory services are reasonable.

According to the Department of Labor:

"Plan fees and expenses are important considerations for all types of retirement plans. As a plan fiduciary, you have an obligation under ERISA to prudently select and monitor plan investments, investment options made available to the plan's participants and beneficiaries, and the persons providing services to your plan. Understanding and evaluating plan fees and expenses associated with plan investments, investment options, and services are an important part of a fiduciary's responsibility. This responsibility is ongoing. After careful evaluation during the initial selection, you will want to monitor plan fees and expenses to determine whether they continue to be reasonable in light of the services provided."

2 Wall Street Fees, Investment Returns, Maryland and 49 Other State Pension Funds by Jeff Hooke and John J. Walters, July 2, 2013. The authors reviewed the Wall Street money management fees of all 50 states and the states five-year annualized investment returns. The information was disclosed in the state pension funds' CAFR.
3 Revealing Excessive 401(k) Fees, The New York Times, June 3, 2011.

American state and local government pensions are exempt from ERISA and are governed by state law. However, because ERISA and state law protections both stem from common law fiduciary and trust principles, best practices for public pensions are frequently similar to those found in ERISA.

At the outset, sponsors of government as well as corporate retirement plans must take steps to understand the sources, amounts, and nature of the fees paid by the plan, as well as the related services performed for such fees. After all, a plan sponsor cannot determine that fees are reasonable without understanding how much is paid and what that money pays for.

While American pensions generally neither fully comprehend nor disclose their investment fees, there is far, far less awareness and transparency regarding fees outside the United States. Hidden, excessive, and poorly understood pension investment fees are a global problem largely unrecognized abroad.

A recent scathing report by U.K. Parliament's Work and Pensions Committee stated it is "not convinced" the pensions industry is willing to voluntarily provide clear, transparent information to pension plans about the costs and charges of investments. The committee placed much of the blame for the lack of fee transparency on pension plan trustees. The report stated there is "evidence that some trustees are making investment decisions without a clear understanding of how much those decisions cost."

The report cited Anna Tilba, an associate professor in strategy and governance at Durham University Business School, who said that "... it is near impossible for investors to figure out how much their investments are costing them because additional costs are hidden and too high."

Colin Meech, a national officer for U.K. trade union UNISON, provided an example of the difficulties U.K. pensions have had in identifying fees and costs. He said that in the Netherlands, a template is used across the industry to identify pension costs. When Meech asked five investment managers to complete similar cost templates like the ones used in the Netherlands, they questioned the importance of knowing the costs as they insisted it was only the performance that matters.[4]

---

4 Recall that the Dutch, nevertheless, came to America to learn more about their pensions' investments.

Recently I took a peek at the British Columbia Investment Management Corporation,[5] a $153.4 billion provider of investment management services to British Columbia's public sector workers.

This manager of public monies worries me and, if I were a participant in a pension managed by BCI, I'd be asking lots of questions.

According to its Annual Report 2018-2019,[6] the manager is in the process of transforming from a passive investment model that was historically in place to an active in-house investment manager, shifting its investment focus to private markets and global equities.

Shifting from passive investing to active investing is a terrible idea, in my opinion. Shifting from transparent, liquid, public markets to opaque, illiquid, private markets is another colossally bad idea.

And banking upon developing in-house expertise in private markets—good luck with that high-stakes gamble!

Two things are certain: moving from passive public investments to active, private investments will result in mushrooming risk and skyrocketing investment fees.

Recently, for nearly a month, I repeatedly asked the firm to fully disclose the fees it pays for investment management related services.

(I include the entire email exchange below because I want you to be aware that even when dealing with one of the world's leading pension experts, pension overseers are hardly forthright. You can expect a chilly, even hostile response to your questions and eternal evasiveness.)

Here is my initial carefully-worded query:

> Please disclose all fees, expenses and other costs related to the pension's investments, including but not limited to, asset-based investment advisory fees and performance or incentive fees, as well as (in the case of any fund of funds) any underlying manager asset based, performance and incentive investment advisory fees. Please provide this comprehensive fee and expense information by manager and for the pension as a whole.

---

5 https://www.bci.ca/who-we-are/
6 https://uberflip.bci.ca/i/1149539-bci-f2019-corporate-annual-report/3?m4=

An anonymous email from Corporate & Investor Relations responded:

Information pertaining to our operating costs is disclosed in our Corporate Annual Report and the financial statements for our pooled funds. These documents are available on our website and for ease of reference, the hyperlinks are as follows: https://www.bci.ca/publications/ and https://www.bci.ca/investments-performance/pooled-funds/

That's a great answer to a question I didn't ask. And a terrible answer to the question I did ask.

I responded with the following:

Please confirm the pension, as a good steward of participant retirement savings, already discloses fully all of the information I have requested. Again, please refer me to the existing disclosures that specifically answer my questions. Since all of this information is apparently already disclosed, I look forward to your prompt response.

Then silence.

So, I wrote:

Please confirm that you do not intend to disclose the information I have requested.

In response, I was referred to the following passage from page 11 of the Corporate Annual Report:

This year our total costs were $873.2 million or 58.4 cents per $100 of assets under management (2017-2018: $919.7 million or 65.4 cents per $100), consisting of internal, external direct, and external indirect costs, all of which are netted against investment returns. Internal costs are operating costs directly paid by BCI and include salaries, rent, and technology and consulting fees, representing 24.1 per cent of costs for the fiscal year. External direct costs are investment management fees paid to third parties to manage assets and include fees to asset managers, auditors, custodian, etc., where BCI has discretion over the buy and sell decision of the asset, representing an estimated 27.2 per cent for the fiscal year. External indirect costs are investment management fees incurred on our behalf by BCI pooled investment portfolios to general partners, who *have discretion over the buy and sell decision of the asset. These costs are disclosed for transparency based on underlying reports provided by these third parties and are 48.7 per cent of costs for the fiscal year.*

This is one of the largest Canadian pension managers—and a manager who is shifting to a much riskier, more complex, costly and confusingly investment program. For example, not only are pension assets invested in tons of private equity limited partnerships, they are also in private equity fund of fund investments involving multiple levels of hefty fees. My forensic investigations have revealed recurring private equity fund of fund fees of as much as 10 percent annually.[7]

The fees BCI discloses are already high at 58-65 basis points. If I am correct and underlying private equity fund of funds and other fees are not included in the disclosed fees, then someone's getting rich—and it ain't the pensioners. At a minimum, the disclosure of investment fees and expenses to stakeholder should be improved.

---

7 https://www.forbes.com/sites/edwardsiedle/2012/06/26/jp-morgan-hedge-fund-of-funds-out-of-this-world-fees-and-egregious-conflicts/#47b1390b2e50

The Ponzi Scheme That's Stealing from our Children

Sometime ago, I was walking past a local bookstore and on the newsstand was a copy of *Barron's* magazine. On the cover was a photo of a person I knew, sitting on a sandy beach under a large beach umbrella. Immediately, I said to myself, *I know that guy*. At first, I was excited, thinking that I knew a celebrity... until I read the headline. It read:

"Would You Trust Your Money To This Man?"

My silent answer, to myself, was *Yes*. I had just given him $150,000. Unfortunately, as I learned from the magazine article, the man was far from trustworthy.

No, the man on the cover was not the infamous Bernie Madoff, who swindled investors out of $65 billion perpetuating the biggest Ponzi scheme in history. And it wasn't the scheme's namesake, Charles Ponzi (1882-1949) a swindler and con artist in the United States and Canada. The person on the cover of *Barron's* was from pre-Madoff time. This guy was small potatoes compared to Bernie.

The Biggest Ponzi Schemes

A more realistic definition, in my opinion, of a Ponzi scheme is this: Ponzi schemes take from the young. Let me explain.

The biggest Ponzi schemes are government Ponzi schemes.

For example, Social Security is going broke because the World War II generation, who contributed little to that Ponzi scheme, will reap Social Security benefits that were funded by *their* children, the Baby Boomers. Baby Boomers will not be as fortunate as their parents.

America's Medicare program is also a government Ponzi scheme, destined for bankruptcy.

What is a Ponzi Scheme?

Investopedia offers this definition: A Ponzi scheme is a fraudulent investing scam promising high rates of return with little risk to investors. The Ponzi scheme generates returns for early investors by acquiring new investors. This is similar to a pyramid scheme in that both are based on using new investors' funds to pay the earlier backers.

"Obamacare," aka The Affordable Healthcare Act, is also a Ponzi scheme. It is destined to implode as well—because younger, healthier workers do not want to pay for older workers' healthcare.

Ted writes about the DB pensions for public sector workers.

> *"State pension funds, including Maryland, have succumbed for years to a popular Wall Street sales pitch: 'active money management beats the market.' As a result, almost all state pension funds use outside managers to select, buy and sell investments for the pension funds for a fee. The actual result—a typical Wall Street manager underperforms relative to passive indexing—is costly to both taxpayers and public sector employees."*

The parallel: Higher fees, lower results.

Also, earlier in this chapter, Ted wrote:

> *"Paying higher fees for active traditional or alternative asset management does not guarantee and, in fact, negatively correlates to superior investment performance. Indeed, the overwhelming majority of active managers fail to outperform market indexes over time net of fees. The higher the fees, the greater the drag on investment returns.*
>
> *Forget the old adage, 'you get what you pay for.'*
>
> *When it comes to investing, generally, the more you pay, the less you get."*

While pensions, both DB and DC, are not (technically) true Ponzi schemes, below the surface there are obvious and terrifying similarities.

Who will pay for the collapse of the public and private pension systems—as well as Social Security and Medicare? No surprise here: It's the children and grandchildren of Baby Boomers will pay for these looming crises.

Ayn Rand

Ayn Rand, (1905-1982) was born in St. Petersburg, Russia and was forced to escape the west. Her experience of being a child as Lenin rose to power influenced her ideas expressed in her books *Atlas Shrugged* and *The Fountainhead*. Two relevant ideas from her work are:

1: *"Evil requires the sanction of the victim."*

2: *"We can evade reality, but we cannot evade the consequences of evading reality."*

How I Got Taken

I got taken in a Ponzi scheme because I was too lazy to learn. Kim and I were pretty successful in business and real estate. Wanting to expand my financial education, I began taking classes on options trading. For three years, I religiously studied and practiced. The instructor kept encouraging the class to be patient, telling us that it usually takes about five years to make money trading options.

One day, this hot-shot options trader came to teach. He shared with our class his track record and how much money he was making for his clients. I took the bait—hook, line, and sinker. I was tired of learning. I just wanted to give him my money and let *him* make me rich.

He was the guy on the cover of *Barron's*.

When I saw that magazine cover, Ayn Rands words came back to me:

"Evil requires the sanction of the victim."

"We can evade reality, but we cannot evade the consequences of evading reality."

I gave the guy on the cover of *Barron's* my money because I was lazy.

As Ted writes:

"You get what you pay for."

Rich dad would say:

"There are no victims in this world. Only volunteers."

I have, voluntarily, paid to be a victim many times in my life. Our children and grandchildren, I fear, will be the ultimate victims—and it won't be voluntary.

Default to Truth

Have you ever had someone *you trust* steal from you?

Unfortunately, over the years, I have had friends, business associates, CEOs, CFOs, and Presidents of my own businesses—people I trusted—steal from me.

My first big heist was by CFO Stanley, my accountant in my nylon wallet company, in 1976. Our start-up was burdened with old debt owed to earlier investors, and we were always short of operating capital. One day, I walked into our offices in Honolulu, handed Stanley a check for $100,000 from an investor, and asked him, "Will this solve the problem?" Stanley smiled. "Yes," he said as he took the check. Both he and the money disappeared, as soon as the check had cleared. It took me eight years to pay back the $100,000 to the investor.

When I talk to entrepreneurs, many have stories of once-trusted friends, partners, employees, accountants, or attorneys running off with the money. In real life, there are few emotional scars deeper than a betrayal after trust.

In his latest book, *Talking to Strangers*, Malcom Gladwell vividly and painfully describes how "good people" allow "bad people" to get away with lying, cheating, and stealing.

Gladwell cites many well-known examples of how these crimes amongst friends and trusted people occur. It is a psychological category known as *default to truth*. In other words, *good people choose to believe another person is "good" rather than face the truth.*

Gladwell's book is painful, interesting, sensational, sordid, and lurid. Here are a few examples he mentions:

> **Bernie Madoff:** For years, Madoff, a prominent and respected figure in the world of investing, was suspected and accused of running a Ponzi scheme. The SEC, Securities and Exchange Commission, investigated and found nothing. No one in the SEC wanted believe Madoff was a crook. This is an example of default to truth.

> Harry M. Markopolos, a former securities industry executive and a forensic accounting and financial fraud investigator, began sounding the alarm in May of 2000. On multiple occasions, Harry warned the SEC that Madoff's wealth management business was a Ponzi scheme. In May of 2000, Bernie's fund had less than $7 billion in assets under management (AUM). By the time Bernie was caught, authorities estimated the fraud and heist of the AUM at $64.8 billion.

Jerry Sandusky, an American college football coach, who was convicted of rape and sexual abuse. Sandusky served as an assistant coach for his entire career, mostly at Pennsylvania State University under Joe Paterno, from 1969 to 1999.

Sandusky was an extremely popular figure at Penn State, as a football coach and for his charitable work with children, primarily children from single-parent, fatherless homes.

A friend of mine from State College, Pennsylvania, said, "For years there were rumors, about Sandusky, but no one wanted to believe a role model for thousands of kids could have a dark side as a sexual predator." Another example of *default to truth*.

Dr. Larry Nassar, the former USA Gymnastics national team doctor and osteopathic physician at Michigan State University. For years young girls would question Dr. Nassar's medical procedures… but here again: *default to truth.* Much like Madoff and Sandusky cases, if more people (parents and coaches, in this case) had listened, Dr. Nassar would have been arrested earlier and fewer young girls would have been molested. In this case, the *default to truth* was so strong that some of the parents, medical doctors themselves, would not believe their daughters. They could not believe the doctor of the USA Gymnastics team could be a bad person—or a serial pedophile.

When a pension, a union, or a government agency decides to bring Ted in, they are no longer willing to default to truth. They trust their intuition, the bad feeling in their gut. They are tired of the B.S., the "Blue Sky" and the lack of answers and transparency.

If more of those responsible for pensions are scrutinized and held accountable, the roaches and rats of Wall Street, the Fed, and thousands of government officials will be taking early retirement, before the pension they have been stealing from, goes bust.

If more of those responsible for pensions are scrutinized and held accountable, the roaches and rats of Wall Street, the Fed, and thousands of government officials will be taking early retirement, before the pension they have been stealing from, goes bust.

In 2002, *Rich Dad's Prophecy* was published, sounding the alarm—a default to truth— about the flaws inherent in DC pension plans, such as the 401(k) plans in America, the Super in Australia, and the RRSP in Canada. Once again, I took a good bit of heat for my take on the future and my predictions from both *The New York Times* and *Wall Street Journal*.

It has not been easy. No one wants to hear that something they believe is good—in this case, their pension and the retirement promises made—is really bad. So bad, in fact, that pensions may bring down the world economy.

Today's young people are not stupid. They are better informed than any generation before them with a world at their fingertips (literally). It's unlikely that they will blindly "do as they are told" and "donate" to Ponzi schemes. And if the young stop "donating"—i.e. funding Social Security and Medicare—the game, for their parents and grandparents is over. Money needs to come in... before it can be paid out.

When I talk to young people across America, I discover that they know that government-sponsored social programs like Social Security and Obamacare are Ponzi schemes. And that they hold the cards... on the future of those houses of cards.

Two School Teachers – Two Pensions

A number of months ago, Ted and I did a talk in Miami to a group of real estate investors. Ted talked about the looming failure of city and state employee DB pensions, and I talked about the failure of DC pensions.

Later that day, two schoolteachers, a husband and wife, came up to me and expressed their concern about the security of their teachers' pension. After I explained their DB pension was probably secure, they sighed a breath of relief.

I then added that, unfortunately, while *their* retirement might be secure, young people, the future taxpayers, are destined to lose via higher taxes and fewer government services.

Not missing a beat, the teachers replied, "We don't care. Just as long as our retirement is secure."

Stealing from Children

All Ponzi schemes steal from children. That is why Social Security and Medicare are Ponzi schemes and facing insolvency. Ponzi schemes do not work without the new money coming in… young paying for the old.

To be clear: DB and DC pension plans, technically, are not Ponzi schemes. They do not steal directly from children. But they might.

The reason I mentioned the two schoolteachers I met in Florida is because they did not care about future retirees. They do not seem to care if their retirement security robed taxpayers and kids of their future.

I explained to the two teachers that the depression I see coming may be caused by the collapse of pensions. Again, they didn't seem to care. Their dual teachers' pensions would put them in the millionaire category.

I pushed forward explaining that, if the pensions collapse, GRUNCH and the Creature would bail out the retirement of Baby Boomers. And bailing out their teachers' pensions would steal from the young.

Again, they didn't seem to care. All they cared about were golf courses and cruising the world.

Finally, they asked, "Why do you say Ponzi schemes steal from the young?"

I responded with a question of my own: "Do you know much about student loans?"

They nodded their heads in unison.

"Aren't student loans stealing from the young?" I asked.

Their response was immediate and defensive: "But it's for their education."

"Yes, it is," I replied. "But these student loans are the most onerous loans in the world. I have millions of dollars in loans, but I would never sign up for a student loan."

I didn't hesitate to share with them other thoughts I have on the subject: Student loans, in my opinion, are criminal, preying on kids of middle class and poor families. Student loans entice teenagers without financial education to sign up for a loan that may hang around their neck like an albatross, ruining their credit for life… and, if the loans aren't paid, they will follow them to the grave.

Nobody challenges this because of the *default to truth*. Nobody wants to criticize education's Ponzi scheme. Nobody wants to say student loan debt is bad—because everyone wants to believe education is good.

Are you hearing, as I am, the words of Ayn Rand…

"Evil requires the sanction of the victim."

I have been ripped-off and screwed more times than I can count—because I wanted to believe that the people I worked with were good people. My laziness and incompetence and trust blinded me, my personal default to truth, and I refused to see the dark side of those people I wanted to trust.

The guy on the cover of *Barron's* did me a big favor. I finished my options trading course, which prepared me for the crash of 2008. Finishing the five-year options trading course gave me the insight to be on CNN in a segment with Wolf Blitzer when I called the crash of Lehman Brothers six months before the start of the 2008 depression.

In 2020, student loan debt in the United States is over $1.6 trillion. Student loan debt now exceeds credit card debt.

In 2009, President Barack Obama changed the laws, taking student loan debt away from banks and gave the business of student loans to the U.S. Treasury.

In 2020, student loan debt is the number one asset of the U.S. government.

Instead of panicing, my partners, Kim, and I moved millions of dollars into a crashing real estate and the crashing interest rate market.

You may be thinking: *How is the options trading course related to this?* A down payment on real estate is an *option*. In this case, a *call option*, a bet that real estate prices would go back up. For a few million dollars, we optioned hundreds of millions of dollars of real estate in a hot market… at rock-bottom prices.

When interest rates, the cost of money, kept falling from 7.5 percent to 2.5 percent, the leverage multiplier of low real estate prices combined with low interest rates was astronomical.

My $150,000 Ponzi scheme loss turned into a priceless and lucrative life lesson.

The Best Lesson

The best lesson I gained from my options trading class was not to fear market crashes. Once I grasped that lesson, I realized I would make more money when markets crash, because markets crash faster than go up. Hence the saying:

> *"The bull goes the stairs…and the bear goes out the window."*

For me, investing five years in study to learn to trade options was a step in securing my future. It took some time and effort, but it was a better plan than following the tired, obsolete advice to

> *"Invest for the long term in a well-diversified portfolio of stocks, bonds, mutual funds and ETFs."*
> … *only to risk losing everything when the bear goes out the window.*

In the next chapter, I will go into more detail on why the bear will go out the window, and why the bear may not get up again… for years.

When the next collapse comes, the young will be robbed. Again.

CHAPTER SEVENTEEN

Your Pension Is Lying About Its Investment Fees

Your pension is lying about how much money it pays Wall Street investment firms to manage its assets. It's paying exponentially more—perhaps 10 times—than it's telling you.

In countless investigations, I have proven that the fees pensions disclose to the public are just the "tip of the iceberg." Most often this is due to alternative investment fee complexity. That is, alternative investments impose multiple levels of hefty fees which are not fully disclosed to even to pensions, much less participants. The problem is exacerbated by the fact that (1) pension overseers lack investment experience and, hence, don't know how to ferret out fees and (2) pension overseers have agreed to withhold documents related to fees from participants and the public—so no one has the opportunity to verify whether fees are fully disclosed.

Why should you care? Because the more your pension pays Wall Street, the worse its net (after fees) investment performance is and the less it has to pay you.

From the beaches of sunny South Florida, I took a quick peek at the website[1] of the distant—nearly 1500 miles away—$7 billion Employee Retirement System of the State of Rhode Island and concluded that the investment fees the state pension was paying to Wall Street were suddenly skyrocketing. Worse still, these escalating fees were not being fully disclosed to the public. Rhode Island politicians and pension officials were dramatically understating the totals.

At that time, April 2013, the total investment management fees disclosed on the state pension's website was **$11,563,979.**

Remember that number.

A hastily-penned article in Forbes entitled *"Rhode Island Public Pension 'Reform' Looks More Like Wall Street Feeding Frenzy"*[2] stating my alarming findings drew an immediate and harsh response from the

---

1 http://investments.treasury.ri.gov/
2 https://www.forbes.com/sites/edwardsiedle/2013/04/04/rhode-island-public-pension-reform-looks-more-like-wall-street-feeding-frenzy/#61d5bdde879d

clueless politician responsible for the pension (and the Wall Street feeding frenzy), Rhode Island General Treasurer Gina Raimondo.

The following day, Raimondo claimed in an interview/article entitled, *"Raimondo Fires Back After Forbes Contributor Attacks Her"*[3] she did not know the amount of the fees the pension paid to its investment managers. Despite her lack of knowledge, she assured readers that the undisclosed fees were reasonable.

The article could have been more aptly-titled *Raimondo Misfires* because, as mentioned earlier, sponsors of public and private retirement plans have a fiduciary duty to ensure that the fees the plans they oversee pay money managers for investment advisory services are reasonable. If Raimondo and the pension officials *did not even know* the amount of fees the pension paid, they could not possibly have concluded the fees were reasonable and consistent with their legal duties.

Within months the disclosure regarding investment expenses on the pension's website was swiftly modified in response to growing criticism. By August, **$47.5 million** in total fees was disclosed—a 400 percent exponential increase.[4] By September, the disclosed fees mushroomed to **$70 million**.[5] Today total annual fees disclosed by the pension are nearly **$80 million**.

To recap, amid growing scrutiny by independent experts, the fees disclosed to the public have ballooned from **$11.5 million to $80 million a year**.

These totals are *closer* to the truth.

But as I concluded six years ago in the findings of my October 2013 forensic investigation, *Rhode Island Public Pension Reform: Wall Street's License to Steal*,[6] "the total investment expenses may already, or in the near future, amount to a staggering almost **$100 million** annually." Tragically, state workers' benefits were forcibly cut 3 percent to pay the exorbitant 4 percent fees to Wall Street billionaires.

The pension did not get what it paid for—investment performance has faltered as fees have soared.

---

3 https://www.wpri.com/blog/2013/04/05/qa-raimondo-fires-back-after-attack-by-forbes-contributor/
4 https://www.providencejournal.com/article/20130803/NEWS/308039987
5 https://www.providencejournal.com/article/20130925/News/309259970
6 https://www.forbes.com/sites/edwardsiedle/2013/10/18/rhode-island-public-pension-reform-wall-streets-license-to-steal/#4e94799e7659

The $87 billion North Carolina state pension is ten times bigger than tiny Rhode Island's. Surely the eleventh largest public pension fund in the United States providing retirement benefits for more than 875,000 North Carolinians, including teachers, state employees, firefighters, police officers and other public workers has the resources to properly calculate and disclose the investment fees it pays? Sure, assuming, of course, it wanted to tell the public the truth.

My 2014 forensic investigation of the state pension entitled *"North Carolina Pension's Secretive Alternative Investment Gamble: A Sole Fiduciary's Failed 'Experiment,'"* concluded the State Treasurer had withheld from public disclosure a massive portion of the fees the pension paid its highest-risk money managers, resulting in the dramatic understatement of fees and risks related to certain investments, as well as the pension as a whole. Indeed, it appeared that the massive hidden fees she failed to disclose in many instances dwarfed the excessive fees disclosed to the public.

The limited investment fee information provided to me by the Treasurer indicated that disclosed fees had ballooned over 1,000 percent since 2000, as the pension moved away from low-cost, low-risk internally managed investments to high-cost, high-risk alternative funds managed by Wall Street. The total disclosed investment fees were projected to climb to over **$500 million**. I estimated the total *undisclosed* fees would comparably climb to approximately **$500 million**.

Thus, I estimated total state pension annual fees would amount to approximately **$1 billion** in the near future—almost twice the figure projected and disclosed by the then-Treasurer.

Since pension underreporting of fees paid to Wall Street money managers has been exposed repeatedly in recent years—at least in the United States—at this point in time demands by participants for greater transparency and accountability regarding fees should be taken seriously by pensions.

Since pension underreporting of fees paid to Wall Street money managers has been exposed repeatedly in recent years—at least in the United States—at this point in time demands by participants for greater transparency and accountability regarding fees should be taken seriously by pensions.

In my opinion, no pension should be confident it is properly disclosing all fees and summarily dismiss participants' concerns.

In my opinion, no pension should be confident it is properly disclosing all fees and summarily dismiss participants' concerns.

You owe it to yourself and your pension to tenaciously ask questions about fees. You must be persistent and not be dissuaded by quick answers and reassurances because—remember—your pension overseers, like Rhode Island Treasurer Gina Raimondo, probably don't even know the full extent of the fees.

Why?

Gross malpractice generally practiced.

The Coming Depression

There are two countries in an economic depression as of 2020. They are Zimbabwe and Japan. The facts are, both countries have been in depression for over 30 years, since the 1990s.

In 1990, Japan entered the "Lost Decade," now the "Lost Decades" as it nears the 40-year mark.

In 2008, America entered its "First Lost Decade" and I would argue that, in 2018, America entered a second "Lost Decade".

Ray Dalio, American billionaire investor, hedge fund manager, and philanthropist is the founder of Bridgewater Associates, one of the world's largest hedge funds. He has this to say about the two types of depressions.

1. *Deflationary Depressions* occur in countries where the debt is financed in local currency.

2. *Inflationary Depressions* occur in countries where the debt is financed in foreign currencies.

Japan's debt is financed in Japanese yen. Japan is in a *deflationary* depression. Prices keep falling. At one time, the Japanese had the highest savings rate per capita in the world. When interest rates went sub-zero, rather than stop saving, the Japanese ran out in mass and bought safes to keep saving at home, in the hope of stocking away a few more yen.

I am fourth-generation Japanese-American. I do not speak Japanese, but I do remember a few words, spoken by my grandparents. One word is *baka*, which means *fool or idiot.* You may have guessed, that word was often directed at me, a little boy who was always doing something he should not have been doing.

Zimbabwe's debt is financed in foreign currencies, such as the dollar, euro, and yen. Zimbabwe is in an *inflationary* depression. Prices keep rising. Not long ago, it took 300 trillion Zimbabwe dollars to buy an egg. That's inflation.

Most people think the definition of inflation is simply that "prices go up." It is not. Inflation is money coming into the system, like a flood after a dam fails. Inflation occurs when *money* fails.

Zimbabwe went into hyper-inflation when trust in the Zimbabwe dollar had eroded to the point that it was non-existent. People had to spend it as fast as they got their hands on it.

Rich Countries

A very important point is that both countries are rich countries.

Zimbabwe, once known as Rhodesia, was the Breadbasket of Africa. Today, Zimbabwe is the basket case of Africa. Japan, on the other hand, is a very rich, high-functioning, productive country. And yet it's been in depression for 30 years.

The problem is the differences in their governments' fiscal and monetary policies.

And the fact that Japan's debt is financed in Japanese currency, the yen.

What About America? Many people think the United States is headed for a depression. I think it will be a deflationary depression, with a slight difference.

The U.S. dollar is the reserve currency of the world, which makes America a little different. The U.S. dollar became the reserve currency of the world in 1944, at the Bretton Woods Conference. The problem is that in 1971 the United States broke its promise to keep the U.S. dollar backed by gold. Today, the world is in debt to the United States.

> The U.S. dollar became the reserve currency of the world in 1944, at the Bretton Woods Conference. But in 1971 the United States broke its promise to keep the U.S. dollar backed by gold. Today, the world is in debt to the United States.

In other words, the U.S. dollar is strong because of the hundreds of trillions of dollars of global debt is in U.S. dollars. Good for the United States; bad for the countries whose debt is in U.S. dollars.

This is GRUNCH... the heist in action. And this heist couldn't take place unless the U.S. dollar was the reserve currency of the world. The world's reserve currency is fake money.

The Failure of Money

It is important to understand the difference between money flooding a system (i.e. QE, quantitative easing, the printing of money) and the failure of money.

So, is America in a depression? Yes, in my opinion. But rather than admit America is in a depression, the experts have been calling it The Great Recession.

It's also important to understand the difference between a Great Recession and a Great Depression? That's where definitions come in.

Jim Rickards, author of the *Currency Wars, Road to Ruin,* and *Aftermath* has this to say about the American depression:

"This is a depression. This is not a normal recovery."

"America is in a depression, a continuation of a global depression that began in 2007."

Jim uses John Maynard Keynes definition of *depression* to support his statement:

According to Keynes, a depression is "years of below trend growth." In other words, there could be growth, but very low growth.

For example, let's say you were earning $50,000 a year in 1980. If you were still earned $50,000 a year in 2020, a wage stagnation that millions experienced, with no income growth, you would be in below-trend growth.

In other words, **you can have growth in a depression.**

Utilizing Malcom Gladwell's term *default to truth,* many "financial experts" use words like *growth, green shoots,* and *longest economic recovery in history* to keep people from the truth.

As Jim Rickards and many others point out, this *"longest economic recovery in history"* has not turned into the *Greatest Depression in History,* simply because the Fed, the Treasury, and Wall Street have kept the economy floating, via the *greatest money printing heist in history.*

The only questions are:

1: When will the *default to truth* become truth?

2: What happens if the U.S. dollar fails?

What Will Cause the Depression?

The primary reason Ted's investigative reporting is so important, is that he allow us to see what most people cannot see.

One possible cause of the next depression are pensions, both DB and DC.

Ted's work uncovers the corruption inside failing pensions. As he states;

> "A hastily penned article in Forbes entitled Rhode Island Public Pension 'Reform' Looks More Like Wall Street Feeding Frenzy[7] stating my alarming findings drew an immediate and harsh response from the clueless politician responsible for the pension (and the Wall Street feeding frenzy), Rhode Island General Treasurer Gina Raimondo.

> "The following day, Raimondo claimed in an interview entitled, Raimondo Fires Back After Forbes Contributor Attacks Her[8] she did not know the amount of the fees the pension paid to its investment managers. Despite her lack of knowledge, she assured readers that the undisclosed fees were reasonable.

> "The article could have been more aptly titled Raimondo Misfires because, as mentioned earlier, sponsors of public and private retirement plans have a fiduciary duty to ensure that the fees the plans they oversee pay money managers for investment advisory services are reasonable. If Raimondo and the pension officials did not even know the amount of fees the pension paid, they could not possibly have concluded the fees were reasonable, consistent with their legal duties."

The Plot Thickens

Ted sent me this additional bit of info from his files:

> "Two years ago, Rhode Island's state pension fund fell victim to a Wall Street coup. It happened when Gina Raimondo, a venture capital manager with an uncertain investment track record of only a few years—a principal in a firm that had been hired by the state to manage a paltry $5 million in pension assets—got herself

---

7 https://www.forbes.com/sites/edwardsiedle/2013/04/04/rhode-island-public-pension-reform-looks-more-like-wall-street-feeding-frenzy/#61d5bdde879d

8 https://www.wpri.com/blog/2013/04/05/qa-raimondo-fires-back-after-attack-by-forbes-contributor/

elected as the General Treasurer of the State of Rhode Island with the financial backing of out-of-state hedge fund managers.

Raimondo's new role endowed her with responsibility for overseeing the state's entire $7 billion in pension assets. In short, the foxes (money managers) had taken over management of the hen house (the pension).

For Raimondo, a 42-year-old Rhode Island native serving as state treasurer was a major career boost. It also has presented her with an opportunity to enrich herself and her hedge fund backers at the expense of the state's pension fund, the public workers who are counting on it to finance their retirements and the taxpayers who could be stuck for millions, or billions, of dollars if it's mismanaged.

Further, a significant portion of the Treasurer's wealth and income relates to shares she owns in two illiquid, opaque venture capital partnerships she formerly managed at Point Judith Capital— one of which she convinced the state to invest in on different, less favorable terms. Unlike the state, which paid millions for its shares in one of the Point Judith funds, the Treasurer was granted shares in both of the venture capital funds for free. Worse still, the venture capital industry is noted for its lack of transparency and, once the Treasurer assumed office, she refused to disclose virtually any information regarding the investment fund in which she and the state pension remain co-investors.

For example, the Treasurer refused to release documents which would reveal whether she (or any other investor) had been granted any special rights more favorable than those granted to the state, or other limited partners in the fund.

Point Judith Capital, the Treasurer's former employer, is a firm which is substantially funded by Tudor Investment Corp., a multi-billion-dollar private equity and hedge fund conglomerate controlled by the secretive billionaire Paul Tudor Jones. Without Tudor as a strategic partner, possessing a substantial investment performance history, Raimondo's Point Judith would not have been a contender for a $5 million venture capital commitment from the state. In a very real sense, today Rhode Island's leading investment fiduciary is largely compensated by an out-of-state hedge fund investor—and, worse still, she is paid indirectly and secretly."

As Ted said to me, this is just the tip of the iceberg. Pension funds are filled with "Gina Raimondos," fronts for private capital markets. Ted also said that 25 percent of all public pension funds, which are supposed to be public, are in secret off-shore accounts.

A reasonable conclusion is that the world of money, not just pension funds, is filled with "Gina Raimondos," funded by secretive Wall Street billionaires.

This is GRUNCH and the Creature in human form.

This is why the coming depression will be the biggest ever.

The depressions in Zimbabwe and Japan are nothing compared to what I see as the coming U.S. Depression, a collapse caused by the crash of pension funds.

No one knows how long the coming depression will last. The Great Depression that began with the stock market crash of 1929 lasted for 25 years, until 1954. The most important question is: Will you have sustainable cash flow and be able to survive and thrive for what could be several decades?

CHAPTER EIGHTEEN

Your Pension Is Lying About Its Investment Performance

Over the course of my 35-year career examining thousands of pensions, I have never seen a pension openly acknowledge that its investment performance is poor. Obviously, there have to be some pension laggards, but you'd never guess it from reading the glowing performance reports they provide to participants and the public.

So, how can every pension claim to have superior investment results?

They lie—or, to put it more kindly, they don't tell the complete truth.

Since your pension managers can be counted upon to continue to lie to you about the pension's investment performance, you need to know how to look beyond the performance puffery and get to the truth about how it's really doing.

For example, the overseers of the Rhode Island state pension claim to "deliver strong long-term returns and reduced risk for the state's investments." The fund's website indicates that for 5-year and 10-year periods it has beaten the Total Plan Benchmark which supposedly represents the hypothetical performance of an average fund with the same asset allocation as Rhode Island and a 60/40 Blend hypothetical portfolio benchmark that consists of 60 percent U.S. stocks and 40 percent U.S. fixed income.

Beware of meaningless or misleading benchmarks—selected by pensions themselves—against which to gauge their performance!

The Rhode Island pension may have beaten a convoluted "Total Plan Benchmark" it created for itself (to easily beat), but that's irrelevant. If it hadn't beaten its Total Plan Benchmark long enough, the pension would have simply changed it—which is exactly what it did a few years ago. Further, the pension is not remotely invested 60 percent in publicly traded stocks and 40 percent in bonds—its portfolio is far, far riskier. Thus, whether it beat a 60/40 hypothetical portfolio benchmark is equally irrelevant.

So, you need to dive deeper. The performance of the pension should be compared against a relevant benchmark which you can readily determine—like the S&P 500 or Russell 3000.

When held up against these unbiased benchmarks, Rhode Island's performance doesn't look good at all.

For the 10-year period that ended June 30, 2019, gambling at the Rhode Island state pension resulted in a mere 8.75 percent return, massively underperforming the 14.41 percent return of the far less costly, far less risky Russell 3000 Index. For all other periods—one-, three-, and five-year—the pension significantly underperformed the Index. In other words, the pension took on greater risk for which it was not only *not rewarded*, but punished severely.

There have been volumes written on the best ways to evaluate investment performance. You probably don't wish to spend years becoming an expert on the subject. So, keep these simple points in mind.

Whenever presented with investment performance results for your pension, you should be suspicious. Due to gross malpractice generally practiced, almost all pensions will consistently perform poorly compared to an appropriate benchmark index. Thus, pensions are always searching for ways to make their bad or mediocre performance look stellar. Pensions are assisted in this effort by investment consulting firms which have mastered the art of investment performance chicanery.

Trust me, the people running your pension will never, ever admit to participants or the public that they've done a bad job. If they did, they'd lose their jobs.

Make sure performance is shown for all time periods—one, three, five, and 10 years. Short-term performance is less important than long-term because you'll be in the pension for decades.

The choice of benchmarks and the changing of benchmarks are both telling. It's safe to assume that whenever a benchmark changes, it

The choice of benchmarks and the changing of benchmarks are both telling. It's safe to assume that whenever a benchmark changes, it means performance against the benchmark looks bad. Also, "custom" benchmarks, like Rhode Island's Total Plan Benchmark are always designed to be confusing, easy to manipulate, easy to beat, and used to make the pension's performance look good.

means performance against the benchmark looks bad. Also, "custom" benchmarks, like Rhode Island's Total Plan Benchmark are always designed to be confusing, easy to manipulate, easy to beat, and used to make the pension's performance look good.

Here's the current composition of the Rhode Island state pension's Total Plan Benchmark:

GROWTH

Total Public Growth
40% MSCI ACWI Net

Total Private Growth
11% ILPA All Funds Index
2.5% ODCE + 2.5%
1.5% ILPA/Cambridge Distressed Securities Index

INCOME

1.5% Alerian MLP Total Return
3.5% Liquid Credit Custom (50% BoA HY/50% CS LL)
3% S&P LSTA Lev Loans + 3%

STABILITY

Crisis Protection Class
4% CS Managed Futures 18% Vol Index
4% Barclays Long Duration US Treasury Index

Inflation Protection
2% CPI + 4%
4% NFI-ODCE Index
1% Barclays 1-10 Year TIPs Index
1% BB Commodity Index

Volatility Protection
11.5% Barclays Agg
6.5% HFRI FOF Composite
3.0% BofA Merrill Lynch US T-Notes 0-1 Yr

Confused? Of course you are, and so am I. That's exactly the intended result.

It's complex, with lots of movable parts overseers can tweak to produce a favorable comparison.

So, when attempting to evaluate the performance of your pension stick with simple, straightforward benchmarks like the S&P 500 for American pensions and the MSCI World Index for foreign pensions.

Finally, as pensions increasingly gamble in alternative funds with hard-to-value portfolios, investment performance claims become all the more suspect. Alternative managers can be counted on to overstate the value of assets they manage to boost their performance-based compensation. Pension performance will, likewise, be inflated when they do so. The managers of alternative investments and pension overseers are complicit in the performance puffery.

The Three Little Pigs

Most of us know the story of the Three Little Pigs and the Big Bad Wolf. As the story goes, the first little pig built his house out of straw, so he could spend more time playing. The second pig built his house out of sticks and ran out to play with the pig that built his straw house. The third pig, spending a lot more time and money, built his house with bricks.

As the third pig labored away, the first two pigs frolicked and played and tried to convince the third pig to join them. The third pig's reply: "The big bad wolf is coming. My house of bricks will protect me."

The first two pigs squealed and chanted, "Who's afraid of the big bad wolf, the big bad wolf, the big bad wolf?"

When the big bad wolf shows up, he huffs and puffs and blows down he house of straw. And then the house of sticks. It's the house built of bricks that keeps the pigs safe.

The moral of the story, I believe, is clear.

KISS: Keep It Super Simple

This has been the hardest chapter for me to write. My challenge has been how to keep "financial complexity" simple. So, I start with the story of the Three Little Pigs—a children's story that everyone can understand. In this chapter you will learn and how and why the giant house of straw, built by the Big Bad Wolf will soon come tumbling down.

The good news is, this chapter starts with a real teacher, who knows the Big Bad Wolf, and knows the house of straw the wolf built, intimately.

YouTube University

I love YouTube. If I had had YouTube in 1983, the year I went searching for GRUNCH, my search for answers would have been easier. Finding out who and what GRUNCH is has been like putting together pieces of a thousand-piece puzzle, a thousand different people, each representing a different piece. YouTube gives me access to people I would never have met—pieces of the puzzle I could never have found on my own.

The first TV interview I did about *Rich Dad Poor Dad* was on *Oprah!* Oprah Winfrey was a voice the world trusted and respected, and my appearance on that show catapulted *Rich Dad Poor Dad* onto the world stage. Since then I have done thousands of interviews all over the world in support of financial literacy. The challenge I always face was that most television interviews, especially in news and finance shows, are only a few minutes long. It's a big challenge to be both relevant and informative in that short a window.

And that's why I love YouTube. YouTube grants adequate time—for real teachers to explain their experience in the real world. Obviously, there are a number of quacks on YouTube, but this free access to real teachers from the real world of money is priceless.

One real teacher I watch is Brian Reynolds. I came across him on YouTube on a Real Vision program entitled *Brian Reynolds – The unfunded pension and retirement crisis.* I have watched and re-watched the program at least 10 times, which is another reason why I love YouTube—I can learn at my own pace and go back over the information again and again. Still wanting to learn more, I invited Brian on the Rich Dad Radio Show and during that interview Brian filled in more pieces of the puzzle.

The Detroit Bankruptcy

Two big pieces of the current financial crisis that Brian Reynolds gave me were:

1. The power of the modern credit market
2. The Detroit bankruptcy

These two events had blown the world into the biggest financial bubble in world history, a bubble some call, The Everything Bubble. I call it a Castle of Straw.

When The Everything Bubble bursts, the world will fall into the Greatest Depression of all time.

Lessons from The Three Pigs

Prior to 1971, the world economy was a house of bricks. The U.S. dollar was the Reserve Currency of the world and backed by gold. The world economy was safe, strong, and secure—like the little pig's brick house. The brick house kept all the pigs safe.

Prior to 1971, a saver could save for the future because the dollar held its value. Even Central Banks of the world, saved the U.S. dollar, because it was as good as gold.

As I covered in a previous chapter, there are three definitions of money:

> Prior to 1971, a saver could save for the future because the dollar held its value. Even Central Banks of the world, saved the U.S. dollar, because it was as good as gold.

1. Unit of account – that's easy to measure

2. Exchangeable – and readily accepted, which is why Bitcoin is not yet money

3. Store of value – something that holds its value

In 1971, the U.S. dollar stopped being a store of value. Sadly, if you look at modern definitions of money, the words *store of value* are no longer included in the definition. More evidence that, today, *savers are losers.*

In 1971, the gap between the rich and poor began to widen. This is why rich dad's lesson #1 is: *The rich do not work for money.* I'll pose the question yet again: Why work for money when the rich are printing it and interest rates are sub-zero?

After 1971, inflation set in. Inflation set in because the dollar was losing value. Stock prices and housing prices began to rise. Real estate flipping and stock trading became professions for the average person. Investing for the long-term was for losers.

In 1974, Nixon opened the doors to China. High paying jobs left America and China boomed. Also in 1974, DB pensions were replaced by DC pensions.

In 1971, the world economy boomed. Unfortunately, it was an economy that was no longer a house of bricks. Today, the world economy is a giant, invisible castle in the sky, a castle made by the Big Bad Wolf, a castle made of straw, a castle to capture the Three Little Pigs.

Also in 1971, the credit/debt market was born. Today, the modern credit/debt market is the foundation for the global castle made of straw.

Since 1987, the Big Bad Wolf has been huffing and puffing, hoping his castle made of straw does not come down. His huffing and puffing has blown the world economy into The Everything Bubble. When The Everything Bubble bursts, everything—stocks, bonds, real estate, gold, and silver—will come down and a global depression will begin.

The real story of the Big Bad Wolf and the Three Little Pigs is found on YouTube and told by Brian Reynolds, a real teacher. Brian begins with the story of the birth of the modern credit market.

Credit: The Start of the Modern Pension Crisis

Brian Reynolds began his career in business, in the 1980s, before there was a credit market.

Ray Dalio defines **credit** as:

> *"The giving of buying power. The buying power is granted in exchange for a promise to pay it back, which is **debt**."*

When Brian began working, the stock market ran on fundamentals, like earnings and valuations. In those days, a strong credit rating—AAA, for example— was important.

Fundamentals are like building a house out of sticks. Why sticks and not bricks? Because our money is fake. Before 1971, the world economy ran on fundamentals and real money, backed by gold. After 1971, credit/debt became money.

Today, many of those once-AAA-rated companies, such as GE, General Electric, and AT&T, are rated BBB, one level above "junk." Today, these once-blue-chip companies are "corporate zombies" loaded with debt. In fact, AT&T is the most indebted corporation in America.

Brian worked in the money market industry, and witnessed firsthand how it evolved into today's modern Shadow Banking system. And as I've mentioned earlier in this book, Danielle di Martino Booth states, in her book *Fed Up*, the shadow banking system is a banking system outside the control of the Fed and other Central Banks. Credit/debit and the shadow banking system built the house of straw.

Baby Bankers

I once heard a speaker describe the bankers at the Federal Reserve as children, sitting in a child's car seat, playing with a toy steering wheel. The baby banker has a lot of fun, making a lot of car noises, turning the toy steering wheel, left and right... while the shadow banking system drives the real car.

That metaphor of a baby pretending to steer a car is fitting, I think. The Fed has been wrong, many times. I do not know why so many people listen to what the Fed says. The Fed "steering the economy" has caused crashes to the left and crashes to the right, wiping out millions of jobs, trillions of dollars in wealth, and destroyed millions of lives. Yet the Fed has never warned anyone of a coming crash.

Today, the world has trillions in dollars earning negative interest rates. How did this happen? Why would anyone save money to get less money back? Why anyone listens to the Fed's highly educated PhD's from our best schools is a mystery to me. If they were real doctors they might have been sued for malpractice.

Brian states that this "tiny credit market" started to grow as "junk," in the 1980s and evolved into a "credit Goliath" in the 1990s.

The Junk Bond King

If you are old enough, you may remember Michael Milken, the Junk Bond King, in the 1980s. He went to jail for securities fraud in the 1990s. Milken was sentenced to 10 years in jail and fined $600 million. To his credit, he turned his life around and today is regarded as a philanthropist with a net worth estimated as $3.4 billion.

Milken continues to invest in private equity, hedge funds, venture capital, and more than one asset management firm. A side note regarding the assets Michael Milken invests in: Those "assets" are central to the theme of this book. Milken is 100 percent invested in shadow banking. I doubt he has a government pension or a 401(k)... or is living off the interest of his savings.

Brian Reynolds also explains that the tiny credit market evolved from the junk bond market, evolving into the modern "investment grade" credit industry.

Today, "junk bonds" are called "private credit." It sounds much more respectable. And is yet another example of a default to truth.

Today the shadow banking, private credit, and private equity markets are more powerful than the public stock or bond markets. Private credit is the tail that wags the dog.

Around 1990, public employee pensions were becoming "the dominant global investor." In 1984, public employee pensions were 60 percent of GDP. In 2019, public employee pensions are 120 percent. Brian says, "Nothing in the world has grown that fast."

There are reasons why public employee pension funds have grown so fast.

One of them is *promises.* Governors and legislatures made pension promises to public employees. The problem: These governors and legislatures did not fund the pensions to match their promises.

> There are reasons why public employee pension funds have grown so fast.

Another reason is *the gap.* The pension board needed to make 7.5 percent returns in the market, to fill the gap.

As Ted has explained:

> *"If the fair value of the plan assets is less than the benefit obligation, there is a pension shortfall."*

The problem: Pension boards are made up of teachers, firefighters and police officers.

And as a solution to the gap problem, in the 1980s, Wall Street began selling pension boards high risk "credit assets." The financially illiterate pension overseers blindly bought up these assets. The free fall started when, in 1990, high risk assets began failing, all over the world.

Hedge Fund (LTCM) Long-Term-Capital Management, a hedge fund many pensions were invested in, imploded. Wall Street ended up bailing out LTCM, fearful that 4,000 other hedge funds, filled with pension money, might fail as well.

In another attempt at a solution, on November 12, 1999, President Bill Clinton signed the Financial Services Modernization Act that repealed Glass-Steagall. The Glass-Steagall Act, was passed in 1933 and sought to permanently end bank runs and the dangerous bank practices that caused panics. The 1933 Glass Steagall Act separated mom and pop savings banks from high-risk investment banks.

But in 1999, President Clinton joined mom and pop savings banks with investment banks, turning mom and pop banks into hedge funds. President Clinton allowed banks to use mom and pop's insured savings as leverage. In other words, your savings could be used as credit and debt the same way hedge funds and investment funds use credit and debt. Mom and pop's hard earned savings are now gambling chips for the banks.

When the bets lose, and the house of straw falls, and mom and pop taxpayers are on the hook for the losses. The big winners: the banks.

In the 1990s, pensions (via Wall Street) had bet on Worldcom and Enron. Their valuations went through the roof, with hot pension money. I remember photos of extravagant, multi-million-dollar toga parties hosted by Worldcom CEO Dennis Kozlowski… reportedly with pension money.

Earlier, I wrote about the accountants who suggested that we convert our real estate holdings into stocks and bonds. The accountants came from Arthur Anderson, once a highly-respected member of the Big 8 Accounting firms. Arthur Anderson went down with the Enron scandal.

Then came another failed and desperate solution: the Greenspan put. The Fed started bailing out the bankers.

And another bubble—the dot-com bubble—grew between 2000 and 2002. In 2002 the dot-com bubble burst.

I've always believed that pictures speak louder than words:

125 YEARS OF THE DOW

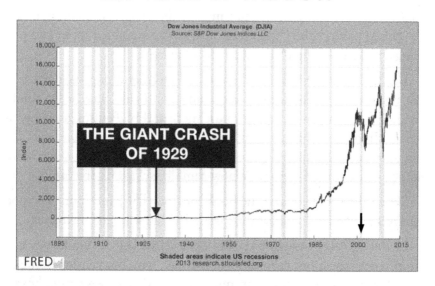

The Greenspan put was used to stop crashes and prevent future depressions. This is why I say the Fed is a criminal organization. The Greenspan put may have saved the bankers, but it screwed "we the people."

The Greenspan put was the Big Bad Wolf, huffing and puffing, doing anything to keep the house of straw from collapsing.

The Everything Bubble

Today as I write, in December of 2019, the world is in The Everything Bubble.

The cost of *everything we want* is cheap. Television sets, clothes, and toys are cheap.

The cost of *everything we need* is expensive. Education, healthcare, housing, and food are expensive.

Lesson

Equity investors are different than credit investors. This is why the growth of the modern credit market, starting in the 1990s, has changed the world of investing.

Public employee pensions and the modern credit market have caused once blue-chip, AAA credit companies of the 1980s to become BBB rated—"pre-junk" zombie companies... yet valued at the highest prices in the world.

The Biggest Crash in World History

As I write, in December of 2019, the stage is set for the biggest crash in world history.

When will it happen? No one knows. Maybe tomorrow, maybe five years from today. Maybe 10 years. The straw castle will collapse when all the public employee pension funds want to get out of the shadow banking system at the same time.

That is what happened in 2008. When that day comes, *everything* will crash. Stocks, bonds, real estate, commodities, even gold and silver.

It's tough to say what will trigger it. It could be anything, much like the single snowflake setting off an avalanche. It could be a military war, a trade war, or a small country declaring bankruptcy and defaulting on its debt.

The House of Cards Crashes

As Brian Reynolds explains, equity investors are always going in and out. Credit investors only go in. When they come out... they all come out at the same time. Again, that is what happened in 2008.

If just one, former blue-chip company, bank, or country defaults its investment grade BBB credit rating and is down-graded to "junk," the exodus will begin.

When investment-grade credit turns into "junk," there will be no one around to buy it.

Why? Because funds that invest in investment grade credit, BBB and above, must sell when BBB turns to junk.

There are not enough businesses that invest in "junk." When the shadow banking system begins dumping "junk," it will turn into "super-junk."

It will be like yelling "fire!" in a crowded theater. The burst of The Everything Bubble will look like a one-lane dirt road filled with hundreds of cars all trying to get out of town at the same time.

I am concerned that the end is near. The biggest crash in world history and the next great depression may be just one snowflake away.

Which begs a series of questions: What can a person do? How do you avoid getting crushed when The Everything Bubble bursts? What will be safe?

I will answer these questions in the final chapters of this book. The final chapters are dedicated to how you can build your house of bricks.

CHAPTER NINETEEN

Your Pension Is Lying About Whether It Has Enough Money to Pay You

A recent survey of government pensioners in the United States revealed they are generally unaware as to whether their pension is underfunded or not as well as the risks any such underfunding poses to them.

You need to know whether your pension is adequately funded to pay the money it's promised you.

An "underfunded" pension plan is a retirement plan that has promised to pay more money than it has. The more underfunded a pension is, the less assurance that future retirees will receive the pensions they were promised or that current retirees will continue to get their previously established benefits. Certain pension plans, such as corporate pensions in America governed by the federal ERISA law, are required to inform pensioners if the plan is seriously underfunded.

The federal government has different warning labels for pension plan underfunding. The government's alert system is:

- Critical – This is code red for pensions, meaning that your plan is less than 65 percent funded and faces either a funding shortfall in the next five years or insolvency within five to seven years.
- Severely Endangered – The next level down, this translates into less than 65 percent funding and a shortfall within seven years.
- Endangered – This is akin to a yellow alert, meaning the plan is less than 80 percent funded and will face a shortfall within seven years.

Whether a pension plan is underfunded can be as simple as comparing the fair value of plan assets, which includes plan assets that the sponsor estimates it will have in the future, to the accumulated benefit obligation, which includes the current and future amounts owed to pensioners. If the fair value of the plan assets is less than the benefit obligation, there is a pension shortfall.

However, there is the risk that corporate and government pension sponsors, as well as others, may use investment return assumptions to reduce, or increase, the need to add money their pension funds. Assumptions can be made in good faith, or they can be used to minimize, or maximize, any adverse impact on corporate earnings or government budgets.

For example, if a company or government assumes a long-term rate of return on its pension investments of 8 percent, this would increase the money expected to come from investments and reduce the need to add money to the pension. This assumption, however, is overly optimistic if you consider that the long-term return on stocks is about 7 percent and the return on bonds is even lower.

Using inflated or unrealistic investment return assumptions can save corporations and governments money—they are required to put less money into their pensions. That's not good, but it's pretty obvious why sponsors would inflate their investment return assumptions.

Why would a sponsor of a pension want to manipulate, i.e. lower their investment assumptions to make the pension look *more underfunded* or imperiled—closer to running out of money?

The answer is that sometimes corporations or governments want to nudge or push their pensions toward bankruptcy and thereby either eliminate the pension or reduce the benefits that have been promised.

> *Sometimes corporations or governments want to nudge or push their pensions toward bankruptcy and thereby either eliminate the pension or reduce the benefits that have been promised.*

For example, after the city of Detroit filed for bankruptcy in 2013—the largest municipal bankruptcy filing in U.S. history—the actuaries hired by the city's emergency manager concluded that the pension was five times more underfunded than previous estimates.[1]

The pensions fought back, challenging this assessment. But, in the end, the bankruptcy proceedings eliminated $7.8 billion in payments promised to retired workers and the city got off the hook for $4.3 billion in unfunded health-care obligations and future costs. It could have been far worse. At one point during the bankruptcy journey, the city's general retirees were threatened with the possibility of having

1   https://www.bloomberg.com/opinion/articles/2013-08-21/how-underfunded-are-detroit-s-pension-plans-

their pension checks slashed by up to 34 percent and police and fire retirees were looking at cuts of up to 10 percent.

The fact that America's public pensions are spectacularly—to the tune of $1.4 trillion—underfunded has received a lot of national attention.

States with the worst pension fund shortfalls include Colorado, Connecticut, Illinois, Kentucky, and New Jersey which have less than half of the assets needed to pay promised benefits and another 17 states have less than two-thirds. (Many local pensions in well-funded states are less than 50 percent funded.)

Warren Buffett has described America's underfunded public pensions as a "disaster" that companies and individuals should consider when deciding whether to expand or move into a state.

"If I were relocating into some state that had a huge unfunded pension plan, I'm walking into liabilities," Buffett said. "'Cause I mean, who knows whether they're gonna get it from the corporate income tax or my employees—you know, with personal income taxes or what. That liability isn't gonna—you can't ship it offshore or anything like that. And those are big numbers, really big numbers."

"The politicians are the ones that really haven't attacked it in a good many states. And when you see what they would have to do, I say to myself, *Why do I wanna build a plant there that has to sit there for 30 or 40 years?*" Buffett said. "They will come after corporations, they'll come after individuals. They're gonna have to raise a lotta money."

It's anyone's guess what will happen if and when a state pension in the United States runs out of money, but it's indisputable that the amount of money that will be needed to bail out a *single* failed U.S. state pension will be in the *tens of billions*.

The extent to which public pensions are underfunded has been obscured by governmental accounting rules, which allow pensions to eliminate their underfunding, no matter how large, simply by investing in sufficiently risky assets. In fact, investing in riskier assets may allow a pension to raise investment assumptions, but it also increases the probability that existing underfunding will increase.

Gambling on risky investments is never the solution to underfunding.

Gambling on risky investments is never the solution to underfunding.

I can assure you that should one of America's states go bankrupt due to its unfunded pension liabilities, it will be bailed out. Otherwise, it's Armageddon and that's not going to happen in America.

The only question is: Who will pay for the bailout?

All public pension stakeholders—American taxpayers and pensioners—need to get educated *fast* as to the causes of coming pension collapses and learn what they can do about it now.

The bottom line is you need to know whether the pension that has promised to provide for your retirement security has sufficient money to pay you over the decades of your retirement. You also need to be aware that pensions, with the assistance of paid professionals such as actuaries and investment consultants, manipulate their finding levels in furtherance of their ever-shifting goals. Your fully-funded pension may, overnight, suddenly be deemed "code red."

In order to find out whether your plan is underfunded, ask for any reports related to your pension's funding level, such as the plan's most recent annual report summary.

Look at the '"funding ratio" section of your plan's annual report. This figure is a ratio of assets to liabilities. If the funding ration is above 100, the plan is over-funded. If the funding ratio is below 100, the plan is underfunded. The higher the ratio, the better funded the plan is.

An underfunded pension should not be ignored. If a company's pension is underfunded, the company should revise its cash flow plans and reduce spending. Further, when a company informs employees the pension plan has become underfunded, this may attract the attention of investors, vendors, lenders, and rating agencies, which may cause the company further financial trouble.

An underfunded pension does not necessarily mean that you will not get the benefits you have been promised. Government pensions are safer than corporate pensions because a government can increase taxes to cover the pension shortfall. However, if your plan's funding ratio is well below 100, you should join with other participants and demand changes to the plan. You may wish to contact the plan administrator and representatives of any union to which you belong.

Pensions with growing underfunding—not uncommon—are especially worrisome.

The Gold Standard: A House of Bricks

As I mentioned before, I quoted the Robert Frost classic *The Road Not Taken* in my first book *Rich Dad Poor Dad* more than 20 years ago. In that poem—in its entirety in Chapter One—these words from Frost in the closing verse spoke to me and influenced the path my life would take…

> *I shall be telling this with a sigh*
> *Somewhere ages and ages hence:*
> *Two roads diverged in a wood, and I—*
> *I took the one less traveled by,*
> *And that has made all the difference.*

In 1973, I returned home to find my poor dad without a job, paycheck, or pension.

When he suggested that I follow in his footsteps—which was to go back to school, get my Master's degree, possibly my PhD, and get a job in corporate America or with the government—was when those "two roads diverged" for me… and I took "the one less traveled." With 20/20 hindsight I can confidently say: "… that has made all the difference."

I chose to follow in my rich dad's footsteps. Choosing to forsake job security and a pension meant I had to build my own house of bricks.

Houses of Straw and Sticks

In his book *The Road to Ruin*, Jim Rickards tells a story about giving a talk at a public library in New York City, warning of the impending financial disaster. A man raised his hand and asked, "I have a job and a 401(k). What should I do?"

Jim wanted to say, "Quit your job." But instead he offered suggestions of what a person could do to prepare for the coming financial meltdown.

In his book Jim continues on with a poem from *Cat's Cradle*, a novel by Kurt Vonnegut:

> *Oh, a sleeping drunkard*
> *Up in Central Park,*
> *And a lion-hunter*
> *In the jungle dark,*

And a Chinese dentist,
And a British queen—
All fit together
In the same machine.
Nice, nice, very nice;
Nice, nice, very nice;
Nice, nice, very nice—
So many different people
In the same device.

Jim's warning in *The Road to Ruin* is the same warning Bucky Fuller' gave in *GRUNCH of Giants* and G. Edward Griffin gave in *The Creature from Jekyll Island*…:

"Nice, nice, very nice… So many different people, in the same device."

In simplest terms, most people are living in financial houses made of straw and sticks… and the Big Bad Wolf is coming.

As Ted writes:

"Confused? Of course you are, and so am I. That's exactly the intended result.

"Finally, as pensions increasingly gamble in alternative funds with hard-to-value portfolios, investment performance claims become all-the-more suspect. Alternative managers can be counted on to overstate the value of assets they manage to boost their performance-based compensation. Pension performance will, likewise, be inflated when they do so. The managers of alternative investments and pension overseers are complicit in the performance puffery."

If I had followed in my poor dad's footsteps and not taken a different path, I, too, would be confused and living in a house made of straw or sticks.

In the remaining chapters, I will share with you how I built my house of bricks, and how you can too.

Build Your House of Bricks

Jim Rickards and I come from nearly opposite life paths. Yet when we get together, we share very similar solutions for building a house of brick.

In *Road to Ruin*, Jim tells the story of Palazzo Colona, a private palace in the heart of Rome, Italy. The palace has been owned by one family for 31 generations, over 900 years. The family controlled the palace and its wealth through political changes, religious battles, and war after war. Jim writes:

> *"On a cool Roman evening in the fall of 2012, I joined a private dinner in the Palazzo, with a small group of the world's wealthiest investors. My dinner companions were mainly Europeans, some Asians, and relatively few from the United States. Amid marble, gold, paintings, and palatial architecture, I mused on the meaning of old money compared with the new money crowd that congregated for cocktails near my Connecticut home. These phrases distinguish between old family fortunes like the Rockefellers, Vanderbilts, and Whitneys, and the new fortunes o Greenwich hedge fund mavens and Silicon Valley CEOs. Implicit in this distinction is that old money has proved they know how to preserve wealth while the jury is still out on new money busy buying yachts, jets, and sharks in formaldehyde.*
>
> *"Still, old money in the United States is perhaps 150 years old, or slightly older for families like the Astors and Biddles. Yet in Rome, I was ensconced in a nine-hundred-year-old fortune, still intact. Here was a family fortune that had survived the Black Death, the Thirty Years War, the wars of Louis XIV, the Napoleonic Wars, both world wars, the Holocaust, and the cold war.*
>
> *"I knew the Colonna family were not unique; there were other families like them throughout Europe who kept a low profile. These families are only too happy to be overlooked by the Forbes 400. This type of wealth and longevity could not be due merely to good luck. In nine hundred years, too many cards are turned from the deck for luck alone to be sufficient. There had to be a technique.*
>
> *"I turned to a striking Italian brunette to my right and asked, "How does a family keep it's wealth for so long? It defies the odds. There*

must be a secret." She smiled and said, "Of course. It's easy. A third, a third, and a third." She paused knowing I needed more, and continued, "You keep one third in land, one third in art, and one third in gold. Of course, you might have a family business as well and you need some cash for necessities. But land, art, and gold are things that last."

Things That Last

Rich dad's definition of intelligence is:

"If you agree with me, you're intelligent. If you disagree, you're an idiot."

If rich dad were alive, he would say Jim Rickards is a very intelligent man. The only thing that rich dad did not have was "museum quality artwork." Rich dad only invested in things that last. Today, Kim and I do the same.

In my 2019 book *FAKE* I write about buying my first gold coin, a South African Krugerrand, in Hong Kong for about $50. I still have that gold coin and today as I write, it is worth about $1,500.

This is because, since 1971, the U.S. dollar has lost nearly 97 percent of its purchasing power.

This is why I say that savers are losers and why Kim and I save gold and silver coins, not dollars.

In 1972, rich dad recommended I start buying gold.

In 1973, poor dad recommended I return to school to get my MBA… and possibly my PhD.

That same year rich dad recommended I take real estate investment courses, so I could learn about debt, taxes, and cash flow.

Building Your House of Bricks

In 1971, Nixon took the world off the gold standard. That event was a milestone. If you are serious about building your house of bricks, start with a foundation of gold, not paper.

If gold is too expensive, start with silver coins. Personally, in 2019, silver is the smarter buy. An investor with $2.00 can start investing in investment grade silver, pre-1964 dimes. Everyone in the world can afford $2.00.

Gold and silver are god's money and will last much longer than cash or paper assets.

The gold and silver you buy today can be held by your family for generations.

Your Pension Is Not Fully Protected Under Law or By Law Enforcement

It has been said that the law is a blunt instrument, incapable of dealing with all shades and circumstances, with little or no regard for individual situations.

Management of pensions is doubly complex because equal parts of law and investing are involved. Typically, those knowledgeable in pension law, lack investment expertise and vice versa. Lawyers, judges, and regulators rarely understand investment theories, strategies, and practices well enough to sort through the nonsense and make sound decisions. They are regularly misled by savvy Wall Streeters intent on selling dicey financial products. Even well-intentioned investment experts rarely grasp nuances which can have severe legal consequences.

Again, pension overseers are often the most clueless of all regarding both pension law and investing.

Further, the world of investing is fluid and ever-changing. New investment products and practices emerge and old schemes come back into vogue every few years. The law moves slowly—it does not, and possibly cannot, supply clear, timely answers for every pension management question that arises.

Derivatives? Bitcoin? Even where the most comprehensive legal and regulatory framework exists and answers are crystal clear your pension is at risk because enforcement or policing of the law is lacking. I teach U.S. Department of Labor pension investigators. As trained and committed as they are, they're hopelessly out-gunned by the investment industry. Wall Street runs circles around regulators charged with enforcing pension laws.

However, the vast majority of pensions are not subject to any comprehensive law.

The world of investing is fluid and ever-changing. New investment products and practices emerge and old schemes come back into vogue every few years. The law moves slowly—it does not, and possibly cannot, supply clear, timely answers for every pension management question that arises.

For example, as hard as it is to believe, explain, or justify, the approximately $4 trillion in America's government pensions is not protected by any comprehensive federal or state law.

The Employee Retirement Income Security Act of 1974 (ERISA), the federal law that establishes minimum standards for pension plans in private industry, *does not* apply to public pensions.

ERISA was enacted to protect the interests of employee benefit plan participants and their beneficiaries by requiring the disclosure of financial and other information concerning the plan to beneficiaries, establishing standards of conduct for plan fiduciaries, and providing for appropriate remedies and access to the federal courts.

Since ERISA doesn't apply to public pensions, none of the above-mentioned protections exist with respect to America's state and local government pensions.

Further, both investment managers hired to manage public pension assets and public pensions themselves often get confused as to what legal standards apply.

For example, my 2015 forensic investigation of the Jacksonville Police and Fire Pension Fund revealed that while the city pension was not subject to federal (ERISA) pension law, it had voluntarily adopted the highest ERISA legal standards and then failed to enforce those standards. Therefore violators could be subject to personal liability for any ERISA fiduciary breaches. In short, this non-ERISA government pension voluntarily became ERISA governed, much to the confusion of all involved.

So, if ERISA does not cover state and local pensions in America, what law does?

In short, there is no comprehensive law. Public pensions are regulated by a thin patchwork quilt of state and local laws. Many of the most significant issues related to managing state and local pensions are unanswered in these statutes. Anything that's not clearly illegal under applicable law can probably be done without consequences.

For example, another investigation of a government pension I undertook revealed that while local law prohibited the pension from investing in hedge funds, the pension had secured a twisted legal opinion from a local firm that an investment in a trust that, in turn, invested exclusively in hedge funds was permissible.

An investment in a fund that invested exclusively in hedge funds was not an investment in a hedge fund—got that?

The pension overseers were obviously hell-bent upon gambling in hedge funds. Some Wall Street huckster had sold them on a complex hedge fund investment they neither understood nor would have selected on their own. The overseers weren't about to let the law get in their way. They didn't outright break the law—they just bent it in their direction.

Another problem with state and local government pensions in the United States is that no federal or state regulator, or law enforcement agency, is monitoring or policing these plans. Crooks need not worry about the feds—the Department of Labor or FBI—coming after them and even state Attorneys General are reluctant to get involved in public pension matters due to political concerns.

For example, in both Rhode Island and North Carolina my forensic investigations exposed billions in state pension looting amounting to the largest financial crimes in the histories of these states. My clients and I referred these findings to both the FBI and state Attorneys General.

In Rhode Island, then-Attorney General Kilmartin responded that his office had "limited investigatory authority" and "did not investigate issues involving the solvency of the pension fund." Imagine that, the state's top cop—who claimed on his website to "fight to enhance the economic security of Rhode Island and restore the public trust in state government by fighting corruption"—lacked the authority to delve into a multi-billion-dollar heist.

"If you have general questions regarding the fund's solvency, contact the pension," said Kilmartin. "If your complaint concerns an allegation of criminal misconduct, you should contact the Rhode Island State Police or your local police department."

Refer to a local police department to investigate complex, multi-billion-dollar financial crimes?

With all due respect, Kilmartin's office didn't have anything more important to do than investigate allegations of wrongdoing related to the largest pot of money in Rhode Island—billions in the underfunded pension that thousands of state workers depend upon for their retirement security.

In closing: to protect your retirement security you need to have some knowledge of the law that governs your pension—and the law's strengths and weaknesses. While American pension laws are often regarded as the most comprehensive, as we have seen there are significant loopholes—such as federal ERISA law not covering public pensions—and monitoring and enforcement by regulators and law enforcement is hardly foolproof.

Many foreign countries lack the regulatory and financial capacity to thoroughly ensure the integrity and solvency of foreign pensions.

However, if pensioners globally take an active role in scrutinizing their pensions, asking probing questions, identifying irregularities, funding investigations through crowdfunding, and sharing all they have uncovered with regulators and law enforcement, regulators and law enforcement will become more familiar with pension matters and more likely to make pension protection a priority.

Infinite Returns: Print Your Own Money

In *Rich Dad Poor Dad*, I wrote about "making money" by melting down used toothpaste tubes, and forging (illegally, I later learned) nickels, dimes and quarters. In many ways I continue the practice, legally, today.

In financial literacy, printing my own money is known as *infinite returns*, aka money for nothing. Money that is created from pure knowledge.

In 1973, I followed my rich dad's advice and took a 3-day real estate investment course. In that course, for an investment (in myself) of $385, I learned the secret of "infinite returns."

As I said, I continue the practice today, using Other People's Money (OPM) to create money from nothing.

ROI: Return on Investment

A major reason why both DB and DC pensions are in trouble is because the ROIs, the returns on investment or the yields, are low.

As stated earlier, government employee DB pensions are unable to achieve 7.5 percent yields in their pensions. But why? Why can't DB pensions achieve such low yields?

As Ted states:

> *"Over the course of my 35-year career examining thousands of pensions, I have never seen a pension openly acknowledge that its investment performance is poor. Obviously, there have to be some pension laggards but you'd never guess it from reading the glowing performance reports they provide to participants and the public.*
>
> *So, how can every pension claim to have superior investment results?*
>
> *They lie—or to put it more kindly, they don't tell the complete truth."*

So, what is the truth?

The answer, as I see it, is the default to truth. We all know humans have the potential to lie, cheat, and steal, yet most of us would rather believe the people we trust our money understand and respect with fiduciary responsibility. DB pensions can't achieve even the low return of 7 percent because they are lying to themselves, and everyone else, about the health of the pension.

The definition of fiduciary is:

> *Person or a legal entity (firm, bank, credit union) holding assets (cash, property, securities) or information as an agent-in-trust for a principal (stockholder, customer, member). A fiduciary owes (among other obligations) the duty of loyalty, full disclosure, obedience, diligence, and of accounting for all monies handed over, to the principal. A fiduciary must not exploit his or her position of trust and confidence for personal gain at the expense of the principal. Law demands a fiduciary to exercise highest degree of care and utmost good faith in maintenance and preservation of the principal's assets and rights and imposes compensatory as well as punitive damages on the erring fiduciary.*

In 1971, the U.S. dollar became fake money and the word *fiduciary* seemed to go right out the window.

In 1974, the year ERISA was passed, which led to the introduction of 401(k)s and IRAs, the Fed and Wall Street became a den of thieves, preying on the innocent and uninformed. Fuller explained it best in his book *Cosmography*, published 1992, nearly 10 years after his death:

> *"The Dark Ages still reign over all humanity, and the depth and persistence of this domination are only now becoming clear. This Dark Age prison has no steel bars, chains, or locks. Instead it is locked by misorientation and built of misinformation. Caught up in a plethora of conditioned reflexes and driven by human ego, both warden and prisoner attempt meagerly to compete with god.*
>
> *All are intractably skeptical of what they do not understand. We are powerfully imprisoned in these Dark Ages simply by the terms in which we have been conditioned to think."*

I'll admit that I've read (and re-read) Fuller's words more than a few times and thought about what they mean. What do those words mean to you? Powerful words like these mean different things to different people.

Fuller passed away on July 1, 1983. This book, *Cosmography*, was not found or published until 1992. I understand that it was completed prior to his death and found on a shelf in his office. When I read the book, I knew I had to do my best to become a writer, although I really enjoy writing and failed high school English because I was "a poor writer."

Each time I have read that passage from *Cosmography*, I found myself focusing on these words:

> *"This Dark Age prison has no steel bars, chains, or locks. Instead it is locked by misorientation and built of misinformation."*

And these:

> *"We are powerfully imprisoned in these Dark Ages simply by the terms in which have been conditioned to think."*

Fuller, like my rich dad, believed humans lived in a prison, trapped by the words,

> *"Go to school, get a job, work for money, pay taxes, save money, get out of debt, and invest in the stock market."*

Each time I have read that passage from Cosmography, I found myself focusing on these words:

"This Dark Age prison has no steel bars, chains, or locks. Instead it is locked by misorientation and built of misinformation."

And these:

"We are powerfully imprisoned in these Dark Ages simply by the terms in which have been conditioned to think."

During the three summers I studied with Fuller—1981, 1982 and 1983—he often said,

> *"Who says you have to earn a living?"*

He questioned the very idea of working for money. Reading *Cosmography*, I could hear him saying,

> *"Animals do not earn a living. Trees, birds, fish, do not earn a living.*
>
> *Only humans are conditioned, taught to earn a living, working for money."*

He encouraged us to "think for ourselves," and ask ourselves:

> *"What does god want done? Then decide if we wanted to do what god wants done. Not do what you want to do. Do not do what you love. Do what god wants done."*

Infinite Returns

Once you understand the words *infinite returns*, you will never have to work for money again. I teach financial literacy because, if you have a command of the words of money, you too will never have to work for money.

In *Rich Dad Poor Dad*, rich dad's lesson #1 is "The rich don't work for money."

I have taken this lesson to heart—and not worked for money—since 1973, the year I returned from Vietnam. Instead, I have been studying and learning to be an entrepreneur and an investor, creating my own assets. I create assets that achieve infinite returns, so I do not have to buy assets from Wall Street or be a prisoner working for money to earn a living. I am free to do... not what I want to do, but what I think god wants done. Even, sometimes, when it isn't something I want to do.

Here are some examples of how I achieve infinite returns.

- Kim and I founded the Rich Dad Company in 1996. We raised $250,000 from investors. The investors received a 200% return of their money in three years. Today The Rich Dad Company, a private company, produces millions of dollars a year—all infinite returns since Kim and I do not have any of our own money in The Rich Dad Company.

- Rich Dad is an international brand. The business licenses the use of the Rich Dad brand to book publishers and approved education companies all over the world. The revenue this generates represents a 100% infinite return.

- In *Rich Dad Poor Dad*, I wrote about Ray Kroc, founder of McDonald's, asking an MBA class at the University of Texas, "What business is McDonald's in?" The class responds, "The hamburger business." To which Ray answered, "McDonald's is a real estate company." The high-margin fast food business gives McDonald's the earnings to purchase the most expensive and valuable real estate in the world.

Rich Dad is also in the real estate business. The following diagram explains the cash flow pattern in real estate.

$1 million

$5 million ($1 + $4 million of debt)

Let's say Rich Dad earns $1 million in the B quadrant. That $1 million is invested into a $5 million apartment complex as $1 million equity plus $4 million debt.

The cash flow, the income, is tax free.

The IRS allows three tax incentives that we take advantage of. They're not loopholes, because the government created them expressly because it wants and encourages Inside investors to invest. The three incentives are:

1. Appreciation: The price or value of the property goes up tax free.

2. Depreciation: Tax write-offs, for the wear and tear on the property.

3. Amortization: The payment of the principal on the loan, tax free.

The net effect: Infinite returns and no taxes, legally. Money— literally—for nothing… and zero taxes. There are no taxes on debt because the government wants qualified individuals and entities to borrow. If you and I did not borrow, money is not created. Remember, after 1971, the U.S. dollar became debt.

"You Can't Do That Here"

Wherever I teach, in the United States or anywhere in the world, someone will stand up and say, "You can't do that here."

To which I reply, "Do you have McDonald's here?" Obviously, the answer is most always, "Yes."

And then I say, "You may not be able to do this here, but someone is."

Again, in Fuller's words:

> *"We are powerfully imprisoned in these Dark Ages simply by the terms in which have been conditioned to think."*
>
> *And:*
>
> *"The Dark Ages still reign over all humanity, and the depth and persistence of this domination are only now becoming clear. This Dark Age prison has no steel bars, chains, or locks. Instead it is locked by misorientation and built of misinformation.*

Structured Finance

Explained in simplest terms, structured finance uses the leverage of:

- Money: equity
- Leverage: credit/debt
- Tax incentives

Mom and pop and most pension funds do not have the advantages of structured finance. That is a factor in why their returns, their ROI and yields, are so low. That is why they struggle and take great risks to achieve a 7.5 percent yield.

Yield, by definition, refers to the cash return to the owner of a security or investment.

Mom and pop and pension returns are low because Wall Street keeps the fees and the gains that should go to the investor or employee's pension fund.

As Ted states:

> *"Typically, those knowledgeable regarding pension law lack investment expertise and vice versa. Lawyers, judges and regulators rarely understand investment theories, strategies and practices well*

enough to sort through the nonsense and make sound decisions. They are regularly misled by savvy Wall Streeters intent upon selling dicey financial products. Even well-intentioned investment experts rarely grasp nuances which can have severe legal consequences.

"Again, pension overseers are often the most clueless of all regarding both pension law and investing."

When the next crash arrives, DB pensions will bring down the stock market wiping out mom and pop's DC pensions.

We already know the Fed will bail out the banks. The Fed will probably bail out employee pensions. The question is, will the Fed bail out mom and pop?

I'll leave you with this powerful promise: If you have real financial education, seek out real teachers, and learn from real-life experience, you will live and understand the the words *infinite return*... and how they can change the game of investing.

> Here's what I see happening: When the next crash arrives, DB pensions will bring down the stock market wiping out mom and pops DC pensions.
>
> We already know the Fed will bailout the banks. The Fed will probably bailout employee pensions. The question is, will the Fed bailout mom and pop?

You will never again say, "It takes money to make money." You will discover that you already have all the god-given power to make money... without money. If you do not need fake money to make (more) fake money, then you will be able to go back on to your own gold standard, saving real gold and silver... god's money.

CHAPTER TWENTY-ONE

Your Pension May Never Have Been Audited

One winter morning in 2011, a select group of senior US Airways pilots from all over the country descended upon my seaside home in Florida. The purpose of the meeting was for the pilots to give me background information on their multi-billion-dollar, now-bankrupt pension and discuss my upcoming forensic investigation of the pension on behalf of their union, the US Airline Pilots Association. The pilots sat around the long formal dining room table and helped themselves to Dunkin' Donuts coffee and donuts I had laid out. Captain Dave Westberg opened the discussion by casually asking, "You do realize that our pension was never audited?"

"That's not possible," I quickly responded with great confidence. "All corporate pensions are required under the federal law protecting pensions, ERISA, to have an annual audit."

"Oh no, they're not. And ours never was audited," said Captain Westberg speaking with even greater confidence for the group as they all nodded in agreement.

Well, Captain Westberg was right and it was news to me—even after decades specializing in pensions—that corporate pensions were not required to be audited.

ERISA, I soon learned in subsequent research, permits companies to instruct auditors *not* to perform any auditing procedures with respect to a pension's investments under certain circumstances. Instead, a "limited scope audit" is legally permitted where the auditor does not perform the normal procedures designed to provide certain basic assurances about the existence, ownership, and value of a plan's assets held in trust. In a limited scope audit, the auditor disclaims responsibility for fraud or mismanagement of the excluded investments, i.e. all or virtually all of the pension's assets.

In fact, about 60 percent of all corporate pensions in the United States are not audited.

While limited-scope audits of pensions are commonplace, the dangers related to these audit opinions have been widely recognized for decades. The very year I was investigating the failed US Airways Pilots Pension, in 2011, the Inspector General for the U.S. Department of Labor recommended a repeal of ERISA's limited-scope audit exemption, stating, "These 'no opinion' audits provide no substantive assurance of asset integrity to plan participants or the Department."[1]

You might be wondering, *even if* the law permits corporations to instruct the auditors of their pension plans *not* to look for fraud or mismanagement of the pension's investments, why on earth would a corporation ever request, or agree to, a "no-opinion" audit that the Department of Labor itself says is worthless to plan participants and the Department?

Clearly, auditors might prefer and recommend limited-scope audits where they are permitted to pretend to audit but then disclaim responsibility for fraud or mismanagement. But why would companies that sponsor pensions go along with the ruse?

Let's call it another example of the "gross malpractice generally practiced" that pervades pension management.

Likewise, many public or government pensions—including some of the largest—are not audited annually by independent certified public accountants.

At a 2014 press conference, I stood in front of a room full of reporters and executives of the State Employees Association of North Carolina, the South's leading public employees association comprised of 55,000 state employees and retirees, to announce the key findings of my forensic investigation of the North Carolina state pension. Lack of an audit was on the top of the list.

"Remarkably, there were no audited financial statements for the state pension, the seventh largest public pension in the nation with in excess of $87 billion in assets. The lack of audited financials for the state pension is indefensible. An audit which would improve oversight and management of pension investments, reveal deficiencies (including fraud and other wrongdoing), and produce savings, is decades overdue.

---

1 Semiannual Report to Congress, Office of Inspector General for the U.S. Department of Labor, Volume 65, October 1, 2010-March 31, 2011.

"The State Lottery, Turnpike Authority, Housing Finance Agency, State Education Assistance Authority, University of North Carolina System, Supplemental Retirement Income Plan, or the cash basis claims and benefits of the Health Plan—all were audited by independent auditors.

"Contrary to the dictates of common sense, the largest state fund, upon which hundreds of thousands of state workers and retirees depend for their retirement security, failed to be audited.

"Remarkably, there were no audited financial statements for the state pension, the seventh largest public pension in the nation with in excess of $87 billion in assets. The lack of audited financials for the state pension is indefensible. An audit which would improve oversight and management of pension investments, reveal deficiencies (including fraud and other wrongdoing), and produce savings, is decades overdue."

"In an unprecedented state of affairs, the pension entered into agreements with Wall Street to keep secret 35 percent or $30 billion of pension assets. Where is the money? No one knows for sure."

As a participant in a pension, you need to be certain of the integrity of the assets in your pension—i.e. where the assets are and if they are vulnerable to mismanagement, fraud, or abuse. For your protection, you need to find out whether your pension has ever been audited. Ask for and read your pension's audit to determine whether the auditor expresses an unqualified opinion on the integrity of the financial statements (that's good) or if it's a worthless "no-opinion" audit.

There are reasons why elected politicians, auditors, and corporations might prefer limited-scope, no-opinion audits or no audits at all.

There is no reason you should accept anything less than a true and complete audit of your pension to safeguard your retirement savings.

There are reasons why elected politicians, auditors, and corporations might prefer limited-scope, no-opinion audits or no audits at all.

There is no reason you should accept anything less than a true and complete audit of your pension to safeguard your retirement savings.

The Future of Money

As I mentioned in Chapter One, Buckminster Fuller was best known as a futurist. John Denver dedicated his song *What One Man Can Do* to Fuller, a man he called The Grandfather of the Future.

Looking back from 2019, I can see many of Fuller's predictions coming true. One of his most significant prediction was that "there will be a new technology, entering upon this earth, before the end of this decade." In 1989, six years after his passing, today's Internet was released to the public as ARPANET. ARPANET sent its first message in 1969, for the Defense Department and was turned over for civilian use in 1989. Fuller also predicted the end of the USSR, which also occurred in 1989.

The year 1989 marked the end of the Industrial Age and the birth of the Information Age.

Living Longer

Another Fuller prediction was that the life expectancy for Baby Boomers, if they did not smoke, overeat, or do drugs, was 140 years in excellent, youthful, health. His reasoning was tied to breakthroughs in medical technology that would eliminate diseases that kill us as well as give us better health and life expectancy.

As you know, stem cells, medical lasers, mapping of the human genome, medical robots, and other breakthroughs, have greatly enhanced health, youthfulness, and longevity. The problem is affordability. These treatments are expensive and not generally covered by health insurance.

Health is much like education. The rich can afford the best education for their kids. The poor and middle class often receive sub-standard education. In America, there are thousands of kids on waiting lists to get into charter schools. That is a sad testimonial to the quality of public education.

The bigger problem I see is how a person will support themselves if they live to be 140 years old—in a world without jobs. Will governments raise taxes to pay for healthcare, housing, and food for humans to live longer? Or will they just print more money?

CHAPTER TWENTY-ONE

Super AI

Fuller also predicted the end of jobs. His reasoning on this was that the rise of super-artificial intelligent machines that would replace humans. As I've mentioned, Fuller thought the idea of going to work for money was obsolete. He predicted "Super AI Machines" would soon free humans from work that was drudgery.

The October 5, 2019 issue of *The Economist* had this as it's cover story headline: *Masters of the Universe*. Rather than picture of Michael Douglas, who played Gordon Gekko in the 1987 movie *Wall Street*, the image was not of a human, but of a robot. The subtitle read: "How machines are taking over Wall Street." I don't see many employers who'd want to hire an out-of-work Wall Street executive who is used to making $10 million a year when they could have efficient AI technology do the same job.

Fuller also predicted *people would be paid to not work*. That idea was not well received 60 years ago, but has pervaded the current 2020 presidential election.

The Rise of Socialism

Today there is lots of talk about UBI, a Universal Basic Income.

Presidential candidates tout socialist agendas, such as free education, free medical, free housing, and on and on. The question that few seek to address is, in my view, the most important: Who is going to pay for it?

Another popular idea is MMT, Modern Monetary Theory, or Magical Money Tree. Ben Bernanke was called "Helicopter Ben" for his MMT ideas. The difference between Helicopter Ben's ideas and MMT is that Ben's money went to the rich. The MMT money would go to everyone.

Freedom to Solve Our Planet's Problems

Fuller's optimism for paying people not to work was based on his theory that people would then be free to solve our planet's problems rather than go to work.

Fuller asked our class over and over: "What does god want done?" He reminded us that it is not, "What do I want to do?" Or, "I want to do what I love." He challenged us to look to the future and imagine what god wants done.

And, it's been said, that he often asked himself, "What can I do? I'm just a little guy."

Paying people to not work would free people to ask themselves these same questions. *People*—innovators, entrepreneurs, visionaries—would solve our problems, not governments, politicians, or bureaucrats.

With those thoughts in my head, Kim and I took our leap of faith in 1984. We asked ourselves, *What does god want done?* And *What can we do?* We, too, were just we're just "little people."

In 1984, Kim and I began teaching, outside the school system. Since I loved learning, but hated school, Kim and I began teaching the way my rich dad taught me, playing games and having fun, learning about money, business, and being an entrepreneur. We used music, sang songs to inspire our spirits, and focused on solving problems, rather than making money. That model of education has carried us all over the world.

Predictions Come True

In December of 2013, Venture Capitalist at Redpoint posted this article about Fuller's Predictions coming true.

A 47-Year-Old Prediction Comes True

"On January 8, 1966, *The New Yorker* profiled Buckminster Fuller for the first time. During a trip to a Maine island with the journalist Calvin Tomkins, Fuller said something tremendously prescient:

"Fuller proposed a worldwide technological revolution...[that] would take place quite independently of politics or ideology; it would be carried out by what he calls 'comprehensive designers' who would coordinate resources and technology on a world scale for the benefit of all mankind, and would constantly anticipate future needs while they found ever-better ways of providing more and more from less and less.

"Fuller's prediction has come true. The founders of the tech companies embody the values of the comprehensive designers and enact the changes Fuller predicted. From Google investing $100M behind Calico, a life extension research company to Khan Academy which extends high-quality education into the hands of hundreds of millions of people to Twitter which has become the mouthpiece of revolutions and countless others to SpaceX which has dramatically decreased the cost of space transport to Oxford Nanopore which sequences DNA on a chip the size of a USB drive, these products and the comprehensive designers behind them have benefitted mankind tremendously.

"The most important part of the quote for me is the last phrase: the constant improvement and disruption, innovation and change. Welcome to the era of the comprehensive designer."

Welcome to the era of the comprehensive designer? I'm sure you're thinking: *What is a comprehensive designer?*

As Fuller said to our class time and time again, "I do not work for me. I work for everyone." A comprehensive designer works for everyone, doing what god wants done.

Repeating Bucky's words: "… 'comprehensive designers' who would coordinate resources and technology on a world scale *for the benefit of all mankind.*" [Emphasis added.]

The Future of Money

In 1927 Fuller was in a deep depression due to the tragic loss of his young daughter, he came close to committing suicide. On the shores of Chicago's Lake Michigan Bucky's plan was to swim out into the water and eventually drown. Just before taking his life, Fuller had what he referred to as a "spiritual revelation." Coming out of his spiritual *satori*, moment of enlightenment, Fuller decided never to work for money again and dedicate his life working for everyone.

Rather than go to work, Fuller and his wife rented a tiny apartment in Chicago. After breakfast, Fuller would sit at the breakfast table and did only what his "intuition" guided him to do. Rather than panic when money ran out, Fuller, who referred to himself as Guinea Pig B, just kept working. And always and just in the "nick of time," some form of life support, such as food or money, would show up.

Not convinced, I questioned him further on this "nick of time" hocus pocus. He replied, "If things showed up, in the nick of time, that was the universe's way of saying, 'You're on the right track.' If nothing appeared in the "nick of time," that was universe's way of saying, "You're heading in the wrong direction. Time to make changes."

Rather than press him for further clarity, I decided I would have to find out for myself. I would experiment to see if "nick of time" could work for me. Three years later, in 1984, Kim and I held hands and took our leap of faith, leaving Hawaii with nothing for San Diego, California. It was a test to find out if "nick of time" would work for us. Kim and I experienced some long periods when nothing was working and nothing was showing up.

While sitting at his kitchen table in Chicago, Fuller began experimenting with toothpicks and dried peas, discovering the building blocks of the universe—the same building blocks my poor dad had me building from thin sticks and glue when I was kid. Those building blocks led Fuller to discover that the mathematical system we were teaching our kids was wrong. His conclusions let to the admonishment: "How dare we lie to our children."

Using his "mathematics of god" led Fuller from toothpicks to the design of the geodesic dome, a structure that would be showcased as the U.S. Pavilion at Expo.67, the World's Fair of the Future. And I was there to see it.

In 1988, Kim and I met Bucky's second daughter Allegra in Aspen, Colorado at an event with John Denver. Eventually, I found the courage to ask her, "How did you and your mom and dad survive all those years without working?" Her answer, "Patents, books, and honorariums for his talks."

It dawned on me then that Fuller had become wealthy from the cash flow from his assets—his intellectual property—not a job. In the Industrial Age, there was real property, such as real estate. In the Information Age there is *intellectual property*.

After we retired, Kim and I expanded our focus to creating intellectual property, patents, and books. We also focused on creating and building assets. Today, Kim and I receive royalties (cash flow) from books, games, and business licenses for the use of our brand, Rich Dad… one of our biggest assets.

Brands have real value—which is why companies spend to much time and money to create, drive awareness to, and protect their brands. Coca-Cola is one of Warren Buffett's most prized assets. When he sells rights to the Coca-Cola brand, he is leveraging his intellectual property asset. McDonald's does the same thing… and so does Heinz and thousands of other top-of-mind brands.

So here's the good news: anyone can create a brand. Especially in today's Information Age… the Age of Infinity. I like to think about it as infinite returns on infinity.

Why don't more people create world-class brands? There are many reasons, I'm sure, but one is certainly the lack of real financial education. Most people go to school to learn to work for money, pay taxes, get out of debt, and invest in assets that make Wall Street rich—instead of how to create and secure their futures through entrepreneurial innovation.

My rich dad encouraged me to become an entrepreneur, *to take real estate classes so I could learn to use debt as money,* and to learn to sell. He cautioned me that using debt can be extremely risky and insisted that I first invest in my financial education. To learn to sell, I worked for Xerox for four years, selling copiers door to door. If you cannot sell, it is tough to build a brand, because a brand must sell itself and its products. That's what brands do.

A Diversified Asset Column

Pictured below is the Kim's and my financial statement:

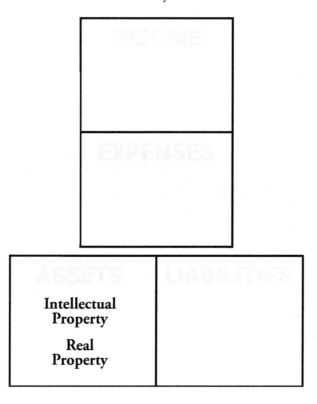

Kim has become an expert in developing real property. I am the expert in developing intellectual property. Our wealth continues to grow via both types of properties as well as commodities like gold, silver, and oil.

Fake Money

Money as we know it—fake money—is dying. That includes the U.S. dollar.

Historically, the average life expectancy for a fiat currency is 27 years, with the shortest life span being one month. Established in 1694, the British pound sterling is the oldest fiat currency in existence. At the ripe old age of 317 years it must be considered a highly successful fiat currency. However, success is relative. The British pound was once defined as 12 ounces of silver, so today it's worth less than 1/200 or 0.5

percent of its original value. In other words, the most successful long-standing currency in existence has lost 99.5 percent of its value.

Since 1971, the U.S. dollar has lost 97 percent of its purchasing power.

The United States has already had two currencies fail, the Continental died during the Revolutionary War and the Confederate Dollar died during the Civil War.

Bitcoin and other cryptocurrencies are now challenging the hegemony of the U.S. dollar and other fiat currencies. It will be interesting to see how long the Central Banks will tolerate the competition from cyber-money before there is a showdown.

I would say that it's doubtful that GRUNCH will allow cyber-money to steal their show. Waiting in the wings is the dollar's replacement, the IMFs SDR, or Special Drawing Rights. After Nixon took the U.S. dollar off the gold standard in 1971, the IMF created the SDR in 1973, standing by to replace the dollar. The SDR has already been used in a number of emergencies.

Another possibility is that the Central Banks will start issuing gold-backed currency. Some say that would send the price of gold past $10,000 an ounce. China, Russia, and many of our enemies are stockpiling gold, preparing to destroy the U.S. dollar's control over the world. When other currencies are issued as backed by gold, the dollar will be dethroned, and the U.S. economy will spin out of control. Global currency wars will most likely replace terrorist wars.

What Is the Future of Money?

I meet and talk with people from all over the world. One thing I hear over and over again is: "I'm just an average person… how does an ordinary person—without a lot of training or skills or financial literacy—prepare for the future and the future of money?"

In my opinion, the best way to prepare is to not need money.

How does a person learn not to need money? That path and process starts with seeking real financial education. That is why Kim and I created the CASHFLOW board game in 1996, followed by The Rich Dad Company and the publishing of *Rich Dad Poor Dad*—all intellectual property assets that came out of our heads. They were simply ideas that we turned into assets. And that is why we do not need fake assets from Wall Street.

Million-Dollar Ideas

All of us, at one time or another, have had a million-dollar idea. The problem is that without real financial education, a person cannot turn that idea into millions of dollars.

The *CASHFLOW* game, and the rest of our IP, intellectual property, has been created to empower ordinary people like you and me to turn our ideas into IP that becomes your personal assets.

I meet and talk with people from all over the world. One thing I hear over and over again is: "I'm just an average person... how does an ordinary person—without a lot of training or skills or financial literacy—prepare for the future and the future of money?"

In my opinion, the best way to prepare is to not need money.

Millions around the world have done this, including Fuller, Kim and me. You can do it, too.

I know I may make it sound simple, but for me, it was not easy. What is easy is going to school to get a job and then work for money, pay taxes, save money, and invest in the stock market. It's choosing the road less traveled that can make all the difference.

The word education is a derivative of the Latin *educe*, which means *to draw out*. I have always thought that our current education system got this wrong—as it seems focused on what it *put in* to students' heads. Today's education tells people what to do, instead of challenging students' thinking in ways that will draw out their ideas and creativity.

A Lesson from Oprah

When I was on *Oprah!* a member of the studio audience raised her hand and asked me, "I have $10,000. What should I do with my money?" Oprah stood and said, "Let me handle this question." Turning to the young woman, Oprah said, "Don't ask Robert what to do with your money. Your job is to *learn what you should do with your money. Never ask anyone else what to do with your money.* If you do not know what to do with your money, people will tell you to do with your money. They will tell you to give your money to them." Her answer didn't surprise me, and

I knew I had met a kindred spirit—someone who knew that education is the cornerstone of taking control of our financial futures.

If not for my experiences in 1973—seeing my poor dad without a job, without a paycheck, without a pension—today I could well be like my friends who went on to be pilots... the people asking Ted "Who stole our pension?"

CHAPTER TWENTY-TWO

Join Others to "Crowdfund" an Investigation of Your Pension

Hopefully, at this point in our book, it is clear to you that:

1. The world is faced with a retirement crisis;
2. The pension benefits you have been "promised" during retirement are in danger;
3. The people overseeing your pension are not knowledgeable about pensions or investments. They are incapable of making sound decisions and cannot be trusted to tell you the complete truth about how the pension is doing;
4. The Wall Street firms that have been hired by your pension to manage its assets are profiting at the expense of your pension (aka looting);
5. You can and should get involved in scrutinizing the pension you will be relying upon to provide your retirement security.

But there is something much more powerful you can do.

Imagine this: You and your fellow pensioners can get together to fund a forensic investigation of your pension by a pension expert. In other words, hire your own expert to review—and get a second opinion—on whether the pension overseers and Wall Street "helpers" they have hired to manage your pension are doing a good job.

For the cost of dinner for two at a middle-of-the-road restaurant, say $100, you and your fellow pensioners can retain an expert to investigate and provide a written report with recommendations to improve your pension and stop the looting. Is it worth a one-time contribution of $100 to protect a pension of, say, $1,000 a month for life?

My investigations of the New York State Teamsters, US Airways Pilots, North Carolina and first Rhode Island state pension were all funded by large established groups (associations and unions) of pensioners. If no large, organized group exists for your pension, there's an alternative.

Four years ago I speculated that crowdfunding—the practice of funding a project or venture by raising monetary contributions from a large number of people via the internet—was emerging as a game-changing way of empowering pension participants.

I wrote that the time was ripe for using crowdfunding to disrupt the fundamentally-flawed pension and retirement plan paradigm that had failed retirement savers for decades. The existing paradigm, which specifically excludes the very individuals whose money is at risk from having a voice in decision-making, has never made sense.

Through crowdfunding, retirement plans can be dramatically improved virtually overnight. The optimal time for change would have been years ago—before the collapse of thousands of corporate pensions, severe public pension underfunding, and the failure of 401(k) s to deliver retirement security as promised. For sure, a paradigm shift in retirement planning has been long overdue.

In March 2015—after a mere 29 days of fundraising—the first-ever crowdfunded investigation of a state pension was successful. A total of 349 backers contributed $20,464 for a second forensic review of the Rhode Island pension, proving that stakeholders no longer had to remain helpless, hopeless, and voiceless as their pension was fleeced.

> Through crowdfunding, retirement plans can be dramatically improved virtually overnight. The optimal time for change would have been years ago—before the collapse of thousands of corporate pensions, severe public pension underfunding, and the failure of 401(k)s to deliver retirement security as promised. For sure, a paradigm shift in retirement planning has been long overdue.

A year later, lightning struck again—107 backers contributed $20,130 for a follow-up investigation focused upon the Rhode Island pension's worst-performing investments in real estate.

Each crowdfunded investigation into the state pension's investments resulted in a substantial, credible expert report which was made publicly available, as well as submitted to regulators and law enforcement.

Transparency was enhanced and, despite formidable opposition from pension overseers, hedge fund and real estate gambling was exposed. Within months of the final investigation, after years of racking up $500 million in losses, the state pension dumped its hedge funds.

That's a real result and only the beginning for what we'll call "pensioner empowerment."

For a successful investigation, your expert will need to have access to pension investment information. While forensic experts can usually connect the dots in overcoming lack of access to key documents, easier access usually results in more definitive conclusions and lower review costs.

Second, to succeed, the cost of the analysis must be easily affordable. This is important because there seem to be limits as to how much can be raised through crowdfunding.

An effort to raise substantial funds ($750,000) to have my firm investigate the largest public pension in the nation ($300 billion CalPERS) failed, despite the fact that 1.72 million members rely upon CalPERS for retirement benefits and the pension had a funded status of only 69.8 percent at the time. Prudent management of the state pension's investments, I thought, would have been of paramount concern to all stakeholders—including California's 11 million taxpayers—and it would have been a lengthy multi-year inquiry. I suspect a more modest initial investigatory scope and crowdfunding financial goal would have been successful.

Finally, if you decide to crowdfund an expert investigation, be sure to clearly define the deliverable—the scope and length of the expert analysis that will be provided. Your expert must agree to the publication of his or her findings and you will need to create a strategy for maximum impact upon the release of your expert's report.

If you can find even 10 like-minded folks willing to pledge $50 each, as well as each recruit 10 others for a credible pension investigation that they deem important, you're off to the races.

Helpless and hopeless? Hardly.

CHAPTER TWENTY-THREE

Join the Global *Stop Pension Looting* Network

I encourage all pension stakeholders and financial advisers to join together to create a global network to monitor and improve pension investment practices before millions more lose the retirement security they have been promised. Coming together may be the only way to ensure that promises made are, in fact, kept.

Pension stakeholders, including participants and taxpayers, should make their voices heard by joining www.stopensionlooting.com.

In addition, there are tens of thousands of financial advisers globally who could help active workers and retirees monitor and evaluate the strengths and weaknesses of their pension investment programs. (Obviously, some advisers are more skilled in pensions than others.) My advice to every financial adviser around the world is to spend some time studying local pensions and commenting on the investment programs. It's a great way of responding to the needs of potential clients who participate in pensions and your efforts will help address growing global concerns.

Improving pensions will not only help preserve existing plans but will also encourage expansion of pension coverage to include more workers as it becomes apparent that well-managed pensions are efficient and sustainable.

To repeat what I said in the opening chapter of this book:
You—all of us—deserve a safe and secure retirement.
This book was written, in collaboration with Robert, to bring you one step closer toward that goal.

REFERENCES AND RESOURCES

Trifecta of Imprudence: Forensic Investigation of "Critical and Declining" New York State Teamsters Pension Fund

I.   Executive Summary

The New York State Teamsters Conference Pension and Retirement Fund ("the Fund" or "the Plan") is a multi-employer pension plan which is failing.

With a funded percentage of 45.8 percent and liabilities exceeding its assets by approximately $1.7 billion, the Fund is projected to become insolvent and require financial assistance from the Pension Benefit Guaranty Corporation ("PBGC"), the federal agency that backstops corporate pensions, by 2027.

Many of the over 34,000 participants in the Fund have asked how this could happen to their retirement savings plan—a pension that was nearly fully-funded in 1999.

As recently as Fall 2014, a Fund Newsletter reassured participants in response to the question "whether there will be sufficient money to pay pension benefits that have been earned and promised:

The simple answer remains: Yes!"

Key Finding:

A massive $767 million gamble on high-cost, high-risk, illiquid and opaque "alternative" investments—a losing wager that has already cost $400 million-plus in investment underperformance and excessive fees—is inappropriate for a struggling pension that is only 45 percent funded, in "critical and declining" status and poised to suspend benefits to workers dependent upon the Fund for their retirement security.

[1]

Trifecta of Imprudence: Forensic Investigation of "Critical and Declining" New

This forensic investigation funded by the Teamsters Alliance for Pension Protection, a non-profit organization with hundreds of active and retired participant donors, examines whether mismanagement of plan investments (including fiduciary breaches, conflicts of interest, undisclosed or excessive fees and wrongdoing) has contributed to the demise of the Plan.

- **Time to Examine Causes of Pension Failures Long Overdue**

At the outset, we note that while the need to examine failing pensions is great, forensic investigations of such plans are rarely undertaken. Nationally, there are over 10 million workers/retirees in 1,400 multiemployer plans. Approximately 150 to 200 of these plans are projected to run out of money within the next 20 years. The PBGC, which has become responsible for almost 4,800 failed single-employer and multiemployer plans, has never once conducted a forensic investigation into the demise of any pension—despite repeated demands by participants, as well as litigation brought against the agency to compel such investigations.

The time to examine what causes pensions to fail is long overdue, in our opinion.

- **"Critical" Status Determination**

Since 2008, the Pension Protection Act of 2006 ("PPA") has required an annual actuarial status determination for multi-employer pension plans, including the Plan. A pension generally is in "endangered" status if its funded percentage is less than 80 percent; in "critical" status if the funded percentage is less than 65 percent; or in "critical and declining" status if it is in critical status and is projected to become insolvent (run out of money to pay benefits) within 15 or 20 years.

[2]

The Plan operated in "endangered" status since 2008 and was certified by its actuaries to be in "critical status" (also known as the "red zone") beginning 2010. The Plan was certified in critical status each plan year thereafter until 2016.

For the 2016 Plan Year the actuaries certified the Plan as in "Critical and Declining" status under the Multiemployer Pension Reform Act of 2014 ("MPRA").

As a Notice sent to participants in February 2016 explained, a plan in Critical and Declining status does not have enough money to pay all the benefits that have been promised and is headed toward insolvency unless action is taken. The Notice also stated that benefit suspensions "are almost certainly necessary in the near future. "

In summary, for at least the past 9 years, the Fund has been in acute financial crisis—a fact which until recently has been misrepresented in communications to participants by the Board of Trustees of the Fund, such as the Fall 2014 Newsletter cited earlier.

Through March 2014—four years after the Fund had been certified in "critical status"—the Trustees, investment advisors, counsel, and actuaries continued to incur annual travel expenses for January and March four-day meetings held in Florida because, according to the Executive Administrator, "It is too difficult to have meetings at this time in Syracuse due to snow." Only after the U.S. Department of Labor ("DOL") opined that the travel expenses were improper for a plan in "critical status" was the Florida travel curtailed—to one week-long meeting a year outside of the Syracuse area.

[3]

- **Multiple Rehabilitation Plans Fail to Address Needed Investment and Administrative Improvements**

The PPA requires the Board of Trustees of a multiemployer pension plan that has been certified by its actuary as being in critical status to develop a "Rehabilitation Plan." The Trustees adopted a Rehabilitation Plan effective January 1, 2011 and updated it twice effective June, 2012 and January 1, 2015.

Simply put, there are three major components to the health of a pension plan—how much money is contributed into the plan; how the money in the plan is invested over the decades; and how much money is paid out in the form of benefits.

Rehabilitation Plans generally include information such as reductions in future benefits and increases in contributions, if agreed by the parties. However, such Plans are not required to include information regarding any needed improvements in the management of the pension's investment portfolio, such as:

1. Enhanced disclosure/transparency;

2. Reductions in investment/administrative fees and expenses; and

3. Limitations on illiquidity or other risk reduction measures, including mitigation, or elimination of, conflicts of interest.

None of the Fund's Rehabilitation Plans have included any information regarding such needed improvements in the management of the pension's investments.

Absent critical information regarding management of the pension's investments it is impossible, in our opinion, for participants in a failing plan to evaluate whether plan fiduciaries are acting prudently, as well as

4

the likelihood they will ever receive the retirement benefits they have been promised.

- **Trifecta of Imprudence**

In fact, as detailed in this report, it appears that (a) opacity; (b) fees and expenses; and (c) illiquidity, conflicts of interest and related risks, have all *dramatically increased* as the Fund's financial condition has worsened—all contrary to prudent fiduciary practice.

In our experience, such a *trifecta of imprudence* is all-too-common among failing pensions.

In light of the lack of government/regulatory review of mandated Rehabilitation Plans, incomprehensibility to participants, and failure to address the critical issue of improvements to pension investments, in our opinion, Rehabilitation Plans (such as the Fund's) frequently provide minimal benefit and add to the costs of operating financially-strapped plans.

- **Application to U.S. Treasury for Approval to Suspend Benefits**

On August 31, 2016, the Fund submitted a proposed Pension Preservation Plan to the U.S. Department of the Treasury under the MPRA, which includes benefit reductions for New York State participants. If Treasury approves the Preservation Plan, then participants and beneficiaries will be given the opportunity to vote on the proposed reductions. Unless a majority of all participants and beneficiaries vote to reject the Preservation Plan, it will go into effect on July 1, 2017.

The Application includes numerous statements about the Plan's current investments, including asset allocation percentages and related performance (over the past seven years only). In addition, there is discussion of the Fund's alternative investment strategy adopted and

5

implemented in 2005 to supposedly reduce risk and increase returns, as well as the "devastating" loss of 36 percent in asset value the Fund experienced in 2008.

As detailed in our report, statements regarding the Fund's investment performance over the past seven years in the Application to Treasury differ dramatically from the Fund performance reports we have reviewed. That is, the performance stated in the Application is significantly higher.

In our opinion, Treasury should investigate further the actual investment performance of the Fund over extended periods of time, as opposed to accept the limited performance figures included in the Application.

Finally, we disagree with the representation in the Application that the Trustees have taken all reasonable measures to avoid insolvency. As detailed below, we estimate $400 million-plus in avoidable underperformance losses and over $500 million in excessive investment and administrative fees and expenses.

- **Misrepresentations to Participants by Trustees**

Since 2013, the Board of Trustees has made representations to participants in newsletters and on the pension's website regarding actions taken to improve management of the investments. The Board of Trustees has repeatedly represented to participants:

1. A "sophisticated," "bold" private placement investment strategy was necessary if the Fund was going to meet its long-term funding requirements;

2. The alternative investment strategy is expected to result in greater returns over time and has, in fact, already resulted in greater returns; and

6

3. These investments have allowed the Trustees to appropriately continue a higher ("aggressive") interest rate assumption than other plans.

In our opinion, none of the above statements is accurate.

Similarly, from 2013 through 2015 the Board of Trustees emphatically assured anxious participants that "there will be sufficient money to pay pension benefits that have been earned and promised." Suddenly, in the fall of 2015, the "simple" reassurances were gone.

The time had come—in the words of the Trustees—to "be realistic about the long-term financial stability of the Plan."

- **Unreasonable "Aggressive" 8.5 Percent Investment Assumption**

The Fund has an 8.5 percent assumed rate of return on its investments. Further, the Fund acknowledges in its communications to participants that its investment return assumption is "higher" and even "aggressive."

The Fund's assumed rate of return is *significantly higher* than the average cited in a 2016 Milliman Multiemployer Pension Funding Study for all 1,300 multiemployer plans. According to Milliman, multiemployer assumed returns are generally between 6 and 8 percent, with an average of just below 7.5 percent. It is noteworthy, says Milliman, that about 200 plans have *decreased* their assumed rate of return over the last several years.

The Fund, on the other hand, *increased* its investment return assumption from 8 percent to 8.5 percent in 2007 and has maintained that higher assumption since then. Within months of the increase in the assumption, the Plan was certified as being in "endangered status" by its actuary for the Plan Year beginning January 1, 2008.

We note in our report that the Oracle of Omaha, Warren Buffett, in an oft-cited 2007 annual letter to Berkshire Hathaway shareholders, explained that it was unlikely that pensions could achieve the investment return assumptions they had set, which averaged 8 percent in 2006—i.e., well before the 2008 market collapse.

According to Buffett, the equity portion of pension assets—allowing for expenses of .5 percent—would produce no more than 7 percent. Buffet notes that .5 percent may well understate costs, given the presence of layers of consultants and high-priced managers he refers to as "helpers."

The fees the Fund pays its external advisers to manage approximately $767 million, or 64 percent of its portfolio invested in alternative hedge, private equity, real estate and infrastructure funds are *exceptionally high*—an estimated annual 2 percent asset-based and 20 percent performance fees, plus additional underlying and operating fees and expenses (as much as 6 percent).

We conservatively estimate the Fund's equity-related expenses are closer to 4 percent, or eight-times-greater, than Buffet's .5 percent estimate. Plus, the Fund has paid millions to multiple costly consultant and manager "helpers."

Buffett's Berkshire Hathaway uses an assumed rate of return of 6.5 percent, down from 6.7 percent in 2014 and 2013.

In conclusion, it appears that the Trustees, the investment consultants and actuaries of the "critical and declining" status pension all have steadfastly agreed it will outperform legendary investor Warren Buffett's pension estimates by an astounding 2 percent, net of all fees and expenses—fees and expenses which are easily eight times greater than Buffett's .5 percent estimate.

In our opinion, based upon the Fund's risky asset allocation, high investment-related expenses and actual sub-par investment experience, there is no reasonable basis to conclude the Fund will outperform Buffet's estimates by 2 percent. Rather, the high-risk, high-cost asset allocation virtually ensures the Fund will consistently underperform on a net basis.

- **"Bold" $767 Million Alternative Investment Gamble**

The Fund has allocated (including both committed and invested capital) **$767 million,** or approximately **64 percent** of its assets to alternative investments, including hedge, private equity, infrastructure, natural resources and real estate funds.

This $767 million is invested in a staggering **170 or more** alternative funds.

In our opinion, allocating $767 million or 64 percent of the troubled Fund's assets to 170 or more alternative investment funds makes no sense. While a certain amount of portfolio diversification is prudent, with such small balances invested in dozens of alternative funds it is impossible for any single manager to significantly add value. In addition, the task of monitoring dozens of high-risk, opaque managers is arduous.

It is likely the vast number of alternatives will result in, at best, a market rate of return with significantly greater fees, investment and operational risk.

Further, the Fund's hedge fund of fund investments appear to have provided little to no downside protection.

We note seven years ago Warren Buffett and, more recently, John Bogle, Founder of the Vanguard Group, warned against these investments.

9

- **$400 Million-Plus Alternative Investment Underperformance**

We estimate that underperformance of alternative investments has cost the Fund approximately $340 million over the past seven years—assuming the Russell 3000 is the appropriate benchmark for all of these assets. However, in our opinion, a more appropriate private equity benchmark used by pensions is the Russell 3000 *plus a premium of 4 percent* for the risk related to the leverage (2 percent) and illiquidity (2 percent) features of these funds.

Using the more appropriate Russell 3000 plus 4 percent benchmark for private equity, alternative investment underperformance losses amount to **$400 million-plus** over the past seven years.

In conclusion, it appears the Fund has paid exponentially greater fees, incurred massive risk and dramatically underperformed with respect to its "bold," "sophisticated" alternative investments gamble over the past 7 years.

- **Massive Risks Related to Alternative-Private Market Investments**

We agree with the warnings of the Fund's investment consultant, Meketa, regarding the significant risks related to private market investments. We note certain of the Trustees' representations in newsletter and website communications to participants regarding risk related to Fund's private market investments appear to be inconsistent with the consultant's formidable warnings. That is, the Trustees have generally characterized the private market investments strategy as reducing, not increasing, the risk of financial insolvency.

For all of the reasons cited by Meketa, as well as additional risks detailed in the report, we believe a massive $767 million gamble on high-cost, high-risk, illiquid and opaque alternative investments—a losing wager that has already cost $400 million-plus in investment underperformance and excessive fees—is inappropriate for a struggling pension that is only 45 percent funded, in "critical and declining" status and poised to suspend benefits to workers dependent upon the Fund for their retirement security.

In our opinion, further investigation into the recommendation to pursue the alternative strategy, as well as disclosure of the related costs and risks, is advisable.

- **"Bundled" Custody Arrangement Creates Risk of Overcharges, Even Fraud, By Custodian of Plan Assets**

The Fund has entered into a contract with a global custodian bank, State Street Bank and Trust, to purchase a range of services, including custody of its assets, on what is commonly referred to in the industry as a "bundled" fee basis. In a bundled fee arrangement, the global custodian safekeeping pension investments also may provide investment management (including cash management), securities lending and trading, foreign exchange, and other services. Bundled fees lack transparency and obscure the prices pensions pay for any given service included in the bundle. As a result, pensions are exposed to potentially excessive, or even fraudulent, expenses. Therefore, in reviewing a pension's relationship with its custodian, bundled fees must be unbundled to determine the prices paid for services provided and any potential overcharges.

We were not provided with any contracts or agreements between the Fund and State Street.

On July 26, 2016, the bank agreed to pay at least $382 million, including $155 million to the Department of Justice, $167 million to the SEC and at least $60 million to ERISA plan clients in an agreement with the Department of Labor, to settle allegations that it deceived some of its

11

273

custody clients when providing them with indirect foreign currency exchange services. The bank also agreed to pay $147.6 million to settle private class action lawsuits filed by bank customers alleging similar misconduct.

- **$8.5 Million in Excessive Investment Consulting Fees**

The investment consultant to the Fund, Meketa, discloses in its regulatory filings with the SEC that it also serves as a discretionary investment manager. As a result, a potential conflict of interest exists because the firm both recommends money managers to its clients and is itself a money manager. Under these circumstances a risk arises that the consultant-gatekeeper may recommend itself as an investment manager to the pension based upon the compensation it will receive in that capacity, as opposed to investment merits.

Many plan fiduciaries specifically exclude investment consultants subject to such conflicts from consideration for their plans due to risk that the advice provided regarding asset allocation and manager selection may not be objective.

In our opinion, the fees paid to Meketa for investment consulting are unusually volatile, high and excessive. Based upon our experience, total investment consulting fees for a pension of this size should not exceed $250,000 annually.

Thus, in our opinion, the excessive investment consulting fees amount to almost **$8.5 million** over the past nine years.

To the extent that the Meketa fee may relate to discretionary investment management services (as opposed to non-discretionary consulting services), in our opinion, the arrangement is imprudent due to conflict of interest concerns, as well as the excessive compensation to Meketa and the alternatives managers.

Trifecta of Imprudence: Forensic Investigation of "Critical and Declining" New

12

274

According to the Fund's Forms 5500 filed with the DOL, Meketa was paid both investment advisory and "soft dollar" commissions. However, according to the firm's current Form ADV filed with the SEC, the firm is not registered as a broker-dealer and does not receive any portion of commissions.

Using plan commission dollars to pay for investment consulting services, referred to as "soft dollaring," can be highly problematic. We recommend further review of the Meketa compensation arrangement by the DOL and Securities and Exchange Commission, in light of the soft dollar arrangement involving the firm disclosed by the Fund in its Form 5500s.

- **$510 Million in Excessive, Largely Undisclosed Investment Fees**

It is well established that ERISA trustees have a fiduciary duty to ensure that the fees their plans pay money managers for investment advisory services are reasonable. Further, in recent years such fees have come under increased scrutiny because of class action litigation, Department of Labor regulations, and congressional hearings.

The amount of investment fees the Fund discloses it pays its managers has substantially increased since 2004 (more than doubled in certain years)—even as assets under management have fallen almost in half and the Fund's financial status has deteriorated.

In our opinion, the amount of fees the Fund *discloses* it pays its managers could easily be significantly reduced—cut in half or more, saving the pension **$5 million- $9 million** annually.

However, based upon our experience (and other experts identified in the report) we estimate additional *undisclosed* fees related to

13

alternative investments may range from a low of **$21 million** (3 percent) to over **$42 million** (7 percent) annually.

We estimate as much as **$51 million** annually in *excessive* fees related to the Fund or **$510 million** over the past decade—since the Trustees approved the high-cost alternatives gamble.

With respect to $229 million the Fund has committed to private market partnerships, but not actually invested, we estimate the Fund pays fees of approximately $4.5 million annually. That is, the Fund is paying these managers **$4.5 million for doing nothing**—not actually managing any of its assets.

In our opinion, paying $4.5 million in fees to Wall Street for doing nothing is unreasonable.

In conclusion, based upon the limited reports we have been provided and have reviewed, it appears that the investment management fees and expenses the Fund pays its managers have not been adequately disclosed to and reviewed by the Trustees for reasonableness, consistent with their fiduciary duties.

- **Potential Excessive Administrative Expenses**

Like the Fund's investment expenses, its administrative expenses have almost doubled in recent years and are excessive.

In our opinion, the Florida travel expenses deemed improper by the DOL in 2014 are a significant "red flag." While winter meetings may have been held in Florida in the past, as the Trustees claimed, when a plan has been certified in "critical and declining" status unnecessary expenses should be eliminated. Further investigation is required to determine whether the doubling in administrative expenses is

14

consistent with the representation in the Treasury Application that the Trustees have taken all reasonable measures to avoid insolvency.

- **Bonding and Fiduciary Liability Insurance**

Finally, according to the DOL, the Plan does have an ERISA Bond in the amount of $500,000 with Fidelity and Deposit Company of Maryland and there is a Fiduciary Liability Policy in place with Illinois National Insurance Company for $20 million.

End Executive Summary

15

II.   Introduction

The New York State Teamsters Conference Pension and Retirement Fund ("the Fund" or "the Plan") is a multi-employer collectively bargained defined benefit pension plan, established in 1954, with approximately $1.2 billion in assets today. Its purpose is to provide pension benefits to members with union agreements calling for contributions to the Fund. The Fund is located in Syracuse, New York, and covers participants in the central, upstate and western regions of New York State, but not New York City, as well as northern New Jersey.

The Plan currently has about 200 contribution employers. The total number of participants in the Plan is approximately 34,526. Of this number, 11,678 are active participants, 16,064 are retired or separated from service and receiving benefits, and 6,784 are retired or separated from service and entitled to future benefits.

The Plan is subject to the provisions of the Employee Retirement Income Security Act of 1974 ("ERISA"), the federal law that establishes minimum standards for private retirement plans to protect employees.

Nationally, there are more than 10 million workers and retirees in 1,400 multiemployer plans. The majority of these pensions, covering most multiemployer plan participants, are said to be in sound financial condition. However, just under half of all *participants* are in plans certified by their actuaries to be in the critical, or critical and declining status.[1]

According to the Pension Benefit Guaranty Corporation ("PBGC"), the federal agency that backstops corporate pension plans, approximately 150 to 200 plans covering 1.5 million workers and retirees, could run out of money within the next 20 years.

16

---

[1] https://www.segalco.com/media/2574/spring2016zonestatus.pdf

Sovereign Wealth Funds Embrace Gross Malpractice Generally Practiced

by Edward Siedle

In recent years the colossal investment screw-ups of another group of supposedly savvy investors—sovereign wealth funds (SWF)—have been in the news.

"The largest kleptocracy case in U.S. history," is what a former U.S. attorney general called the billions allegedly stolen from the Malaysian fund, 1 Malaysia Development Bhd (1MDB)—a fund set up to promote economic development in a country where the median income stands at approximately $400 per month. Malaysia filed criminal charges against New York investment bank Goldman Sachs seeking $7.5 billion in compensation.

An Abu Dhabi SWF also filed a lawsuit against Goldman Sachs for its losses tied to the 1MDB embezzlement scandal.

According to a recent report, Goldman is close to reaching a near-$2 billion settlement with the U.S. Department of Justice over the 1MDB matter. The settlement is said to require its Asian subsidiary, rather than the parent company, pay a multibillion fine and admit guilt for having allegedly turned a blind eye while $4.5 billion was looted from its client, 1MDB.[1]

Concerns have arisen regarding how Africa's SWFs, including Morocco, Botswana, Nigeria, Libya and Rwanda, are being managed, following the news in 2018 that the son of the former Angolan president and former chairman of the $5 billion Angolan SWF had been charged by his country's prosecutors for fraud over the transfer of $500 million from the central bank's account.

Concerns have arisen regarding how Africa's SWFs, including Morocco, Botswana, Nigeria, Libya and Rwanda, are being managed, following the news in 2018 that the son of the former Angolan president and former chairman of the $5 billion Angolan SWF had been charged by his country's prosecutors for fraud over the transfer of $500 million from the central bank's account.

---

1   https://www.msn.com/en-us/money/news/goldman-sachs-close-to-2bn-settlement-over-1mdb-scandal/ar-BBYaz6C

SWFs are not pensions—they do not provide retirement benefits to any employees or retirees.

Rather, an SWF is a state-owned investment fund comprised of pools of money derived from a country's reserves. Reserves are funds set aside to be invested for the benefit of the country's economy and its citizens.

Some countries have massive SWFs. For example, Norway's SWF is the largest in the world with assets exceeding $1 trillion since 2017. That amounts to nearly $200,000 per Norwegian citizen. Other SWF heavyweights include China Investment Corporation, Abu Dhabi Investment Authority, Kuwait Investment Authority, Hong Kong Monetary Investment Portfolio, GIC Private Limited (Singapore), National Council for Social Security Fund (China), SAFE Investment Company (China), Temasek Holdings (Singapore), and Qatar Investment Authority.

The top 86 largest SWFs have combined assets of over $8 trillion.

At the outset, it is difficult to assess how good SWFs are at investing citizens' wealth because many of these funds do not publish their returns. Even those that do report their financial performance cannot be relied upon to do so truthfully. There is a profound lack of accountability, as well as transparency. After all, how likely is it that someone with access to the fund's actual results would be willing to accuse the sovereign of fraudulently misrepresenting fund investment performance?

The wave of SWFs also gives rise to concerns regarding mismanagement of investments, corruption, pursuit of noneconomic or economic-power objectives, financial protectionism, local financial market instability, excessive fees, and conflicts of interest. The structure and governance of SWFs can also be troubling.

These burgeoning governmental investment funds—unaccustomed to the wiles of Wall Street—appear to be making all the wrong moves, such as blindly trusting the very same investment powerhouses whose toxic financial advice and corrupt business practices were exposed, most recently, in the 2008 market meltdown.

Worse still, SWFs (like U.S. state and local pensions) get seduced into funding bespoke "strategic partnerships" with Wall Street—tailor made, *by Wall Street*, to transfer SWF citizen wealth *to Wall Street*.

None of this fleecing of the lambs is particularly surprising. After all, amateur investors get ravaged by the wolves of Wall Street all the time. (Ironically, a producer of the film *The Wolf of Wall Street* was charged with 1MDB linked money laundering in Malaysia.)

However, SWFs are hardly run-of-the-mill rank amateurs. They have virtually limitless resources to retain globally recognized experts, well-versed in the ever-shifting investment fraud landscape and easily avoid even the most sophisticated scams. Yet they don't educate themselves about Wall Street abuses and how to protect their assets.

Having failed to do their homework—investigate before they invest—SWFs pay the price.

In another notable example, a few years ago Libya's SWF filed suit against Goldman Sachs alleging devastating losses of 98 percent of a $1.3 billion bet on currency movements and other complex trades done with Goldman in 2008. The Libyan Investment Authority claimed that Goldman took advantage of the LIA's financially illiterate staff and seduced them with gifts and bribes.

The LIA claimed that they completely trusted Goldman and believed that its former head of North Africa was "their very close friend." Last I heard Goldman had won the legal battle.

SWFs are seemingly willfully ignorant of the concerns that are paramount to forward-thinking institutional investors in America today such as conflicts of interest, breaches of fiduciary duties, corruptive industry practices, undisclosed and excessive compensation arrangements, fraud and misrepresentation and their impact upon net investment performance.

Scrutiny of the integrity of investment firms SWFs hire is lackluster, at best.

Like American state and local government pensions, SWFs have been criticized for allowing political considerations to drive investment decision-making.

The acceptable investments included in each SWF vary from country to country, depending upon the country's liquidity, debt, and projected growth needs. Countries with liquidity concerns have historically tended to limit investments to only very liquid public debt instruments. Most SWFs prefer returns over liquidity, making them more likely to allocate ever-greater amounts to high-risk, high-cost, opaque alternative investments—the very same Weapons of Mass Financial Destruction (made in America) that have been particularly devastating for America's public pensions.

According to a 2019 Bloomberg article, "the world's second-largest sovereign wealth fund is playing a dangerous game. China Investment Corp. aims to have as much as 50% of its portfolio in alternative investments by the end of 2022. That means the $941 billion fund is diving deeper into illiquid investments including real estate, infrastructure, hedge funds, and private equity just as such trades are becoming increasingly crowded." Bloomberg concludes, "CIC's tilt toward alternative assets may prove ill-judged."[2]

In conclusion, like pensions globally, SWFs are plagued by gross malpractice generally practiced and don't even know it.

If, through reading this book, you have learned that Wall Street investment firms (1) are not to be trusted and (2) are not your friends, then you probably already know more that the self-proclaimed "financial illiterates" running your country's SWF.

---

2 https://www.bloomberg.com/opinion/articles/2019-09-22/china-s-sovereign-wealth-fund-boosts-alternative-assets

CalPERS—America's Largest Public Pension— Is No Role Model

by Edward Siedle

Why would America's largest public pension _not_ want to know about Wall Street ripping it off?

With approximately $354 billion in assets, the California Public Employees Retirement System (CalPERS) is America's largest government worker pension fund, serving more than 1.9 million members. There was a time when CalPERS was regarded as the best managed public pension in the nation. Other pensions around the globe followed its lead.

CalPERS was one of the first public pension systems to tie its investments to social activism, selling its investments in companies tied to South Africa's apartheid system in 1986 and ditching tobacco stocks in 2000. The pension was a key organizer of a coalition of 225 large investors with $26 trillion in assets launched to urge corporations to reduce greenhouse-gas emissions.

Over the past decade, financial scandals and dismal investment returns have eroded its once stellar reputation.

As mentioned earlier in this book, in 2016 the former chief executive of the pension was sentenced to a prison term of 4.5 years after pleading guilty to a conspiracy charge for taking more than $250,000 in cash and other bribes from his friend and former CalPERS board member Alfred Villalobos. Prosecutors said Villalobos, who killed himself weeks before he was due to stand trial, reportedly made $50 million as a middleman for investment firms looking to get a piece of CalPERS' business.

In the words of the _Los Angeles Times_ in 2017:

> "Credibility is an important quality for the California Public Employees Retirement System... At the moment, it hangs by a thread."[3]

CalPERS Patronage Does Not Have the "Good Housekeeping Seal of Approval"

3 https://www.latimes.com/business/hiltzik/la-fi-hiltzik-calpers-jelincic-20170502-story.html

Over the decades I have spent investigating investment wrongdoing, I have found that Wall Street investment firms ripping off pensions, particularly state and local government pensions, are often connected in some way to CalPERS.

The "connection" between a crooked investment firm and CalPERS may be as tenuous as the scammer managing a small account for the pension. That's hardly remarkable given its massive size and the thousands of investment firms the pension retains. However, sometimes the relationship is far more significant. For example, CalPERS may play a role in launching a particular investment fund, product or manager, or may be one of the first major investors, or may have an ownership interest in the shady manager offering the investment.

Unfortunately, other public pensions, institutional investors, and the general public tend to believe having CalPERS as a client or partner amounts to a "Good Housekeeping Seal of Approval" of the manager or investment fund. Other investors may pile into investments that are, in one way or another, seemingly sponsored, endorsed or substantially supported by CalPERS.

Decisions at CalPERS often have a dramatic and far-reaching impact upon the world of investing. When the pension hires or supports investment advisers or managers who are unworthy stewards of capital, the nation and indeed the entire world may suffer. CalPERS truly plays a unique role in the investment ecosystem.

I have known members of the board and staff of CalPERS since the early 1990s. I have been privy to the organization's internal struggles and witnessed its blunders.

Over the years I have urged CalPERS board members to seriously examine the integrity of the pension's current and past managers, investigate how investment managers with horrendous backgrounds succeed in getting hired, and assess the impact corruption of the investment process at CalPERS may have on all investors globally.

CalPERS could be a force for global good, I have long believed, if it took politics out of its investment decisions and prudently invested based upon merit alone.

Finally, in 2013, I sent a letter to the CalPERS board stating, "It is apparent to me, even from a distance that the pension continues to lack many of the safeguards I would recommend to improve management and performance." I received no response to my apparently unwelcomed letter, but one friendly board member suggested I write a follow-up.

My second letter further detailed issues that, in my expert opinion, I thought should be investigated fully by the pension. Included in these issues were specifically "undisclosed fees related to investment providers/vendors" and "private equity and hedge fund conflicts of interest, fee abuses and malfeasance."

When my second letter was discussed at a closed meeting, the Board President responded (according to CalPERS) "How is this letter different from any of the thousands of others we receive offering services?"

Wow... I thought when I heard this remark.

If it's really true that the CalPERS board regularly receives tons of similar letters—"thousands" of them—from world-renowned forensic experts and seasoned, credible whistleblowers alleging potential wrongdoing regarding the pension's investments—allegations of wrongdoing which the board routinely ignores—that's really freakin' scary.

Pension stakeholders, such as taxpayers and state workers, should be hair-on-fire horrified to hear that thousands of dire warnings from leading experts go unheeded by the pension's clueless board.

Most recently, in 2017, I wrote an article for *Forbes* entitled *How to Steal A Lot of Money From CalPERS, The Nation's Largest Public Pension.* My advice to would-be criminals was: If you want to steal millions, escape detection and prosecution, then set your sights on the mother of all pension honey-pots, CalPERS. This pension has no idea whether the fees money managers take out of the pension are legitimate or not.

One board member, who had raised the issue of undisclosed Wall Street fees with the board earlier agreed. "We don't know what fees our private equity managers are taking out of the pension and so we can't possibly know whether all the fees are legitimate. When I've raised the issue, I've been told the managers are our 'partners' in the funds and we should just trust them."[4]

No, CalPERS stakeholders, Wall Street is neither your friend, nor your "partner"—nor trustworthy.

---

4 https://www.forbes.com/sites/edwardsiedle/2017/05/24/how-to-steal-a-lot-of-money-from-calpers-the-nations-largest-public-pension/#6188ccae2c2b

"It's a Trap!"
The "Why" Behind the Pension Crisis

by Phoenix City Councilman Sal DiCiccio

There is a disease spreading across America. The decay can be seen everywhere you turn: streets are crumbling, youth and senior programs are being slashed, there are potholes on every corner, and first responders are lacking personnel and resources. America's cities and towns are dying as this epidemic spreads.

The local governments that should be addressing these symptoms are seeing historic revenue gains each year. Property taxes are at record highs, water and sewer charges continue to grow, and local governments never seem to run out of ways to nickel and dime their constituents with fee after fee. Yet, the services that citizens count on continue to decline. No matter how much we feed this beast, it is never enough.

Local governments are morphing into zombies: nothing more than hollow shells that consume everything in their path to sustain themselves just long enough to find their next meal. The beast needs more tax dollars to survive. Officials push for revenue-focused policies to keep up with the beast's growing hunger but they are only masking the symptoms. The underlying infection is left untreated.

What is this disease that is overwhelming local governments throughout America? Pensions.

In Phoenix alone, where I have fought for years as a member of the City Council to rein in ballooning costs, we currently owe in excess of $4.56 billion in unfunded pension promises. Unfunded means we don't have the money or a way of paying off this debt.

That's more than $3,000 in pension debt alone, for every single man, woman, and child in a city of over 1.6 million souls. It's also more than our entire annual discretionary budget—about four times more. Then you have to add in another $3.66 billion owed for other promises like Cadillac healthcare plans, insurance policies, and the like. All told, that's more than $8 billion in promises that politicians in Phoenix made, but never paid.

The average total compensation is now over $115,000 per city of Phoenix government employee each year. This is for all of our 13,000 employees. A starting clerk, the lowest pay level we have, gets 38.5 days of sick leave in their first year of "service" and that number grows by 10 hours every month. And, it gets to roll over year after year after year. Cadillac Health Insurance that is unheard of in the private sector is the norm for government employees. The more the employee makes and gets in benefits the bigger the pension. Pretty simple, the beast needs to eat in order to grow.

We're not alone. Every government across the country is feasting on our goodwill. According to the Stanford Institute for Economic Policy Research, unfunded state and local pension obligations by the end of 2017 totaled $5.2 trillion. And that number is not even the real number.

State and local governments long ago made a proverbial deal with the devil. Politicians who didn't want to face the music for their bad decisions made a deal with the government unions representing all these various pension funds to deliberately underestimate the average annual cost to taxpayers—so they can keep buying votes with money they don't have. But they're only making the problem, and the bills when they come due, dramatically larger.

How much each city, county, state, or local school district owes for their pension liabilities are determined by how much they have promised, how much money is currently in the fund, and the rate of return that fund is projected to return in the market, along with a host of actuarial assumptions like when each person will retire, and how long they'll live after that. The higher the projected rate of return, the later retirees start collecting their pensions, and less time they'll collect those checks before they pass away, the less a local government is forced to pay into those funds. By artificially negotiating these numbers, instead of using historically accurate market returns and actuarial assumptions, politicians can free up millions, even hundreds of millions, of dollars for new spending and more employees.

In the famous words of Admiral Ackbar, "It's a trap!"

Politically fudging the numbers doesn't free up money. It just piles on more debt. It's like maxing out a credit card, and when the bank sends you a bill for the minimum payment, telling them you're going to pay less than that, then demanding an increase in your credit line so you can spend more money. It's ludicrous. There isn't a bank or credit card company in the world that would take that deal.

Phoenix, for example, assumes that our pension funds will earn an annual average return of 7.3 percent in the market. But over the last decade, the real number is closer to 5 percent annually. That may not seem like much—what's a two percent difference?—but as Albert Einstein noted, "compound interest (is) the most powerful force in the universe." Calculated honestly, Phoenix's $4.56 billion in unfunded pension liabilities would be somewhere in the range of $7 to $8 billion. Which, sadly, is a much better situation than a lot of other cities and states find themselves in. According to California politicians and their pension fund co-conspirators, California's largest pension system (CalPERS) is $308.5 billion short on an actuarial basis. But on a real world, market basis? The Stanford Institute estimates an actual pension shortfall in CalPERS of more than $1.05 trillion. On a per household basis that means instead of the $23,632 per household that California politicians acknowledge, every household in California is really on the hook for something like $80,643 in unfunded pension costs. Of course, these are statewide averages. Families living in the Oro Grande Elementary School District have more than $357,000 in unfunded pension liabilities hanging over them courtesy of their local K-8 schools alone.

All of this would seem to militate that local elected officials have an enormous incentive to address the problem aggressively, now, when times are good, the economy is rolling, and virtually every government entity in the country is taking in record revenues. This is certainly the case here in Phoenix, where we have enjoyed record revenue growth that has increased total City spending more than 25 percent in just the last 5 years.

Given a windfall in new tax revenue, what did the politicians here do to address our pension debt? They made it worse. In 2017 the Council chose to extend the timeline for paying off our past due pension obligations, thereby adding an additional $2.3 billion in costs for the taxpayers of Phoenix. Why did they do that? So they could spend an extra $18 million dollars in 2018, and $9 million more in 2019. That's right: when given a chance to address this massive, looming crisis, our elected officials chose instead to saddle Phoenicians with billions of dollars of additional debt just so they could spend a few million dollars more in the present and keep the beast well-fed. It was, without a doubt, the most irresponsible thing I have seen our Mayor and Council do since I first ran for office in the '90s.

Governments are becoming pension machines. The problem is taxpayers neither understand, nor seem to care about, the coming tsunami about to break over our heads. They are going to suffer for their indifference. The devastation will be real. City budgets for core services like public safety, street and infrastructure maintenance, homeless shelters, housing, neighborhood cleanups and all the other critical things cities do will be cut. Millions of retirees currently counting on generous pension promises to cushion them through retirement will have their lives torn apart when courts start cutting down their benefits as part of the bankruptcy proceedings that will—absolutely—begin to rock city after city across the country.

In the summer of 2019, I backed— with tens of thousands of my own money—a simple initiative to Phoenix voters that would have required us to account for our pension deficits accurately by using the last ten years of historical results (the real returns generated by our pension funds in the market) instead of the politically inflated fantasy returns we're currently counting on. The plan also would have required the City to prioritize paying down our pension debt, without cutting any existing programs. It would even have left room for the City to responsibly increase spending each year by a reasonable amount, only ensuring that future windfalls would be used to keep our promises, rather than make more we can't keep.

The local political elite and their myriad organizational allies, charities, and businesses that rely on the public dole for their livelihoods went ballistic, putting millions of dollars behind a campaign of lies to ensure they wouldn't be restrained by even the most basic concepts of fiscal responsibility. They claimed the initiative would have closed libraries, parks and swimming pools across the city. They claimed it would have shut down public transportation and kicked low-income families to the street. Absolutely none of those things was true—after all, the measure didn't require a single cut to any spending program, and even left room to increase spending gradually over time.

There's an axiom in elections that if you're explaining, you're losing. The measure lost, badly. We were trying to explain a complex problem, the other side resorted to simple lies. And simple lies won. The local press, across the country, has been gutted in recent decades. Arizona's flagship newspaper, the *Arizona Republic*, used to have two full-time, experienced journalists covering City Hall. Now we have one recent journalism school grad. When former Obama administration official Ben Rhodes told *New York Times Magazine* that he relied on inexperienced reporters to create an "echo chamber" that would favor the administration's preferred outcome on the now-defunct Iranian nuclear deal, he noted that he was able to do so because modern reporters "literally know nothing", and that therefore almost all the journalists covering the talks had to call the administration to explain to them the background and fundamental principles of the issue. By relying on the government to explain facts to them, Rhodes noted, the government could essentially present whatever "facts" they chose to share, regardless of whether or not their narrative matched reality. Rhodes and his colleagues were essentially given carte-blanche to lie.

Rhodes had another advantage—one he perhaps didn't fully identify, but which was also working strongly in his favor. Current generations have been raised in an environment where adults, most often in the form of school officials, have stepped in to mediate and solve all their problems for them. They are trained to view bureaucratic authority as absolute; and defer to the truth of their decisions. Because of this, there is a significant tendency among new journalists to view government officials and bureaucrats as the umpires in a contest between political parties. Nothing could be further from the truth. Modern bureaucracies are the furthest thing from impartial political observers. They are another team on the field. And they, too, believe they are the smartest people in the room.

Unlike politicians, who at least face re-election, bureaucrats—so long as they assiduously follow the PC cultures laid out by their human resource departments—are essentially an invulnerable, protected ruling class. Their position makes them both reckless and dangerous. Economic conditions largely don't affect them. They can lose millions of taxpayer dollars on their latest boondoggle, as Phoenix did with our ill-fated trip into the hospitality industry when we built a giant downtown Sheraton hotel, lost millions on operations, and completed the fiasco by selling the property for more than $50 million less than we paid to build it, and still be assured no actual repercussions will come their way.

They're not bad people. In fact, City employees are generally some of the kindest, well-intentioned humans you will ever meet. They are eager, desperate even, to demonstrate their compassion. Until your interest conflicts with their own personal interest.

Which brings us to what will almost certainly be the next great evolution, and expansion of our pension crisis: politicians on the left are now moving in concert to nationalize those state and local debts. Not only will their plan not help the current crisis, it is virtually guaranteed to escalate the problem to the point that our only hope of ever getting away from the tsunami will be to drown in it— hyperinflate our currency and create a Venezuelan-style financial crisis that so utterly destroys the value of the dollar we can "pay" our obligations to public retirees in worthless scrip. The federal government is already experiencing its own crisis, with over $14 trillion in debt and a record annual deficit piling onto the problem every single year despite, you guessed it, record revenues.

Adding the official estimate of around $7 trillion more in state and local pension debt would be beyond crippling to the national economy. And, as discussed above, the real number isn't $7 trillion. When we use the real market returns on these funds, that $7 trillion balloons somewhere into the $14 to $21 trillion range—meaning nationalizing these obligations would more than double our national debt. Worse, nationalizing state and local pension obligations would almost certainly cause cities and counties across the country to immediately inflate their spending, and hire millions more pensioned bureaucrats with the "savings"— thereby feeding the beast and ensuring a vicious escalation of the fundamental problem.

Beyond that, the finances just don't work. Already, over 10 percent of our federal budget is spent paying interest on our national debt; a number expected to increase by another 30 percent over the next few years. And we're supposed to more than double that? Spend a quarter of the entire federal budget just to pay interest on our debt? If that happens, the beast will win and you can kiss this country goodbye.

Phoenix City Councilman Sal DiCiccio has been the taxpayer's champion, pushing for pension reform, exposing waste, favoritism, and public unions finagling huge pay increases during the worst recession in most of our lives. He has pushed for managed competition for non-core city services, more transparency in procurement and in government in general and lower taxes, including ending the recently passed new food tax.

The Pension Crisis Is Here

by John MacGregor, CFP®

People don't always like brutal honesty, but as a financial advisor for over 25 years, sometimes it's what they need. In fact, it's often what they need and the hard, cold truth when it comes to pensions is this: **the pension system in the United States is in dire straits**.

I see it so often with my clients: the absolute certainty and assurance they have that nothing can happen to their pension. In fact, most will say, "It's guaranteed and it's in writing." Well, when there's no money, there's no money. And I don't care what that agreement says, if they don't have it, you won't get it.

Today, we're already seeing numerous court cases challenging organizations' requirements to fulfill their pension obligations. This, in my opinion, is the tip of the iceberg.

We hear so often about Social Security and how the new estimates indicate it will go broke by 2035, well before many of us reach retirement. Yet Congress still refuses to act (aside from stealing from SS for one pet project or another).

Well, the pension system is arguably worse off than SS. I've heard skepticism about this claim, snickering, and had people get furious with my warnings, but at the end of the day it remains true.

What I think people focus on when discussing pensions and Social Security problems is that most people will be completely or significantly dependent on Social Security whereas not everyone is entitled to a pension. Therefore, Social Security *is* the bigger fish in terms of the number of people affected, but the pension crisis is still massive and will be much harder to resolve.

Unlike SS, where Congress can pass laws raising taxes, extending the retirement age, or eliminating payments to those who don't need it ("means testing"), you can't do that when dealing with the thousands of different pension plans. The fix is much too complicated, which is why I say it's a much bigger problem.

You can't ignore the reality: government pensions, union supported pensions, and private pensions are *woefully underfunded*. Workers have been overpromised for generations and while our parents may be enjoying their pensions (for now), the pressure on the entire structure is overwhelming the system to the point of collapse.

In fact, John Maudlin, Senior Contributor to Forbes Magazine, wrote in 2019, "A decade ago I pointed out that public pension funds were $2 trillion underfunded and getting worse.[5]" And it has gotten much worse since 2009.

In the decade since, nothing has been done to address the problem. Nothing. Just as politicians in every government district, town, state, and DC do, the problem has been kicked down the road time and time again.

But the piper is coming and he will demand his dues.

We can't simply point to one problem being the cause of this impending nightmare. And when I say 'nightmare,' I don't mean that figuratively; it's genuinely going to directly affect every American— whether they have pensions or not—because it's going to hit retirees, private companies, insurance giants, every level of government with such force that it has the potential to cripple the entire economy for years.

Think I'm being melodramatic?

What do millions of Americans focus on when it comes to their retirement? Not their 401(k). Not their savings. **Their pension**.

They have a specific amount of money they anticipate receiving every month for their retirement. Due to several pressures placed on employers and government bureaucracies for decades, most men and women who worked 'for a pension' over 20, 30, or 40+ years expect up to 80 percent of their final years' salary or average thereof.

It's during those last few years when a lot of them punch in tremendous overtime and max out what they can, putting even more pressure on the system. If those people expect $75,000+ from their pension for retirement, what's going to happen when the money isn't there? What will happen when these agencies and companies take the problem to court (arbitration) and get a ruling that only 30 percent of the promised funds need to be paid out (and that's thinking generously)?

---

5 https://www.forbes.com/sites/johnmauldin/2019/05/20/the-coming-pension-crisis-is-so-big-that-its-a-problem-for-everyone/#550c2b6837fc

Taxes still have to come out of that and millions of Americans will be completely caught off-guard. Unprepared. You think it's tragic witnessing 80-year-old seniors working at McDonald's or Walmart because they can't afford not to? Just wait.

How Did It Get So Bad?

Mismanagement, greed, vote-buying, unrealistic investment return projections, excessive fees, poorly estimated longevity tables... you name it. A lot of factors have gotten us to this miserable place, but there is still time. The problem is that too many people don't want to open their eyes.

They don't want to see or believe that everything they've worked for over the past several decades or more (all their adult life) could very well go up in proverbial smoke.

No one wants to admit when their financial world is crumbling around them. I've seen it over and over through the years: a spouse keeping their true financial situation hidden from their wife or husband and then when they lose the house and everything else, that other spouse is stunned.

They don't want to admit they failed.

When it comes to this pension problem, people just don't want to believe everything they were promised could very well amount to empty words. They don't want to believe they'll have to work well beyond their planned retirement years.

Unions have been notorious for pressuring companies and governments to promise amazing pension benefits. Civil servants end up piling on the overtime to max out their retirement benefits. Private companies decided to chase after mergers and acquisitions when they should have been paying into the pension fund.

Let's not forget low interest rates for the past decade that have put a huge strain on the future stability of the pension crisis.

The only thing preventing the storm from hitting now has been a rising stock market. We're now going on an 11-year bull market. This party won't last forever. And when that bubble bursts, the train will rocket off the track.

The Coming Superstorm

The best way to describe what's happening is to talk about the weather. *Hey, what a beautiful day it is! But this storm that's coming is going to be **bad.***

You've got a low pressure system building in the warm waters of the Atlantic. Another powerful low is rolling across the northern plains. Two high pressure systems will steer these lows into one another and you'll end up with a storm of catastrophic power and destructive force slamming together.

The two low pressure systems here are the overpromising and underfunding. The high pressure "steering" mechanisms would be "historically low interest rates that have driven up pension liabilities around the world"[6] and companies borrowing billions to cover current pension obligations (but all that's doing is trading one debt for another).

In other words, trying to kick that can down the road isn't really kicking a can; it's shoving a snowball that's just getting bigger down a slope. It's fast approaching the wall and when it does, you'll see millions of people in serious trouble.

Very few financial advisors I've seen are sounding the alarm. Why? It's not lucrative. It doesn't bode well for one's business when you tell people, "Two-thirds of what you've been planning on for retirement might very well be gone before you get there."

But it's coming and it's time to wake up. It's time to get serious. It's not too late to do something about this tremendous pension problem, but it continues to be the 800-pound gorilla sitting in our living room no one wants to acknowledge or even look at.

Make no mistake: that beast won't stay asleep much longer. We either deal with it and get it out of the house now or it'll destroy everything.

John MacGregor, is a Certified Financial Planner and author of The Top 10 Reasons the Rich Go Broke.

---

6 https://money.cnn.com/2018/01/18/investing/ge-pension-immelt-breakup/index.html

ABOUT THE AUTHORS

EDWARD SIEDLE

Edward "Ted" Siedle, is a former attorney with the United States Securities and Exchange Commission and America's leading expert in pension looting. He has spent more than three decades forensically investigating over $1 trillion in retirement plans. In 2018, Ted secured the largest CFTC whistleblower award in history—$30 million and in 2017, the largest SEC whistleblower award—$48 million.

He was named as one of the 40 most influential people in the U.S. pension debate by *Institutional Investor* magazine for 2014 and 2015.

ROBERT KIYOSAKI

Best known as the author of *Rich Dad Poor Dad* —the #1 personal finance book of all time—Robert Kiyosaki has challenged and changed the way tens of millions of people around the world think about money. He is an entrepreneur, educator, and investor who believes the world needs more entrepreneurs.

With perspectives on money and investing that often contradict conventional wisdom, Robert has earned an international reputation for straight talk, irreverence, and courage and has become a passionate and outspoken advocate for financial education.

Rich Dad Poor Dad and its messages, an international bestseller and viewed as a classic in the personal finance arena, has stood the test of time and continues to resonate with audiences of all ages around the world.

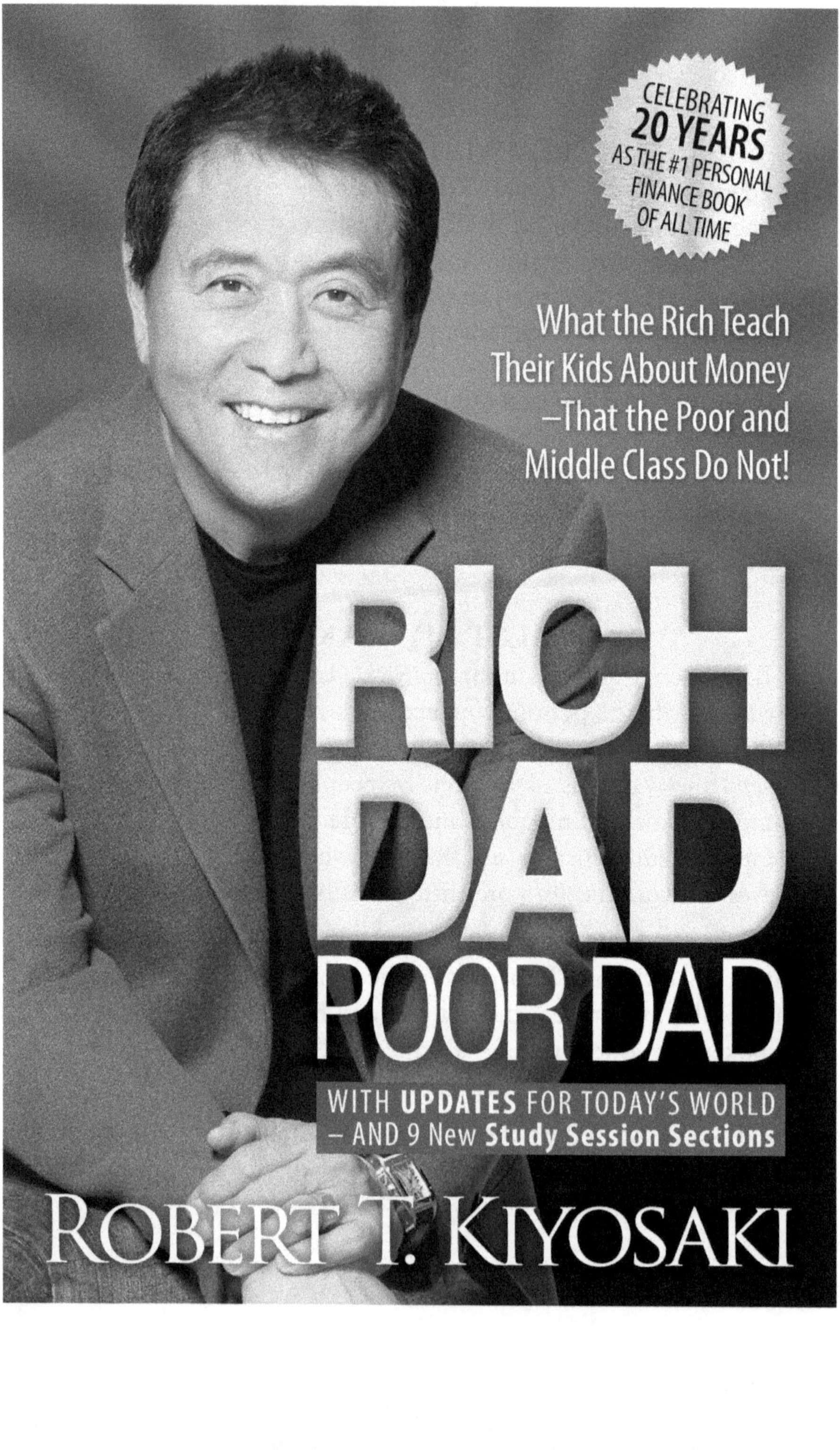
CELEBRATING
20 YEARS
AS THE #1 PERSONAL
FINANCE BOOK
OF ALL TIME
What the Rich Teach
Their Kids About Money
–That the Poor and
Middle Class Do Not!
RICH
DAD
POOR DAD
WITH UPDATES FOR TODAY'S WORLD
– AND 9 New Study Session Sections
ROBERT T. KIYOSAKI

CPSIA information can be obtained
at www.ICGtesting.com
Printed in the USA
JSHW021409150120
3593JS00003B/9